# Globalization and the Distribution of Wealth

*The Latin American Experience, 1982–2008*

The effects of globalization on poverty and inequality are a key issue in contemporary international politics, yet they have been neglected in international relations and comparative politics literatures. Arie M. Kacowicz explores the complex relationships between globalization and the distribution of wealth as a political problem in international relations, analysing them through the prism of poverty and inequality. He develops a political framework (an '*intermestic* model') which captures the interaction between the international and the domestic domains and explains those effects with a particular emphasis upon the state and its relations with society. He also specifies the different hypotheses about the possible links between globalization and the distribution of wealth and tests them in the context of Latin America during the years 1982–2008, with a particular focus on Argentina and the deep crisis it experienced in 2001–2.

ARIE M. KACOWICZ is Associate Professor in the Department of International Relations at the Hebrew University of Jerusalem.

# Globalization and the Distribution of Wealth

## The Latin American Experience, 1982–2008

Arie M. Kacowicz

*Hebrew University of Jerusalem*

CAMBRIDGE
UNIVERSITY PRESS

CAMBRIDGE UNIVERSITY PRESS
Cambridge, New York, Melbourne, Madrid, Cape Town,
Singapore, São Paulo, Delhi, Mexico City

Cambridge University Press
The Edinburgh Building, Cambridge CB2 8RU, UK

Published in the United States of America by Cambridge University Press,
New York

www.cambridge.org
Information on this title: www.cambridge.org/9781107027848

First published 2013

Printed and bound in the United Kingdom by the MPG Books Group

*A catalogue record for this publication is available from the British Library*

*Library of Congress Cataloguing in Publication data*
Kacowicz, Arie Marcelo.
Globalization and the distribution of wealth : the Latin American experience,
1982–2008 / Arie M. Kacowicz.
  pages  cm
Includes bibliographical references and index.
ISBN 978-1-107-02784-8
1. Income distribution – Latin America.  2. Globalization – Latin America.
I. Title.
HC130.I5K33  2013
339.2098′09045 – dc23    2012030787

ISBN 978-1-107-02784-8 Hardback

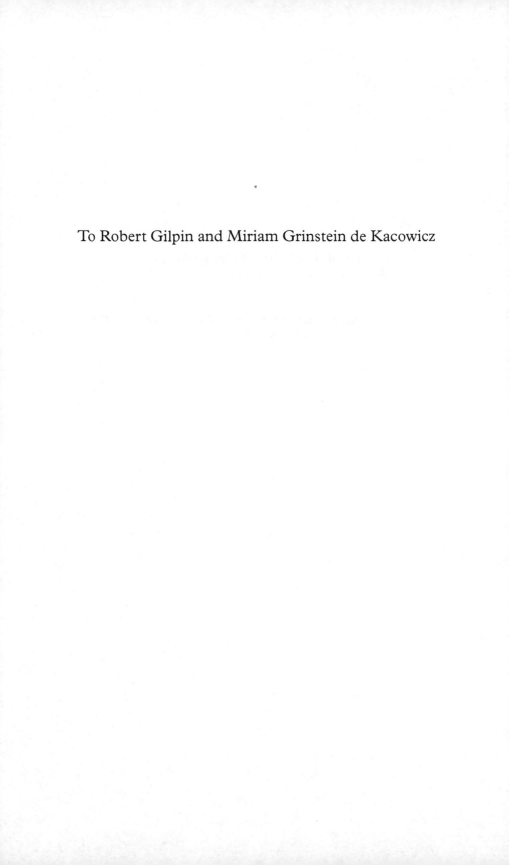

To Robert Gilpin and Miriam Grinstein de Kacowicz

This book was written under the auspices of

the Leonard Davis Institute for International Relations,
Hebrew University of Jerusalem

and

the Harry S. Truman Institute for the Advancement of Peace,
Hebrew University of Jerusalem

# Contents

# Figures

# Tables

# Preface and acknowledgments

This book explores the complex relationships between the phenomena of globalization and the distribution of wealth (with particular emphasis upon the distribution of income), defined in terms of poverty and inequality, as a political problem in international relations. In empirical terms, I focus upon the regional context of Latin America between 1982 and 2008, with a special reference to the Argentine case and the crisis that country experienced in 2001–2, alongside a brief discussion of Brazil and Chile. The empirical evidence is rooted in my reading of Latin America as a fascinating and peculiar historical, political, and sociological laboratory to examine theories and models in social science in general, and international relations in particular.

In 1987, I submitted a Master's thesis that explored the links between the debt crisis that affected Argentina and Brazil in the 1980s and their re-democratization processes. Since then, I concentrated my research on different aspects of peace. Although peace research and issues of poverty and inequality seem very distant one from the other, an eminent Argentine political scientist, Carlos Escudé, explained to me three years ago the rationale for their commonalities in the Latin American case. Paradoxically, while one possible explanation for the 'long South American peace' is related to the relative weakness of states that deter them from waging war, lacking both material means and enough domestic legitimacy, that same weakness explains the relative failure of many Latin American states in dealing with poverty and inequality. Hence, we have to be more cautious about blaming globalization for all the economic and social penuries of the Latin American region and turn our analysis to domestic political explanations as well.

After a hiatus of more than twenty years, in this book I completed a second study on international political economy, partly motivated by the existing confusion about the links between globalization and the distribution of wealth, the effects of the 2008–9 economic crisis, and the peculiarities of the Argentine case (especially with reference to its 2001–2 crisis).

As I started to become interested in the fuzzy concept of globalization in the last decade, I realized that there is a lot of ideological and theoretical confusion about the possible and logical links between globalization, poverty, and inequality. There is an ongoing debate between the proponents of the three major paradigms of international political economy and of international relations (Realists, Liberals, and Marxists), regarding the implications of globalization for the distribution of wealth. In this book, I do not pretend to resolve that discussion, but at least to systematize and contribute to it by developing an *intermestic model*. This model improves upon the alternative and usual explanations for the links between globalization, poverty, and inequality. Although the model stems from a Realist approach in international relations, it enriches it by specifically referring to the interactions between the external and the domestic political domains.

Unlike my previous research that used to tackle issues that were usually under-studied (such as 'peaceful territorial change', 'zones of peace', and 'stable peace'), addressing the links between globalization and the distribution of wealth implies an inter-disciplinary effort, and therefore it runs the risk of reiterating previous works, since perhaps too much material has been published on this subject – especially by economists and sociologists, but less significantly by international relations scholars. At the same time, the subject has been under-explored in the context of Latin America, with the possible exception of the literature on economic development, or in a comparative perspective. This issue merits the intellectual journey I have been undertaking, intermittently, for the last ten years.

This journey started in 2002–3 during my sabbatical year at the Department of Government at Georgetown University, and subsequent summers spent in Washington, DC, where I benefited from the comments and suggestions of Shelton Davis (from the World Bank), Salomon Bergman, Keely Lange, Thomas Wright, Thomas Banchoff, and especially George Shambaugh. Other US colleagues who offered useful suggestions throughout those years include Branko Milanovic (who graciously calculated Gini coefficients for me), Pamela Blackmon, David Pervin, David Blaney, Ethan Kapstein, Sean Reagan, William Thompson, James Mittelman, the late Dennis Goulet, and the late James Rosenau.

Since 2004, I have been visiting Argentina every year, as a guest teacher of the Graduate Programme in International Relations of the Universidad del Salvador (USAL) in Argentina. In Buenos Aires, I managed to meet with many scholars and former officials who offered their comments and suggestions regarding the Latin American and Argentine cases, including

Roberto Bouzas, Carlos Acuña, Federico Merke, Khatchik DerGhaugassian, Domingo Cavallo, Marcelo Cavarozzi, Alexandre Roig, Susana Nudelsman, José Paradiso, Juan Carlos Torre, the late Martín Gonzalez, Fabian Calle, Carlos Escudé, Leonardo Gasparini, Raúl García Heras, Lucas Llach, and Gabriel Kessler. Other Latin American specialists who read and helped me along include Andres Malamud from Portugal, Bruno Ayllon-Pino from Spain, Tullo Vigevani from São Paulo, and Carlos Waisman from UCSD. I want also to thank the librarians at the National Library of Argentina, the Argentine Library of Congress, the Universidad del Salvador (Faculty of Law), and the University of Di Tella Library, all in Buenos Aires.

Some of the ideas and drafts of Chapters 3, 4, and 5 have been presented at the International Studies Association and American Political Science annual meetings since 2001 to the present, as well as in other venues such as Berlin. I want to thank Noemi Gal-Or, Thomas Smith, Raimo Väyrynen, George Sorensen, Sergio Costa, and many colleagues and students, chairs and discussants, who gave me good advice.

At the Hebrew University of Jerusalem, my home institution, many students and colleagues listened to, read, and commented on several versions of the book manuscript, many of them from the Department of International Relations, attending seminars given at my home department, at the Leonard Davis Institute for International Relations, the Harry S. Truman Institute for the Advancement of Peace, and the Liwerant Center for the Study of Spain, Portugal, Latin America, and their Jewish Communities. They include: Yael Krispin, Eytan Meyers, Orit Gal, Steve Kaplan, Luis Roniger, Mario Snajder, Leonardo Senkman, Batia Siebzehner, Shlomo Griner, Asaf Zussman, Avraham Sela, Tomer Broude, Avner de-Shalit, Orit Bergman, Avi Segal, Arie Krampft, Roee Kibrik, Marcia Harpaz, Daniel Schwartz, Nissim Otmazgin, Lior Herman, Reuven Amitai, Eyal Ben-Ari, Yossi Gubi, Henry Lovat, Moshe Bargil, Moses Shayo, Shoham Cosen-Hillel, and Ariel Steinberg. Other Israeli scholars and friends include Hagar Tzameret, Gabriel Elad, Michael Gross, Benito Roitmann, Victor Azarya, Carlos Rozenkoff, and Alex Mintz. The research was facilitated by the generous support of fellowships received from the Davis Institute for International Relations, the Harry S. Truman Institute for the Advancement of Peace, and an Intra-Mural Research award from the Authority for Research and Development, all located at the Hebrew University of Jerusalem. I also want to thank the librarians of the Truman Institute for their help.

In February 2009, I spent two very fruitful weeks at the Munk School for Global Affairs of the University of Toronto as an exchange scholar, enjoying the hospitality of Janice Stein and her wonderful staff. There, I managed to discuss my project and learn from colleagues such as Richard Sandbrook, Judith Teichman, Albert Berry, Lou Pauly, and Emanuel Adler. More recently, David Sheinin, also from Toronto, offered me very useful comments on Chapter 5.

Robert Gilpin, my former mentor and supervisor from Princeton University, wisely suggested to me the title of the book and encouraged me throughout all those years to pursue this research project. Carlos Rozenkoff suggested critical comments, based on his vast expertise about Argentina, on Chapter 5. My spouse Orly and my son Itai provided me with critical insights that I attempted to incorporate in the final version.

I owe my personal gratitude to my colleagues and friends Claudia Kedar, Piki Ish-Shalom, George Shambaugh, and especially Galia Press Barnathan, who read most if not all of the book manuscript in different versions. Gila Weinberger, my research assistant, devised and drew all the tables and statistical material that can be found in Chapters 4–6. Two of my favourite Ph.D. students, Mor Mitrani and Keren Sasson, read the entire manuscript and offered incisive insights, suggestions, and an excellent initial copy-editing.

The inception, thinking, and research for this book took about a decade, while the writing itself was completed throughout 2010 and revised throughout the Fall/Winter of 2011–12. In between, social protests demanding 'social justice' spread out throughout many developing and developed countries, including a memorable summer of discontent in Israel, offering a particular topical perspective to this book, and bringing to the fore arguments about inequality and distribution of wealth. My daughters Ela (14) and Elior (9) got it right when they told me several months ago, 'Daddy, it is time for you to finish that book!'

As with my previous book (*The Impact of Norms in International Society*), again I suggest to the reader, following the model of Julio Cortázar in *Rayuela* (1979), three alternative ways to read this book: (a) from cover to cover, the usual way; (b) those who are interested in the general subject of globalization and the distribution of wealth can read Chapters 1–3, and then move directly to Chapter 6; (c) those who prefer to learn more about Latin America and Argentina might refer also to Chapters 4 and 5, the empirical core of all the research project.

Some excerpts of Chapters 1, 3, and 6 were published in a condensed version in articles that I authored in the *Whitehead Journal of Diplomacy and International Relations* in 2005 (6: 111–27) and in *International Studies Review* in 2007 (9: 565–80; also reprinted as a chapter in *North and South in the World Political Economy* (Oxford: Blackwell, 2008), pp. 19–38). I am grateful to the journal publishers and to Blackwell Publishing for allowing me to use the material for this book.

In the production of this book, I want to thank the thorough comments of two anonymous reviewers for Cambridge University Press who wrote me eighteen pages of comments and suggestions, as well as the wise advice of its editor, John Haslam, and his superb editorial team, including Carrie Parkinson, Karen Oakes, Jo Breeze, and Linda Randall, the excellent copy-editor.

Finally, I want to dedicate this book to two individuals, who are turning octogenarians as this book is being completed. Robert Gilpin, my former teacher and supervisor, has been my intellectual source of inspiration to this project, following the insights he developed about a decade ago on the ambiguous relationship between globalization and the distribution of wealth. Miriam Grinstein de Kacowicz (Zonis), my mother, with her indefatigable sources of energy, and her teachings of perseverance and discipline, deserves the dedication of this fourth book of mine. Both Bob Gilpin and my mother were born in the third decade of the twentieth century, during that 'twenty years' crisis' in between the two world wars that witnessed the end of the first globalization period and the disarray of the 1930s. They both experienced the emergence of the second globalization period, which led us into the twenty-first century. Perhaps the wisdom of their age and their spirit of intellectual curiosity should help me, and the readers, to unfold the puzzles of our own chaotic, fascinating, and complex times.

# 1 Globalization and the distribution of wealth: problems and definitions

The new rich may worry about envy, but everyone should worry about poverty.

(*Economist*, 16 June 2001, 11)

## Introduction

This book explores the complex relationship between the phenomena of globalization and the distribution of wealth, analysed through the prism of poverty and inequality, as a *political* problem in international relations. This relationship is a poorly understood phenomenon, since most of the literature on the subject derives from economics rather than from political science. Moreover, even serious economists are still debating whether the effects of globalization on poverty and inequality are generally positive or negative, which means that they could also be small or not significant at all (see Berry 2003a).

Despite the fact that such debate is one of the key contemporaneous political issues in international relations, it has been under-specified in the international relations and in the comparative politics literatures. In this sense, this book seeks to remedy this deficiency by focusing on a political framework that includes a clear definition and taxonomy of the three major concepts involved in the subject: 'globalization', 'poverty', and 'inequality'. It also specifies the hypotheses about the possible links between globalization and the distribution of wealth and tests these hypotheses in the context of Latin America in general, and Argentina in particular, in the years 1982–2008.

The main argument of this book is that politics plays a crucial role in our effort to make sense of the problematic effects of globalization upon domestic societies, as well as a vital part of the effort to tame globalization and to find proper solutions to its potential negative externalities, including poverty and inequality. Thus, I argue in this book that national governments act as 'transmission belts', mediating the impact of

1

globalization upon their societies and citizenry. The stronger the states (in relation to their societies), the more effective they will be in providing 'good governance' and adequate solutions to cope with poverty and inequality. Consequently, variations in the effects of globalization upon poverty and inequality are best understood by examining the interplay of domestic politics and of international relations.

We need to assess the links between globalization and the distribution of wealth from a *political*, rather than economic or sociological, perspective. Furthermore, poverty and inequality are to be considered as international political problems, or even as global issues, so the debate about the links between globalization, poverty, and inequality should be contextualized within the structure of international relations.[1] In a similar vein, we should emphasize the differences between the economic and political perspectives on globalization, as opposed to the traditional typology of economic globalization and political globalization. Hence, this book offers a *political perspective* on processes of economic globalization and analyses their political manifestations and effects.

Economic globalization, manifested essentially through transnational flows of trade and finance, carries substantial political implications, both in terms of domestic politics (leading to political expressions of social protests and an entire range of social and economic national policies) and of international politics (in terms of global inequality and hierarchy between states, and mechanisms for global governance). As Albert Berry cogently argues, 'Economy theory tells us virtually nothing about the likely benefits of shifting from a situation of substantial trade and capital movements to near-free movement of goods and funds' (Berry 2003a, 24). This quotation emphasizes the fact that globalization and its effects (both political and economic) are in dispute between both practitioners and scholars, partly since it is a political concept and a peculiar political phenomenon loaded with distinct ideological perspectives and interpretations.

The research questions to be addressed in the book include the following. Why should we care about the distribution of wealth, assessed in terms of poverty and inequality? What are the implications in normative and practical terms? What is the nature of the links between globalization, poverty, and inequality and what are their causal mechanisms? Last, as Robert Gilpin (2000, 301) cogently frames the discussion, is it possible to evaluate the contradictory assessments of economic globalization and its consequences?

---

[1] I would like to thank Shelton Davis from the World Bank for his comments on this point.

Although we assume that there are complex and inter-related effects of globalization upon poverty and inequality, those effects are rather uneven and they do not always converge; hence, they should be disaggregated. In other words, globalization's impact on poverty will not necessarily go along with a similar effect on inequality. For instance, paradoxically, one of the major arguments and findings in this book is that globalization might reduce poverty while at the same time increasing inequality and the socio-economic gap between the 'haves' and the 'have-nots' (or 'have-less'). This truism reflects economic and social realities in different countries, such as China, India, Chile, and Brazil.[2]

Regardless of whether we are arguing for it or against it, I suggest that globalization has certainly placed the issues of poverty and inequality back and high on the contemporary political global agenda as *international negative externalities*. As Amartya Sen pointed out, one of the major problems of humanity nowadays is the distribution of potential benefits of globalization between rich and poor countries, and between different human groups within countries (see Sen 2009). In this sense, the distribution of wealth has become a crucial yardstick of the legitimacy and ethics of globalization, since it creates both winners and losers (Väyrynen 2008, 1; see also Munck 2007, 599).

In empirical terms, I examine the links between globalization, poverty, and inequality in the context of the economic and social realities of Latin America in general, and of Argentina in particular, with some further reference to the similar and different cases of Chile and Brazil. Much of the economic debate in Latin America at the turn of the twenty-first century has revolved around the effects of economic globalization and structural reform upon economic growth, poverty, and inequality. Poverty and inequality remain the major socio-economic problems of Latin America, with pernicious political implications and connotations, despite the impressive opening of the Latin American markets to the global economy and the encouraging trends of the 2000s in terms of reduction of both poverty and inequality.

Why is that the case? To what extent can we blame globalization for the exacerbation of poverty and inequality in the region? While there is an assumption that deeper integration into the world economy raises the potential for economic growth and for development, the Latin American experience since 1982 has suggested that growth does not necessarily lead to a reduction of poverty, but rather to pernicious effects in terms

---

[2] I would like to thank Robert Gilpin for his comments on this point.

of social welfare, with an increase of income inequality. Thus, during the 1990s, poverty and inequality have actually worsened in many countries of the region, breeding discontent as to the effects of globalization and economic reform upon poverty, living standards, and income distribution. Whether the exacerbation of poverty and inequality should be causally linked to the forces of globalization or to the (ir)responsibility of the national governments remains an important question to be addressed in the book.

### The problematique *and its current salience*

Is globalization a force for equity or for exploitation? Can globalization bring about progress or backwardness, development or underdevelopment, poverty or affluence? How does globalization affect the distribution of wealth in general terms? What are the possible links between globalization and poverty in general, and between globalization and inequality in particular?

The widespread social and political movements against globalization became fashionable about ten years ago, as we witnessed during the virulent demonstrations against the global economic institutions at Seattle in 1999, Prague in 2000, and Quebec and Genoa in 2001. Although it is not entirely obvious what the vociferous opponents of globalization really demand, their claim that Third World poverty has become one of the most pressing moral, political, and economic issues in the political agenda of the new millennium is a legitimate one.

In addition to non-governmental organizations (NGOs) and other grassroots organizations, mainstream international institutions and organizations have also recognized the realities of Third World poverty and global inequalities as a pressing agenda, at least at the rhetorical level. For instance, the official institutions of the Bretton Woods post-World War II liberal regime, the International Monetary Fund (IMF) and especially the World Bank, have focused their discussions and operative plans in the last two decades on the eradication of poverty, or at least its reduction, as the 'single greatest challenge of the century'.

Speaking about ten years ago at the plenary session of the 2000 Annual Meeting of the IMF and the World Bank held on 26–8 September 2000 in Prague, the governors representing the IMF's 186 members acknowledged that 'although globalization has brought opportunities for growth and development to both rich and poor countries, not everyone has been able to take advantage of the new opportunities'. The task facing the international community, the governors agreed, was to build a successful, truly global economy that works well for all people and addresses the widespread poverty that remains the 'unacceptable face of the global economic situation' (International Monetary Fund 2000, 23 October, 341). Similarly, the World Bank former President, James D. Wolfensohn, characterized 'globalization as an opportunity, and poverty as our challenge', though recognizing that globalization can relate to risks as well as to opportunities (Wolfensohn 2000, 308).

Nowadays, there seems to be a recognized *global* political agenda that focuses upon the importance of the links between globalization and poverty, as epitomized at the Millennium Summit at the United Nations headquarters in New York in September 2000 and the Monterrey Consensus of March 2002, while there is still a normative and even empirical disagreement about the precise nature and direction of those links. Among the values and principles mentioned in the 'Millennium Declaration' the possible links between globalization and poverty were emphasized as follows: 'The central challenge we face today is to ensure that globalization becomes a positive force for all [of] the world's people. Its benefits are unevenly shared, while its costs are unevenly distributed' (quoted in International Monetary Fund 2000, 23 October, 251). Furthermore, in a show of unguarded optimism about translating rhetorical intentions into an operative plan for development and for poverty eradication, the leaders of the world that gathered at New York City about ten years ago committed themselves to the following deadline: 'We further resolve to halve by 2015 the proportion of the world's people who earn less than one dollar a day, who suffer from hunger, and who lack access to safe drinking water' (quoted in International Monetary Fund 2000, 23 October, 251).

This brief sample of declarations of good intentions demonstrates that there has been such an emerging rhetorical consensus within the developed countries that we should seriously consider the links between globalization, poverty, and inequality, with its possible positive and pernicious implications, or at least that the developed countries bear some responsibility towards the alleviation of poverty and the diminution of inequality. Furthermore, there is also a normative consensus that globalization *should* fulfil a positive role as a potential panacea in reducing and eradicating poverty, and in decreasing inequality. At the same time, there is a vast disagreement about whether the link between globalization and poverty and inequality is a positive or a negative one. After all, different interpretations stem from divergent ideological, philosophical, moral, and theoretical approaches to international relations in general and to international political economy in particular, such as the inherent optimism of the Liberals in contrast to the radical pessimism of neo-Marxists (see Chapter 3).

*Existing debates over globalization and the distribution of wealth:*
*ideological and methodological*

The debate over globalization and the distribution of wealth has been greatly distorted by the ideological writings of both hyper-globalists and especially of many radical Third World intellectuals. As a matter of fact, a logical and commonsensical economic analysis would suggest that any form of economic growth propelled by globalization might lead to two fundamental implications for the distribution of wealth.

The first one is that economic growth will create winners and losers. In other words, some well-positioned individuals, entrepreneurs, and states will become wealthier, while others are either not affected or will actually suffer a decline in wealth, becoming more impoverished. For example, the Chinese decision three decades ago to join an increasingly globalized world economy has obviously increased the wealth of many millions of Chinese. At the same time, there have been many who have lost from that decision or have experienced stagnation. Yet, the overall picture has been a substantial growth in the wealth of both China and a large proportion of its population, in terms of poverty reduction, but not of reducing inequality.

The second implication is that economic growth will not take place at all, since many societies, especially in sub-Saharan Africa, the Middle East and North Africa, and in some parts of Latin America, for political and other reasons, have not become part of the globalization process. The reasons are multiple, ranging from political corruption and political culture to a lack of adequate infrastructure and entrepeneurship. In this case, for the millions of individuals in this second group we cannot attribute the lack of economic growth and their poverty to globalization, unless we want to equate globalization with Western imperialism.[3]

Various empirical studies claim to prove that globalization increases both poverty and inequality, whereas numerous others claim to prove the contrary, namely that globalization has reduced poverty and inequality. Those in favour of globalization (the Liberals, represented by such international institutions as the World Bank and the International Monetary Fund) argue that there have been significant steps in the struggle against global poverty, as well as a decrease in inequality, in the last twenty years. For them, the globalization of trade and finance has been responsible for this success by prompting economic integration, lifting millions out of poverty, and closing the inequality gap, such as in the cases of China and India. Conversely, there are the critics of globalization (the Radicals),

---

[3] I would like to thank Robert Gilpin for his insights on this point.

who sustain that globalization has led directly to increases in poverty and inequality, deepening the gap between the rich and the poor within and between countries.

In empirical terms, poverty actually rose during the first stage of globalization (by the end of the nineteenth century), but it continued to increase during World War I and World War II, even when the international economy withdrew from globalization. During the contemporary stage of globalization (since the late 1970s), there is clear evidence that extreme poverty has been gradually falling, mostly in Eastern and Southern Asia, and especially in China and India.

According to World Bank statistics, since 1980 there has been a clearly identifiable trend of declining numbers in extreme poverty; in 1981, the number of people living on less than $1 a day was 1.451 billion, compared to 1.1 billion in 2007, while world population grew at the time by 2 billion people (quoted in Glenn 2007, 157; see also Goldin and Reinert 2007, 21). Bourguignon and Morrison (2002) estimate that the number of people living in absolute poverty (defined as those people who live on less than $2 a day) was reduced by 100 million, between 1980 and 1992. Similarly, Chen and Ravaillon (2001) assess that there was a further fall of about another 100 million between 1993 and 1998.

Moreover, in relative terms, absolute poverty has declined significantly due to a significant population growth between 1970 and 1998. In other words, while in 1970 about 40 per cent of the world's population was living in absolute poverty, that percentage diminished to just 24 per cent in 1998 (De la Dehesa 2007, 110–11). Overall, we could then agree with the World Bank's report of 2007 that 'The last quarter-century, a time of unprecedented integration for the global economy, has witnessed a dramatic rise in standards of living around the world' (World Bank 2007, 29). Thus, the world has seen an unprecedented era of economic growth over the past three decades, which has made people better off, on average, leading to the reduction of world poverty, though not necessarily of world inequality.

Furthermore, economists such as Dollar and Kraay (2002) and Sala-i-Martin (2006) argued that there is ample empirical evidence that economic globalization has also reduced inequality, not just poverty. As a counterpoint to these optimistic assessments, Wade (2002) challenged those findings in his reading of the trends in poverty and income distribution. His strong conclusion about the magnitude and trend in world poverty and income distribution is that we must be agnostic, on the grounds that our current statistics are too deficient to yield a definitive answer in one direction or another.

In contrast to the widely shared notion that world poverty has been falling over the last thirty years and more, there is much more disagreement regarding the empirical measurements of inequality. Some economists might argue that income inequality (within countries) has been on the rise – or stagnant at best – in most countries since the early 1980s. Inequality rose in both developed countries (in sixteen out of the twenty rich Organisation of Economic Co-operation and Development (OECD) countries), as well as in China and other developing countries. Interestingly enough, in key Latin American countries such as Brazil and Argentina, there has been a sustained decrease in inequality over the recent decade (see Milanovic 2011, 7–11).

In sum, the assumption that the structural forces of globalization, including the market, the dissemination of science, and the spread of technology, will resolve the problems of inequality and poverty is not completely convincing, considering the lingering reality of more than a billion people living (or better, surviving) in absolute or even extreme poverty. Conversely, left-wing activism, from the sometimes unfairly discredited approaches of *dependencia* to the romanticism about the universe of the marginalized, has still to offer a serious and convincing answer to the actual links between globalization, poverty, and inequality (Nürnberger 1999, 5).

Both sides of the globalization debate have had a tendency to claim an unreasonable degree of causation between liberalizing policies in trade and financial flows and observed trends in poverty and inequality, while supporting their theoretical claims with their own statistical facts. Yet, economic globalization remains a deeply political controversial process, in the sense that neither the theory nor the empirical evidence on globalization and the distribution of wealth allow us to draw simple (or simplistic) conclusions about those links in any definitive manner.

As Aisbett (2007, 34) argues, people's interpretation of the available evidence is strongly influenced by their values and beliefs about globalization itself. Hence, the statistical debate remains an inconclusive intellectual exercise, so we should turn to other forms of analysis, particularly the *political dimension*, as a more interesting and promising avenue of inquiry (see Goldin and Reinert 2007, 21; Mills 2009, 1; and Neutel and Heshmati 2006, 2). The economic discussion about whether globalization leads to more or less poverty has to be transcended. In general, one can argue that in absolute terms the number of poor people in the world has decreased, while at the same time inequality has increased; both within states and across states, this carries significant political implications.

There are a myriad of studies dealing with globalization and poverty in separate ways, and there is an emerging literature linking globalization, poverty, and inequality in broad terms. Much of this research draws upon studies of political economy and international economics; it is usually conducted by economists and sociologists, rather than by political scientists and international relations scholars. Just to mention a few important studies: (1) Joseph Stiglitz, *Globalization and its Discontents* (2002), and (2) Joseph Stiglitz, *Making Globalization Work* (2007). These two popular books partly focus upon the links between globalization and poverty, suggest policy recommendations (to reform globalization), and are based upon the experience of the author as a former World Bank official. (3) Abhijit Vinakat Banerjee, Roland Bénabou, and Dilip Mookherjee (eds.), *Understanding Poverty* (2006); (4) Machiko Nissanke and Erik Thorbecke (eds.), *The Impact of Globalization on the World's Poor* (2006); and (5) Ann Harrison (ed.), *Globalization and Poverty* (2007). These three collections of distinguished economists focus upon the economic analysis of the links and transmission mechanisms (causal chains) between globalization and poverty, such as trade, financial integration, capital flows, and diffusion of technology, but without emphasizing much of the political context, either domestic or international. (6) Raphael Kaplinsky, *Globalization, Poverty, and Inequality: Between a Rock and a Hard Place* (2005). This original book poses a causal link between globalization and poverty, by focusing on the mobility of investment and the theory of global value chains. But, again, the argument is eminently economical rather than political, and, to some extent, even biased against globalization. (7) Guillermo De la Dehesa, *What Do We Know about Globalization? Issues of Poverty and Income Distribution* (2007). The prevailing approach of this book relies on both the professional economics literature and on empirical evidence. It is a sober assessment of the implications of globalization for poverty and for development. (8) John Rapley, *Globalization and Inequality: Neoliberalism's Downward Spiral* (2004). This book indeed refers to the political implications of globalization and of neoliberalism upon the Third World states. Even though it presents an important political analysis, the author does not put much emphasis upon poverty and inequality.

*The missing link: developing a political* intermestic *model*

In contrast to these economic analyses, I offer in this book a particular political *intermestic* model. I argue that in order to understand the links between globalization, poverty, and inequality we should focus upon the role of the state in relation to both the external and domestic environments, framing the national policies. Those policies act as critical variables to reap the benefits of globalization and to cope with its adverse effects.

Even though the effects of economic globalization along several social dimensions are deemed benign, on balance, rather than malign, we need *political institutions*, first and foremost national governments and state institutions themselves, to confront, monitor, and balance globalization, in order to maximize the positive potential outcomes that it might achieve. Thus, the choice for national governments is not how to confront globalization, but rather how to manage it and channel it for positive results within their own societies (Haass and Litan 1998; and Stiglitz 2002, 218), and among themselves, through mechanisms of global governance.

In this book, I develop an *intermestic* model that improves upon the alternative and usual explanations for the links between globalization, poverty, and inequality. This model stems from a Realist approach in international relations, but it adds to it and transcends it by specifically referring to the interactions between the external and the domestic domains. The *external* domain focuses upon the position of the state in the regional and international structures, especially with reference to the global economy and to globalization processes, and the relationships between a given state and the regional and global institutions. The *domestic* domain refers to the social and economic stratification within societies, as well as to the political divisions within the different states, alongside state–society relations that are mainly characterized by the level of strength (or weakness) of any particular state in relation to its own society (see Holsti 1996; and Kacowicz 1998).

The *intermestic* model has to be spelled out by referring to the state as a critical (but not always effective) *active transmission belt* or intermediary actor, between the structural forces of economic globalization and the structural domestic characteristics of a given society, plagued sometimes by poverty and social and economic inequalities. In this analysis, the state is not merely a conduit but rather an active agent, which absorbs the effects of globalization and other external factors, and then translates and internalizes them into specific ideologies, strategies, and policies articulated by the national government.[4]

In empirical terms, the model has to be examined through different policies (social and economic) adopted by different governments over time in order to cope with poverty and inequality, including welfare, education, health, employment, social security, taxes, and fiscal and monetary policies, keeping in mind the huge differences between what the state would like to do, and what it actually does in practice. Furthermore, states as active 'transmission belts' might *redistribute wealth*, by transferring income, wealth, or property from some individuals to others within societies through monetary policies, taxation, welfare, nationalization, or charity.

---

[4] I would like to thank Mor Mitrani for her insights on this point.

One of the major political variables to consider here is the concept of *state strength* (in relation to its own society, or to state–society relations), as crucial to understand the performance of the state in *intermestic* terms. In more specific terms, I hypothesize that the external forces of globalization tend not to exacerbate poverty and inequality in *strong states* (vis-à-vis their own societies), which manage to institute progressive economic and social policies. Thus, the effectiveness of the state performance in economic and social terms is a function of the state strength as related to its society. A strong state, by definition, will be able to provide 'good governance' and thus to benefit its society in better coping with poverty and inequality. In a nutshell, one can argue that 'greater governance, greater good'.[5] By contrast, globalization tends to exacerbate poverty and inequality in *weak states* (vis-à-vis their own societies), since they are less likely to adopt and implement such policies.

This is an *intermestic* (international + domestic) model of politics that answers the question about the possible links between globalization, poverty, and inequality by referring to the critical role of political actors within those structures, rather than embarking on econometric debates about the effects of globalization upon poverty and inequality. The model depicts a complex representation of the political economy reality, where the links between globalization and the distribution of wealth are a two-way, open-ended relationship. Moreover, I assume for this model my own normative bias of a social-democratic belief that states can perform a positive (meaning by that benign) role in cushioning their domestic societies against the structural forces of globalization. According to this social-democratic belief, it is possible to reconcile the needs of achieving growth and development through globalized markets with the granting of political, social, and economic rights (see Sandbrook et al. 2007).

In the following pages, I define the concepts of 'globalization', 'distribution of wealth', 'poverty', and 'inequality'. Once defined, I turn to a brief discussion of the methodology employed in this study, and introduce the contents of the rest of the book.

## Defining globalization and the distribution of wealth

### *What is globalization?*

Despite the fact that defining globalization as a unique political phenomenon in international relations has been attempted by numerous

---

[5] I would like to thank the first reviewer from Cambridge University Press for his insights on this point.

scholars and policymakers it continues to mean different things to different people. There is a lot of confusion about the term, and about the rhetoric of globalization and the 'new world order' that followed the end of the Cold War. Contemporary globalization preceded the end of the Cold War in 1989 and can be traced back to the 1980s or even to the late 1970s. Globalization can be conceived as a myth, a rhetorical device, a phenomenon, an ideology, an empirical reality, a process, and even the context or structure of current international relations. In both academic and popular discourses, globalization has become one of the catchwords of the new millennium. In fact, globalization is shorthand for a cluster of inter-related processes that bring about economic, ideological, technological, political, and cultural changes.

*Economic changes*, which encompass the most salient and relevant dimension of globalization, include the increasing integration of economies around the world, particularly through trade and financial flows. This takes place through the internationalization and deterritorialization of production, the greatly increased mobility of capital and of transnational corporations, and the deepening and intensification of economic interdependence.

The *economic manifestations* of globalization include the spatial reorganization of production, the inter-penetration of industries across borders, the spread of financial markets, the diffusion of identical consumer goods across distant countries, the (relative) free movement of people and knowledge across national borders, and the extension beyond national borders of the same market forces that have operated for centuries at all levels of human economic activity – village markets, urban industries, and financial centres (see International Monetary Fund, September 2000, 4; and Mittelman 1996a).

*Ideological changes* involve investment and trade liberalization, deregulation, privatization, and the adoption of political democracy in the domestic institutional realm of any given polity (or, alternatively, the spread of religious fundamentalism as a backlash and itself a by-product of globalization). In this context, we should clearly distinguish between the 'neutral' forces and processes of economic globalization and the ideology of market capitalism or neoliberalism, as one possible variant of economic globalization. It is the ideology of neoliberalism (rather than globalization per se) which is contested in its possible consequences upon poverty and inequality.

*Technological changes* refer to information and communication technologies that have shrunk the globe, causing a shift from the production of goods to the production of services. Finally, *cultural changes* involve trends toward a homogenization of tastes and standards, epitomized by a common universal world culture that transcends the nation-state (Li 1997, 5).

Globalization can thus be defined as *the intensification of economic, political, social, and cultural relations across borders*. In this sense, globalization involves more than just the geographical extension of a range of phenomena and issues. It implies not only a significant intensification of global inter-connectedness, but also an *awareness* or consciousness of that intensification (that is, a *cognitive change*), with a concomitant diminution in the significance and relevance of territorial boundaries. Globalization encompasses a qualitative shift. This implies that the idea (and reality) of globalization cannot be quantified. Globalization is more than 'more of the same'; here lies the differentiation, for instance, between 'complex interdependence' and globalization.

Globalization is pushed by several factors: among others, technological change, economic factors, and policy changes articulated by states and other (non-state) actors. In the political, economic, and sociological senses, globalization is better understood as an encompassing cluster of processes that includes a qualitative shift in the conditions of people's lives, for better or for worse. Thus, globalization, considered in structural terms, implies a major transformation in world order, and the revision of the concept of space in geographic terms.

In other words, the principle of territoriality stands in contradiction with the de-territorialization of economic flows, as globalization can be defined as a *shared social space by economic and technological forces* with the relative de-territorialization of social, economic, and political activity, and the relative denationalization of power. We should point out that the new feature of globalization is not only the intensification of political, economic, and social relations across borders; it is rather the alternation of such relations from a merely territorial-based framework to a hybrid one that includes both territorial and non-territorial components.[6]

Globalization may lead to the integration of states, peoples, and individuals through increasing contact, communications, and trade, thus creating the possibility for a holistic, single global system. At the same time, globalization is very uneven in both its intensity and geographical scope, as well as in its different domestic and international dimensions and effects. In this sense, we might identify different types of globalization, across a rich regional variation (see Holm and Sorensen 1995, 1–7; see also Chapter 6 in this book).

To sum up, the concept of globalization is frequently used (and abused) but seldom clearly defined. It means many different things for different

---

[6] I would like to thank Mor Mitrani for her insights on this point.

people. This is why it is imperative to explain globalization as a peculiar political phenomenon and mostly as a complex and multi-dimensional cluster of processes that embodies a significant transformation in the spatial organization of social relations and transactions. Although the focus of globalization is usually upon its economic dimension (also in this book), it includes other, non-economic ones.

Among the possible definitions, most of them neutral and positivist, and others more ideological (the last two in the list below), we might include the following:

- Intensification of economic, political, social, and cultural relations across borders.
- The historical period since the end of the Cold War (our contemporary age).
- The transformation of the world economy, as epitomized by the integration of the financial markets.
- A technological revolution with social, political, and economic implications.
- The inability of nation-states to cope with global problems that require global solutions, such as demography, ecology, human rights, nuclear proliferation, and poverty.
- The triumph of US values, through the combined agenda of neoliberalism in economics and of political democracy in politics.
- An ideology about the logical and inevitable culmination of the powerful tendencies of the market at work. As an ideology, globalization is understood differently in different parts of the world. Thus, for those who possess power and wealth, globalization equates to freedom; conversely, for those at the bottom of the global hierarchy, globalization might imply marginalization and is associated with Western imperialism (see Mittelman 2004).

*Focus on economic globalization*

As mentioned above, globalization encompasses multiple dimensions, including economic, technological, cultural, political, social, moral, and normative aspects. It is important to draw the distinction between the *qualitative* and the *quantitative* dimensions of globalization: more of the same might imply a quantitative change, while qualitative shifts might indicate a quantum leap. Unlike interdependence, which might imply only a quantitative change, *economic globalization* invokes a qualitative shift toward a global economic system that is no longer based upon autonomous national economies, but rather relocates production, distribution, and consumption of goods in a consolidated global single marketplace.

According to the OECD, economic globalization can then be defined as 'free movement of goods, services, labor and capital thereby creating a single market in inputs and outputs; and full national treatment for foreign investors (and nationals working abroad) so that, economically speaking, there are no foreigners' (Wolf 2004, 1). In other words, economic globalization implies the integration of economic activities, via markets, driven by technological and policy changes, including falling costs of transport and communications, and a deliberated liberal policy of greater reliance on market forces. It is then reflected in the increasing amount of cross-border trade in goods and services, the increasing volume of international financial flows, increasing flows of labour, and the globalization of production, through the work of transnational corporations (see Aisbett 2007, 35; Fischer 2003, 3; Goldin and Reinert 2007, 2; Ocampo 1998a, 65–6; and Wolf 2004, 19).

The economic side of globalization, which receives most of the scholarly attention and is particularly relevant for the *problematique* of this book, is found in 'that loose combination of free trade agreements, the Internet, and the integration of financial markets that is erasing borders and uniting the world into a single, lucrative, but brutally competitive, marketplace' (Friedman 1996, 30). In more specific terms, the discussion in the book focuses upon two major dimensions of economic globalization: (1) international trade in goods; and (2) international movements of capital flows, including foreign direct investments (FDIs) and portfolio investment flows.

In logical terms, there is a close relationship between the shift towards economic liberalization and globalization. If by economic globalization we mean the integration of economic activities via markets, it presupposes that both natural and man-made barriers to international economic exchange will continue to fall; hence, it assumes economic liberalization (see Wolf 2004, 14–15).

### *Political effects of economic globalization*

As it will be examined in Chapter 3, the social, economic, and political effects and implications of economic globalization are diverse and somehow controversial. It seems that the vast majority of economists believe that liberalization of trade and technology flows enhance economic growth, and therefore reduce poverty. At the same time, the effects of trade (and probably also of technology) flows upon income distribution (in terms of more or less inequality) are much more ambiguous, and at some times they are even irrelevant.

With regard to capital flows, economic theory certainly argues that it should benefit poor countries and promote economic growth. Yet, it seems that the empirical evidence is rather mixed. However, it makes sense to differentiate between different types of capital flows. For instance, FDIs are more prone to lead to growth than other types of flows, such as short-term foreign currency and bank finance.[7] There is also a significant difference between horizontal and vertical FDIs, so that the two may have different effects on growth and poverty, as well as upon income distribution. For instance, FDIs that are for local consumption are a substitute for international trade. Conversely, FDIs that are linked to international production chains may generate higher add-value plus technology transfers, resulting in skills upgrade, as well as a rise in growth and income.[8]

In social and political terms, as the focus of this book's *problematique* implies, there is no consensus about the effects of economic globalization upon poverty and inequality. It is clear that economic globalization brings about winners and losers, but who are they? Who wins from economic globalization? If the economic cake becomes larger, it seems that everybody could win in absolute terms (for instance, by reducing poverty); while at the same time inequality might expand, as a result of technological factors and capital flows that affect negatively labour wages, while increasing the skill and digital divides, at least in the short term.

Liberals believe that economic globalization has been the inevitable result of technological change; moreover, from their perspective, global economic liberalization will strengthen and lead to political democracy. Globalization will expose societies to democracy, while economic liberalization will provide the material basis for subsequent democratic consolidation. Even if this assertion is true, it conceals a conceptual and normative trap: paradoxically, the economic forces of globalization, by definition, are undemocratic, if not anti-democratic.

There is a serious 'democratic deficit' here. The lack of accountability of global economic forces poses a serious political problem, for both states and individuals alike. By condensing the time and space of social relations, economic globalization transcends territorial states while not being accountable to elected political officials (Mittelman 1996b, 197). The only form of a checks-and-balances mechanism is in the hands of the non-elected market forces, regulated by the logic of economics and efficiency, which resonates with a Darwinist tendency of the economic 'survival of the fittest'.

In this (vulgar) Darwinist world, poverty and inequality can be considered as an unintended consequence, or collateral damage, of the market forces of globalization, as epitomized by the actions of transnational

---

[7] I would like to thank Asaf Zussman for his insights on this point.
[8] I would like to thank Lior Herman for his insights on this point.

business and multinational corporations. There seems to be a contradiction between this Darwinian process and the economic idea of comparative advantage; that is, between the economic and political logics
of globalization, leading to a 'democratic deficit' and to serious market
failures, unless regulated (or distorted) by the intervention of the state.
This 'democratic deficit' ignores the realities of poverty and inequality
as relevant political issues, unless brought to the global agenda by the
state and other social and political actors, such as social movements and
NGOs. Before we can seriously explore the impact of globalization upon
the distribution of wealth, we first need clearly to define the concepts of
'poverty' and 'inequality'.

### Distribution of wealth: poverty and inequality

I refer to the *distribution of wealth* in broader political terms than just the
statistical comparison of the wealth of various members or groups in a
society (within states), or across countries (world distribution of wealth).
'Wealth' is contrasted with 'poverty', where poverty should be measured
not just as lack of income or expenditure to sustain a minimum standard
of living. In effect, poverty amounts to a lack of adequate food, shelter,
education, health, life expectancy, sanitation, and access to safe water.
Thus, poverty also implies deprivations that prevent people from living
lives with a sense of security and expectations for the future.

Whereas 'wealth' consists of items of economic values that we possess,
'income' refers to the inflow of those items of economic value. Thus,
*distribution of income* is a close (yet not identical) concept to that of *distribution of wealth* focusing essentially upon measures of income equality
and inequality, such as the Gini coefficient. Therefore, under the general
rubric of the *distribution of wealth* (either in a given society or across countries in a specific region or worldwide), I will simultaneously refer to the
inter-related though not identical phenomena of poverty and inequality.

The two concepts, 'poverty' and 'inequality', should be kept analyt-
ically distinct, one referring to the *relative* economic wherewithal of an
individual, group, or society (inequality), and the other to some *absolute* measure below which an individual or group can (barely) manage
to survive. Thus, while poverty is concerned with *absolute levels of living*, inequality refers to *disparities in the level of living* (see Glenn 2007,
154).

### What is poverty?

Like globalization, poverty is a loaded and confusing concept in the social
sciences. The common usage of poverty is usually referred in terms of

*income poverty* measured in constant (price adjusted) 'purchasing-power parity' (PPP) dollars, as related to three degrees of poverty: (a) a per capita income of less than $1 a day (or $1.25 since 2005) (*extreme poverty*), which means that poor people cannot meet the basic needs for survival; (b) a per capita income of $2 a day (*absolute poverty*), which might barely meet the basic needs; and (c) *relative poverty*, as defined by a household income level below a given 'poverty line', as a proportion of the national average. These measurements of poverty stem from a conventional economic approach, which defines human well-being in terms of the consumption of goods and services. Poverty is then regarded as a lack of consumption of goods due to a lack of the minimum necessary income for that purpose(s) (De la Dehesa 2007, 111; and Goldin and Reinert 2007, 4).

Yet, this notion of poverty is not as straightforward as it might first appear, due to the fact that it is considered nowadays a multi-dimensional economic, social, political, and normative phenomenon that refers to issue-areas such as income, health, education, empowerment, participation, vulnerability to shocks, and working conditions (see Aisbett 2007, 53; Blackmon 2008, 183; Goldin and Reinert 2007, 3; and World Bank 2001, 34).

For the purpose of this book, I suggest a composite definition of poverty that is based upon several conceptualizations of poverty and that includes both economic and sociological dimensions, as follows: *poverty is a multidimensional phenomenon that includes lack of basic needs, relative and multiple deprivation, lack of human capabilities, lack of empowerment, lack of participation, and vulnerability to external shocks.*

To disaggregate this definition into its different components, we might turn to a brief examination of at least six different definitions for the concept of poverty, which somehow overlap and complement each other. According to Spicker (1999, 151–7) and several other authors, poverty can be defined in terms of:

*(1) Lack of basic needs.* Poverty can be understood as a lack of material goods or services, such as food, clothing, fuel, shelter, and acceptable levels of health and education that people require ('need') in order to live and function properly in society (Spicker 1999, 151; and World Bank 2001, 34). In this regard, we can find two distinct categories of poverty: (a) *extreme poverty*; and (b) *overall poverty*. Extreme poverty (or 'primary poverty') implies a lack of income necessary to satisfy basic food needs, usually defined on the basis of minimum calories requirements. In this case, the total earnings are insufficient to obtain the minimum necessities for the maintenance of merely physical efficiency, as in the extreme case of starvation and famines (Sen 1981, 11). Conversely, *overall poverty*

refers to the lack of income necessary to satisfy essential non-food needs, such as clothing, energy, and shelter (UNDP 2000, 20).

*(2) Lack of an adequate standard of living, or 'relative deprivation'.* In this sense, poverty does not refer to specific forms of deprivation, but rather to the general experience of living with less than others (Spicker 1999, 151). A related definition refers to poverty in terms of *relative deprivation*, as a situation in which income meets the basic essentials but not the level of social expectations, as compared with other social groups. Thus, people are relatively deprived if they cannot obtain the conditions of life that allow them to play a significant role in society (Nürnberger 1999, 61; Townsend 1993, 36; see also Sen 1981, 17).

From a normative or moral perspective, people are held to be poor when their material circumstances are deemed to be morally unacceptable. Poverty is considered as a social aberration, the elimination of which is regarded as morally good (Sen 1981, 17; and Spicker 1999, 157). In this view, poverty is regarded as a social fact, and its elimination is considered as part and parcel of the consensual normative conventions of society, unlike social inequality, which is a much more disputed political concept. As I examine in Chapter 2, poverty is related to the erosion of basic human rights (civil, political, social, and economic) and the lack of entitlements, possibilities, and dignity. Conversely, human rights abuses lead to poverty and to impoverishment. Thus, there is an intrinsic link between poverty and (the lack of) human rights.

*(3) Lack of basic security in terms of human capabilities.* Poverty can be assessed in terms of vulnerability to social risks, as equivalent to need (Spicker 1999, 152). We can then introduce the concept of *human poverty* in terms of a lack of basic human capabilities, within the context of human security. In other words, illiteracy, malnutrition, an abbreviated life span, poor maternal health, illness from preventable diseases, as well as lack of access to goods, services, and infrastructure such as education, communications, and drinking water – all of them indicate a lack of basic human capabilities (UNDP 2000, 20). Martha Nussbaum and Amartya Sen (1993) developed the related concept of a *capabilities approach*, which refers to poverty as a capability-deprivation mechanism.

*(4) Lack of entitlement and destitution.* Both deprivation and lack of resources reflect lack of entitlements, rather than the absence of needed items in themselves. The lack of entitlement becomes then the political and juridical context for poverty; thus, people who have the necessary entitlements are being regarded as no longer poor. In this sense, poverty derives from the relationship between ownership and exchange (see de Soto 2000; Sen 1981 and 2009; and Spicker 1999, 153).

In this context, we should clarify the distinction between poverty and *destitution*. 'Destitution' can be considered as a case of extreme poverty, an extreme want of resources or lack of means of subsistence. Poverty has always been considered as an economic and social phenomenon, while destitution, as a political and legal concept, has become more pronounced only recently, given the assault of development on traditional communities and their life-support. For instance, large parts of Africa, Latin America, and Asia were poor according to the definitions mentioned above well before colonial administrators and development planners *recognized* them as poor. At the same time, they were not considered destituted, in terms of lack of entitlement (Nandy 2002, 107, 115, and 121).

*(5) Multiple deprivations*. According to this definition, poverty implies long-extended circumstances in which people suffer from a constellation of deprivations experienced over a period of time (Spicker 1999, 153). For many people in the developing countries, three relevant dimensions of human poverty in terms of multiple deprivations include: (a) deprivation from a long and healthy life, as measured by the percentage of people not expected to survive the age of forty; (b) deprivation from knowledge, as measured by adult illiteracy; and (c) deprivation in economic provisioning, from private and public income, as measured by the percentage of people lacking access to health services and safe water, and the percentage of children under the age of 5 who are moderately or severely underweight (UNDP 2000, 22). Those measures are directly related to the *Human Development Index* of the United Nations Development Programme (UNDP), which establishes a composite statistical measure of human development in terms of life expectancy, knowledge and education, and standard of living.

*(6) Social exclusion and dependency*. In this sociological sense, poverty can be regarded as a set of social relationships in which people are excluded from participation in the normal pattern of social life (Spicker 1999, 154). As Sen (1981 and 2009) and Nussbaum and Sen (1993) argue, poverty implies the deprivation of basic capabilities and rights of people, like 'genuine opportunities' for an effective functioning in society, in terms of what people are able to do or to be, as a process of social exclusion from enjoying basic human rights (Wolff and de-Shalit 2007, 74).

The social exclusion framework allows us to understand the linkages and interactions between different risk factors (economic, social, cultural, political, and institutional) in a given social formation, and the impact these factors might have upon different social groups (Gacitúa and Davis 2001, 15). As a consequence, poverty might imply a sense of voicelessness and powerlessness with reference to the institutions of state and society (World Bank 2001, 34). Moreover, according to this definition, poor people are those who receive social benefits as a result of their lack of means; therefore, they are 'dependent' (Spicker 1999, 156). This implies a vulnerability to adverse shocks, linked to an inability to cope with them, partly derived from a lack of knowledge, and not only a lack of capital (World Bank 2001, 34).

### *Explaining poverty: two models and three levels of analysis*

These different definitions of poverty can be clustered according to two alternative but complementary models: the *behavioural/economic* model that examines the behaviour of individual actors and emphasizes measures of *absolute poverty* and *relative poverty* in a conventional way; this is usually the approach preferred by Liberals (definitions 1, 2, and 5). Alternatively, there is a second approach represented by the *structural/sociological/political* model that explains poverty as embedded within political and social structures, macroeconomic strategies, and the role of states and institutions; this is usually the approach preferred by Marxists and Realists who emphasize poverty as a relational (or relative) feature (definitions 3, 4, 5, and 6). For the purposes of measuring poverty, we can rely on three basic ideas or concepts of poverty, *subsistence, lack of basic needs and capabilities,* and *relative social deprivation,* as a synthesis of the two models depicted above.

The theoretical and especially the popular and non-academic debates regarding the causes of poverty have tended to polarize around these two explanatory models, the structural (socio-political) and the behavioural (economic) approaches. The *structural model* emphasizes institutionalized systems of inequality, macroeconomic impacts, and political strategies of exploitation and exclusion. Conversely, the *behavioural model* focuses on the individual attributes and behaviour of poor people in economic terms (Pinker 1999, 1–2). To put it simply, both perspectives are relevant to understand the conundrum of poverty.

The application of these two distinctive models to define and explain poverty depends upon different approaches to poverty as a social and political problem, at the domestic, international, and global levels. In this regard, considering poverty can imply three complementary, yet different, concepts: (a) poverty as a national (domestic) problem of underdevelopment, to be resolved within the borders of a given society and state; (b) poverty as an international problem, as part of the agenda in the relations between and among states; and (c) poverty as a global problem, in terms of world order and distributive justice (see Chapter 2). These different levels of analysis also suggest different approaches about how to address poverty. These three levels actually overlap and the distinction between them is somehow blurred, as between the international and the global levels of analysis.

*First level: poverty as a national (domestic) problem of underdevelopment* In one of the most significant shifts in the setting of development goals, poverty alleviation had become a defining feature of development in the late 1960s and 1970s. Poverty was no longer considered only a simple condition of states, but became also a condition of (poor) people *within* states (Finnemore 1996, 89–90). Thus, poverty came to be considered, first of all, a *domestic* problem of (under)development having international and global implications, though the mechanisms for its reduction and eradication remained first and foremost a domestic social, economic, and political issue.

As stated by several documents of the World Bank, poverty is about a lack of voice as well as lack of income *within* states. Market-oriented reforms can deliver economic growth, but growth in itself is not sufficient to eradicate poverty. According to this view, the poor must be able to build up assets of his or her own through access to education, health, and land, so that deep-seated gender, ethnic, social, and racial inequalities should be confronted and eventually eradicated.

The approach to reducing poverty has evolved over the past fifty years, in response to a changing conception of development. This evolution is clearly reflected in the changing views of the World Bank over time, including its policy prescriptions for developing countries in general, and for Latin American states in particular. Thus, the economic and social development policies of the World Bank had evolved from a doctrine of fighting 'absolute poverty' during the 1970s to the neoliberal doctrine of the 1980s.

Neoliberals affirmed that 'good policies' (i.e., the neoliberal ones) would bring both growth and greater equity, though as a matter of fact many developing countries experienced lower growth and rising inequality compared to previous periods. This was reflected in the so-called 'Washington Consensus' of the late 1980s. At the core of that consensus, there were several universal prescriptions, such as getting the prices right and keeping the government out of unneeded interventions, as well as downplaying the political and social context that might facilitate or impede development. Finally, in the late 1990s, the World Bank doctrine shifted again to a more general idea of 'governance', which repudiated political and economic corruption and promoted nation-building (see Gal 2007; and Stein 2008).

For instance, in the 1950s and 1960s, many viewed large investments in physical capital and infrastructure as the primary means to achieve growth and development, and to combat poverty. In the 1970s, awareness grew that physical capital was not enough, so the focus turned to health and education. The 1980s saw another shift of emphasis against the background of the debt crisis and the global recession. The emphasis turned to improving economic management and allowing greater play for market forces, under the aegis of neoliberalism.

In the 1990s, 'good governance' and political institutions moved toward centre stage, with a focus upon issues of vulnerability at the local (sub-national) and national levels, the argument being that the *quality of governance*, rather than democracy per se, was the deciding political factor leading countries out of poverty. Low quality of governance usually implies high incidence of corruption, government incapacity, and political instability. Finally, in the last decade, the World Bank has focused its strategies of fighting poverty upon three major themes: promoting opportunity, facilitating empowerment to political, social, and other institutional processes, and enhancing human security by reducing vulnerability to economic shocks, natural disasters, ill health, disability, and personal violence.

This broader conception of poverty, following the *capabilities approach*, led to a deeper understanding of its causes and a broader range of actions for attacking it, mostly at this first level of analysis (see Blackmon 2008, 198; and World Bank 2001, 6–7, 29, 34). These ideological changes were reflected in the type of projects that the World Bank undertook and financed since its inception. At the beginning, those were projects of physical infrastructure and education; later on they focused on human capital and development, education and health; finally, the contemporary projects emphasize the agenda of strengthening 'good governance' (see Gal 2007).[9]

According to this first level of analysis, the causes of poverty are embedded within the domestic context, including factors such as the narrow or small size of the internal market; inequality in the distribution of income and wealth; limited access to education, health services, and housing; limited access to political participation in the decision-making processes; wrong macroeconomic policies of the government; inequality between the different social strata of the population; lack of education; racial discrimination; unemployment and under-employment; corruption and administrative inefficiency of the state institutions; domestic effects of economic crises; and separation of social policies from macroeconomic

[9] I would like to thank Claudia Kedar for her comments on this point.

policies (Romero 2002, 161–72). Moreover, according to the *capabilities approach* of Sen and Nussbaum, the causes of poverty lie within the countries themselves. The crucial variable to consider here is the domestic decision-making process within the developing countries at the level of national and sub-national institutions, as well as the policies of local and national governments.

The IMF and especially the World Bank have adopted strategies for poverty reduction in the last decade that have focused upon the domestic realm. They have emphasized that a lasting breakthrough in combating poverty would be achieved only if the poorest countries were able to build the fundamentals for sustained growth by adopting the right economic and social policies. The centrepiece of these initiatives has focused on the country's ownership of the strategies to reduce poverty, and on the issue of effective governance. Effective governance is often considered as the missing link between national anti-poverty efforts and poverty reduction. For many poor countries, the external assistance needed is not only on economic aid for development, but also on how to improve governance and build stable political and economic institutions that will reduce, if not eradicate, poverty (UNDP 2000, 5–8).

*Second level: poverty as an international problem (in the relations between states)* The international community does not regard poverty only as a domestic issue of national development or underdevelopment, but also as one of the major issues in the agenda of international relations. Under normal conditions of peace, poverty is related to the dynamics of the international economy, interdependence, and its division of labour. Moreover, in conflict situations of relative deprivation, the problem of poverty is associated with international and civil wars, flows of illegal and legal migrations, refugees, environmental degradation, and threats to the existing international order emanating from demands of international and global justice instrumented occasionally through terrorist and guerrilla activities. This argument fits a very wide and Liberal conception of world order, based on notions of human security and related to the concepts of 'weak states' and of ineffective governance (or 'bad governance').

In this context, an important feature of the contemporary international system has been the emergence and persistence of a group of weak states and economies in the developing world that have not been able to benefit from economic globalization and from political democratization, thus posing increasing challenges to the international economic order, and, even more, to global peace and security (see Chapter 2).

It should be emphasized that the Bretton Woods Institutions (the IMF and the World Bank) traditionally regarded poverty as a national, or at most international, problem, rather than as a global one. Thus, the poverty relief measures favoured by the World Bank and also by the UNDP make provisions especially for international coordination, cooperation, and for economic assistance to the less-developed countries on an inter-state basis (Lumsdaine 1993, 5).

*Third level: poverty as a global problem* Why should the rich countries help the poor ones? Why should the international financial institutions assist poor people in developing countries? If the answers to these questions are not framed merely in prudential terms of rational cost-benefit calculations, including considerations of international security and of international political economy, then we can move our analysis, as we do in Chapter 2, from the rational to the normative dimension, and from the international to the global realm, recognizing a logic of cosmopolitan morality and justice that is hard to implement as a whole across nations and peoples (see Sen 2009, 408–15). Yet, there is a clear discrepancy between the normative tenets of potential global governance and the lingering realities of a Westphalian state system.

Poverty becomes a global problem since it has implications and ramifications for the human community as a whole, similar to the evolution of political and human rights in the direction of universal jurisdiction for international law when there is a gross violation of those rights. In this sense, there is an international, or even global, responsibility for the world's poor, as there is a universal promotion of human rights of various kinds (Finnemore 1996, 26). Poverty is then linked to the more general issues of global equity and distributive justice both within and across borders (see Nel 2000, 1–2; Sen 2009; Wolff and de-Shalit 2007; and Chapter 2 in this book).

Furthermore, as a negative international externality, poverty can also be considered as a global problem, to the extent that it can disrupt and derail the forces of globalization, affecting states, individuals, and non-state actors alike in a transnational fashion. As one of the senior officials of the IMF acknowledged a decade ago, 'growing inequality poses the greatest risk to the future of the global economy. If the majority of the world's population is increasingly marginalized and economically disenfranchised, then globalization will fail' (Manuel quoted in International Monetary Fund 2000, 306). Thus, the eradication of poverty and the reduction of global inequality should be considered as a global project, that is shared by adherents of a cosmopolitan approach, whether Liberals or Marxists.

As for the causes of poverty at the international and especially the global levels, several external and global factors can be mentioned as leading to poverty, as follows: inequalities in the international distribution of labour; the role of financial capital; unequal terms of trade exchange; economic and technological asymmetry among nations; the actual history of colonization of the developing countries; the international financial architecture; foreign direct investment (FDI) that has slowly made the developing economies into appendices of the multinational corporations; the external debt of developing nations; the international rules of the game and the design of the world economic order under the aegis of a neoliberal ideology; the type of institutions and policies other countries adopt (a mimicking process of development); and illegal transfers of resources to the multinational corporations (MNCs) (see Pogge 2005a; and Romero 2002, 147–55).

### What is inequality?

One of the alternative definitions of poverty is that of inequality, as a *relative* conceptualization of poverty. In this vein, people may be held to be poor because they are considered to be in disadvantage vis-à-vis other segments of society. To overcome inequality, it is clear that transfers from the rich to the poor can make a substantial dent on poverty in most societies. Moreover, if inequality is to be considered as a function of the social structure, as we examine in the Latin American context (Chapter 4), then poverty might be associated with a given social class or position (Spicker 1999, 155). In this sense, poverty reflects inequality, though the two concepts are not equivalent and should be disaggregated (see Sen 1981, 14–15, and 2009, 254–60; and Spicker 1999, 155).

*Poverty* refers to some *absolute measures* as specified above (standards of living, deprivation) that can be measured empirically. In contrast, *inequality* implies the *relative* economic wherewithal, social position, and disadvantage of an individual or group, in relation to others, as derived from rules – formal and customary – that literally determine *who shall be poor* (see Glen 2007, 154; Lowi 2002, 54; and Wolff and de-Shalit 2007, 3–6). Hence, *social inequality* is defined as *unequal access to highly valued material and non-material social goods and their unequal distribution, as well as the institutionalization of access to such central goods*, with reference to discrimination and injustice (Suter 2009, 419; see also Harris and Nef 2008a, 3). Similarly, in political terms, inequality refers to a subordinated or peripheral position in a given hierarchical structure, whether regional, international, or global.

This important distinction between poverty and inequality has clear implications about the way to cope with these two phenomena. Thus, for instance, the aim of diminishing *absolute poverty* implies a focus on economic growth as the major mechanism for poverty reduction. Alternatively, if we define poverty in *relative* terms as inequality, changes in inequality should be at the focus of reducing poverty, and this becomes in itself an eminent and prominent political issue. In this latter case, an important puzzle for understanding today's vast inequalities in the world is to understand how and why different countries and regions of the world have grown at different rates during the period of modern economic growth in the second half of the twentieth century and the early years of the twenty-first century (Sachs 2005, 30; see also Berry 2003b, 101; and Stiglitz 2002, 82).

There is nowadays a widespread consensus that poverty is a 'collective bad' (or international externality to globalization) that should be eradicated because it is morally wrong, economically inefficient, and socially undesirable. At the same time, there is no such consensus about the achievement of social equity for plain economic reasons, or of global equality in the broader international society. For example, according to neoliberal thought, inequality has been regarded as the necessary price that a society has to pay in order to achieve economic growth (De la Dehesa 2007, 27; see also Väyrynen 2008, 2).

Yet, since people (and by extrapolation also states) refer to each other in relative, rather than absolute, terms, inequality is considered a *social* and relative condition with clear *political* implications and ramifications. When a disproportionate number of people in any social category are present or absent from an empirically defined poverty class, then inequality becomes a political issue and a cause of unhappiness, envy, resentment, rebellion, instability, and political unrest.

Although the emphasis so far has been on the economic and social dimensions of inequality, we should keep in mind that the concept of inequality carries important political implications at the international level, as related to issues of hierarchy and structural discrimination. Claims about political equality (and inequality) have usually been articulated in relation to the domestic communities within sovereign states. Similarly, processes of economic accumulation and distribution are inherently considered unequal, according to the logic of global capitalism. In other words, the international arena tends to be an enactment of inequality in both economic and political realms, since by definition international politics is characterized by hierarchy and discrimination, beyond the formal (legal) equality of states. In this sense, the very logic of economic globalization creates and requires global duties of justice that should be implemented in a cosmopolitan, global realm (see Ish-Shalom 2008; Pasha and Murphy 2002, 2; and Walker 2002, 8, 13).

*Levels of analysis for the study of global income inequality* One of the most popular approaches to study inequality is the focus upon *income inequality* as a generic economic measurement for understanding

Table 1.1 *Differences between 'poverty' and 'inequality'*

| Category | Poverty | Inequality |
|---|---|---|
| Definitions | Lack of basic needs | Disadvantage |
| | Relative deprivation | Relative social position |
| | Lack of capabilities | Relative economic |
| | Lack of entitlement | wherewithal |
| | Multiple deprivation | Unequal access to goods |
| | Social exclusion | Unequal distribution |
| | Social inequality | Discrimination |
| | Moral deprivation | Injustice |
| | Lack of empowerment | |
| | Lack of participation | |
| | Vulnerability to external shocks | |
| Relational approach | Mostly absolute | Mostly relative |
| Normative consensus? | Yes (morally wrong) | No (claims of justice) |
| | Consensus on human rights | Lack of consensus on |
| | | distributive justice |
| Disciplinary approach | Mostly economic | Mostly political |
| | Sociological | Sociological |
| Levels of analysis | Domestic | Domestic |
| | International | International |
| | Global | Global |
| Measurement | Income poverty | Income inequality |
| | Extreme poverty | Gini coefficient |
| | Absolute poverty | HDI (social indicators) |
| | Relative poverty (poverty line) | |
| | HDI (social indicators) | |

problems of development in the Third World. Inequality in income distribution can be measured at three different levels of analysis, similar to poverty: between individuals in the same country, across countries, and across individuals globally (see De la Dehesa 2007, 115; and Keating 2008, 3).

At the first level, *intra-country inequality* refers to differences between individual incomes within national societies, as measured by the Gini coefficient. At the second level, *inter-state inequality*, the concept takes any given country as the unit of observation and uses its income or GDP per capita, it does not account for intra-country population disparity, and it compares across nations. At the third level, *global inequality*, the reference is to all individuals with their actual incomes, notwithstanding their national affiliation (see Glenn 2007; Milanovic 2005; and Mills 2009, 4).

The differences between poverty and inequality are summarized in Table 1.1. Table 1.1 illustrates the commonalities, overlapping, and differences between poverty and inequality. There is a normative consensus on the definition of poverty as a moral wrong that has to be amended, reduced, and even eradicated. By contrast, the concept of inequality is still morally and politically contested.

## Methodology and preview of the book

This book combines a plurality of research methods to tackle the relationship between globalization and the distribution of wealth, drawing on the disciplines of political economy and international relations within political science. In deductive terms, I posit the possible links between globalization, poverty, and inequality, drawing on the philosophical, theoretical, and ethical origins and backgrounds of those links, as posed by the three grand theories or paradigms of international relations – Realism, Liberalism, and Marxism (see Gilpin 1987; and Chapters 2 and 3 in this book). In inductive terms, I present a descriptive (mainly qualitative) analysis of the main indicators for globalization, poverty, and inequality in Latin America, with a particular emphasis upon the Argentine case, and to a lesser extent the cases of Brazil and Chile, between 1982 and 2008 (Chapters 4 and 5). Moreover, in the concluding chapter, I briefly introduce a regional comparative analysis that epitomizes the possible links between globalization, poverty, and inequality.

With the aim of providing a more complex and richer picture of reality, I adopt different methodologies and scopes for the same comparative method. First, I focus on the Latin American regional perspective (Chapter 4). Second, I examine a particularly illuminating case study; that of Argentina between 1982 and 2008. Third, I briefly compare the Argentine experience to that of the two other members of the so-called 'ABC countries', Brazil and Chile (Chapter 5). Finally, Chapter 6 offers a brief cross-regional comparison between Latin America and other developing regions, including East Asia, South Asia, the Middle East, and sub-Saharan Africa.

### *Why Latin America and Argentina in particular?*

*Latin America* has occupied a marginal place in most of the mainstream theorizing about globalization, despite its close integration into the global economy. This lacuna is more striking against the background of a rich Latin American research tradition on development, such as the *dependencia* (dependency) approach, which explains the Latin American underdevelopment as directly related to the economic hegemony of the North and the transnational links between the Northern economic elites and the Southern political elites (López-Alves and Johnson 2007, 10–11).

Much of the economic debate *within* Latin America at the turn of the twenty-first century has revolved around the effects of globalization and structural reform upon economic growth, poverty, and inequality, taking into consideration the fact that Latin America remains the most unequal region in the world in socio-economic terms, though the region is richer than South Asia, sub-Saharan Africa, and even East Asia. My discussion of Latin America will draw upon both Latin American and Northern (mostly US and British) sources, following a historical analysis and interpretation of the evolution of Latin American society, economy, and politics between 1982 and 2008.

As for *Argentina*, which seems to be a kind of extreme case analysis, I will use a qualitative analysis (single case study), based on Argentine sources, personal interviews, and archival research. The intriguing question for the choice of the Argentine case remains: to what extent can Argentina be considered a useful case study to explore the relevance of the links between globalization and the distribution of wealth? Argentina's road to default and economic and political crisis in 2001–2 has become an example of how complex the global economy has become, and how the dynamics of globalization might have paramount, if not devastating, effects upon particular developing countries.

In 2001 and 2002, Argentina's poverty and unemployment rates soared as the country defaulted on its astronomic foreign debt of about 180 billion dollars, precipitating a social, economic, and political crisis that led the country to the verge of institutional and economic collapse. The collapse of the Argentine economy was one of the most spectacular in modern history (Blustein 2005, 1). Critics of globalization saw the Argentine crisis of 2001–2 as a confirmation of their sceptical view regarding the neoliberal tenets of the 'Washington Consensus'. This extraordinary crisis of 2001–2 should and will be explained within the larger context of the evolution of the Argentine economy and politics since the 1970s, and most specifically after 1982. This fascinating story does not conclude in 2002 since Argentina, like the mythical phoenix, has resurrected again from its economic debacle.

### How to measure globalization?

In methodological terms, a simple measurement of economic globalization is crucial to determine its possible impact upon poverty and inequality outcomes, since *how* globalization is measured would determine *whether* globalization benefits or harms the poor. Although globalization remains a very complicated, broad, and complex construct, it is possible partially to operationalize and examine its impact, by focusing on several indexes of economic globalization, as follows (see Harrison 2007, 5; and Mills 2009, 10).[10]

(1) *The KOF economic globalization index* is a very useful index of economic globalization, composed of two dimensions: actual economic flows on the one hand, and restrictions on trade and capital on the other. The weight in the economic globalization index is a weighted average of *trade* as a percentage of gross domestic product (GDP) (given a 10 per cent in the index), *foreign direct investment (FDI) capital flows* as a percentage of GDP (10 per cent), *FDI capital stocks* as a percentage of GDP (12 per cent), *portfolio investment* as a percentage of GDP (8 per cent), *income payments to foreign nationals* as a percentage of GDP (10 per cent), *hidden import barriers* (11 per cent), *mean tariff rate* (14 per cent), *taxes on international trade as a percentage of current revenue* (14 per cent), and *capital account restrictions* (11 per cent). Next, this index is standardized to a scale of one to a hundred, where a hundred is the maximum value for globalization over the period 1970 to 2008 for all relevant countries, while one is the minimum value.

(2) *Trade*, as a percentage of GDP.

(3) *FDI* net flows, as a percentage of the GDP.

### How to measure poverty and inequality?

Since there are several possible definitions of poverty and inequality, the practical measurement of these two concepts focuses upon several indexes and proxy measurements that reflect both economic and social indicators, in addition to the standard measures of poverty as 'extreme' (less than $1 or $1.25 a day) and 'absolute' (less than $2 a day), as follows.

(1) *Unemployment*, as a percentage of the total labour force.

(2) *Illiteracy rate*, adult total, as a percentage of people aged fifteen and above.

(3) *Life expectancy at birth*, total (in number of years).

(4) *Percentage of poor persons*, as defined by income poverty and the drawing of a poverty national line.

---

[10] The indexes of globalization, poverty, and inequality were all prepared and selected by Gila Weinberger.

(5) *Percentage of indigent persons*, or measurement of *extreme poverty*, as a percentage of people living on less than 1$ a day (or $1.25 after 2005).

(6) As for inequality, I follow the mainstream approach in the literature on globalization and inequality, which focuses upon income inequality, as measured by a change in the *Gini coefficient*, which measures trends in within-country income inequality. The Gini coefficient illustrates the range between a perfectly equal distribution (0) to the highest possible condition of inequality where one person would hold all of the income (1) (see Milanovic 2005, 20; Mills 2009, 3; and Ravallion 2003).

(7) In addition, I utilize the *Human Development Index (HDI)* as a reliable proxy indicator of poverty, which is based on three equally weighted factors, life expectancy, education, and (the logarithm of) a purchasing-power parity estimate of per capita GDP (Fischer 2003, 11). Furthermore, I also disaggregate the measurement of the HDI into its three distinctive components (see Chapters 4 and 5).

### A preview of the book

In this introductory chapter, I have clarified the major concepts and set the *problematique*. In the next chapter ('The ethical and practical implications of poverty and inequality'), I briefly present the ethical and prudential argumentations with respect to the linkages between globalization, poverty, and inequality. The normative context includes a discussion of distributive justice and human rights. Moreover, the pragmatic context refers to issues of international security and international political economy.

In Chapter 3 ('The political dimension of the links between globalization and the distribution of wealth'), I assess the different paradigms of international political economy that underlie and explain the possible links between globalization, poverty, and inequality (i.e., Realism, Liberalism, and Marxism). The core of the chapter centres upon the development of a political, *intermestic* model that emphasizes the role of political actors (mainly states) as intermediaries or active 'transmission belts' between globalization and the international (regional and global) structures, on the one hand, and its domestic political and social consequences within states, on the other.

In Chapter 4 ('The Latin American experience, 1982–2008'), I depict the historical waves of globalization in Latin America, including the debt crisis of 1982, the 'lost decade' of the 1980s, the formulation and implementation of the 'Washington Consensus' in the late 1980s and the 1990s, and the early 2000s. I address the so-called 'Latin American puzzle' of poverty and inequality, and outline the major possible causal links between globalization and the distribution of wealth in the region. Finally, I depict the political *intermestic* model and its possible implementation.

In Chapter 5 ('The Argentine experience in a comparative perspective, 1982–2008'), I locate the Argentine crisis of 2001–2 within the larger temporal context (1982–2008) that preceded and followed it. I address the alternative explanations for the crisis of 2001–2 and reintroduce the possible theoretical links between globalization and the distribution of wealth, applying them to the Argentine case. Furthermore, I examine the different social and economic policies adopted by the Argentine state to cope with poverty and inequality between 1982 and 2008. Finally, I briefly compare the similar and different trajectories of Argentina, Brazil, and Chile.

In Chapter 6 ('Regional comparisons and policy implications'), I ask two additional questions. First, can we extrapolate from the findings in the Latin American context to ascertain similar situations in other developing regions, such as sub-Saharan Africa, East Asia and Southeast Asia, South Asia, and the Middle East? Second, which lessons can be drawn from the harsh realities of Latin America in general, and of Argentina in particular?

## Conclusions

This book takes up the challenge formulated by Robert Gilpin about a decade ago, regarding the difficult, if not impossible, task of evaluating the contradictory assessments of economic globalization and its consequences (Gilpin 2000, 301). The inconclusive debate among economists and social scientists in general about the possible economic and social effects of globalization upon poverty and inequality has obscured the political dimension and relevance of this debate for international relations and political science scholars. The major task in this book is then to stress the political dimension, and to develop a political model that emphasizes the role of states in mediating between the structural forces of globalization and its domestic reverberations.

For that purpose, I present the *problematique* of relating globalization to the distribution of wealth, in terms of poverty and inequality, and develop different operational definitions of these three concepts. To narrow down the already encompassing agenda of the book, I focus on *economic globalization* and point out the different *economic and social* dimensions in the definitions of *poverty and inequality*. While there is a normative (moral) consensus regarding poverty, there is not such an agreement as for inequality, which makes the latter an inherently contested political issue at the domestic, international, and global levels of analysis.

It is evident that globalization produces both winners and losers among the rich and the poor, but who they are and what political implications we might infer from this divide remain moot issues. How much can we generalize from this simple truism across different regions of the developing world (Harrison 2007, 4)? In terms of international relations, the extent of poverty and inequality considered as a *global issue* will eventually determine, among other factors, the legitimacy of globalization as the defining economic and political project of the twenty-first century.

# 2    The ethical and practical implications of poverty and inequality

The moral man is giving way to the commercial man.

(Rabindranath Tagore)

Often the moral thing to do is also strategically correct.

(Paul Wolfowitz)

Eradicating poverty is an ethical, social, political, and economic imperative of humankind.

(Monterrey Conference, 2002)

The analysis of the links between globalization and the distribution of wealth is not just a futile academic exercise for the sake of theorizing in international relations. We should seriously care about the implications and consequences of poverty and inequality in both ethical and practical terms. Coping with poverty is a moral obligation; addressing inequality might be sound politics, even if there is an apparent trade-off between political concerns and economic efficiency. But we cannot allow ourselves the luxury of ignoring them, since they carry both moral and practical consequences that affect the way we think about globalization; and thus, in turn, how globalization affects our lives.

The effects of globalization upon the international system and international relations in general have not only been economic and social in nature; globalization has led as well to major changes of normative and political significance. To a certain extent, the legitimacy and success of globalization have come to depend on its perceived effects on poverty and inequality, especially in the Third World, which remain quite moot and unclear (Väyrynen 2008, 1–2).

The end of the Cold War raised the expectations about the possibility of creating a new and better global economic order, a 'new world order', based on lofty ideas of social and economic justice at the global level, in order to reduce poverty and inequality. Unfortunately, this New International Economic Order never fully materialized, and a significant part of the blame has been pointed at the tenets of the neoliberal ideology as a particular version of globalization, known as the 'Washington Consensus' or 'market fundamentalism', in favour of privatization, liberalization, and the shrinking of the welfare state (Stiglitz 2008, 71).

It is not necessarily the case that poverty and inequality have increased as a consequence of globalization in the last twenty years, but it is rather a fact that nowadays we are more aware, both in normative and in practical terms, of its potentially pernicious consequences, especially in the context of North–South relations.[1] The more people interact with each other, see on their TV screens, and navigate through the Internet the vastly different levels of wealth enjoyed by humankind in different countries, the greater is their awareness of poverty and inequality gaps.

In other words, the technological digital revolution and globalization have created a revolution of rising expectations, and have contributed to the sharpening of the perceptions of poverty and especially of inequality, regardless of whether poverty and inequality have actually increased or not (Milanovic 2005, 155). Moreover, the fundamental change in the international order at the end of the Cold War suggests a political explanation of the growing attention for global issues, such as poverty and inequality, or at least facilitates their framing as potential global issues.

In this context, we should also differentiate between the two related, though different, problems of poverty and inequality. While there is a general moral consensus among the rich countries that poverty must be eradicated because it is economically inefficient, socially undesirable, and morally intolerable, the same level of agreement is lacking with reference to inequality, which is a much more politically, economically, and socially contested phenomenon (see De la Dehesa 2007, 127; and Väyrynen 2008).

From the preliminary analysis of Chapter 1, we infer that the links between globalization, poverty, and inequality are complex and ambiguous, due to the potential mutual effects of the relationships (Anan 2000, 22). In other words, it is not only globalization that might affect poverty in positive or negative directions, but also the other way around. Poverty is considered nowadays as a 'global bad' (or ill) that calls for concerted collective action. In a globalized world, national societies everywhere might gain from a reduction in poverty, due to the negative externalities associated with it, such as social and political conflict, the spread of diseases, and harm to the environment (World Bank 2001, 1). Thus, before we turn to a detailed analysis of the nature and causal effects of the links between globalization and the distribution of wealth in Chapter 3, we should pause and ask the crucial question: why should we be concerned with poverty and inequality in the first place?

---

[1] I would like to thank Claudia Kedar and Eytan Meyers for their comments on this point.

There are two possible answers to this question: normative (moral or ethical), and prudential (pragmatic and practical). I argue that the answers to the question must first be framed in normative terms, and only then in prudential and pragmatic ones. Although any attribution of normative values in politics tends to be pragmatic and policy-oriented, I believe that we should first determine our values and principles, so the normative should take priority over the prudential.[2]

The normative answer to our discussion of globalization, poverty, and inequality follows the debates about redistributive justice and economic and social human rights of the 1970s and 1980s, against the background of the Third World demands for a New International Economic Order (NIEO), which eventually failed and did not affect substantially the North–South relations. Quite independently from the failed demands of the Third World then, a vibrant debate exists nowadays in political philosophy and international ethics regarding the issue-area of 'duties beyond borders' and redistributive justice in our globalized world.[3]

At the same time, the prudential or pragmatic answer focuses on the possible disruptive effects of poverty and inequality upon the international system and society, including issues of war and peace, national and regional conflicts, humanitarian emergencies and other human and natural disasters, political stability and democratization, environmental deterioration, and new security issues and threats, such as terrorism, illicit drug trafficking, spread of diseases, population resettlement, and refugees and illegal migration flows.

Beyond the positive utilitarian interest in the economic well-being, growth, and development of the Third World, the rich countries of the North have an obvious stake in neutralizing and avoiding the security threats that partly stem from poverty, inequality, joblessness, and social disintegration. Thus, as globalization and interdependence have transformed the global security agenda, poverty and inequality have emerged as one of the most pressing contemporary issues in world politics (see Mansbach and Rhodes 2003; and Speth 1999, 324). In sum, in a cost-benefit analysis, poverty and inequality might be costly to economic, social, and political stability (see Frank 2010).

From a normative (ethical) standpoint, the persistence of poverty, increasing inequality, and human deprivation diminishes us all as human beings. Poverty as destitution and lack of entitlements stands against human decency, human rights, and basic claims of distributive justice.

[2] Noemi Gal-Or, personal correspondence with the author, 1 April 2006.
[3] I would like to thank Piki Ish-Shalom for his thorough comments throughout this chapter.

Moreover, from a practical standpoint, poverty and extreme inequality are an international externality that can disrupt and derail the economic forces of globalization, promote political violence, translate into political instability and social unrest, and therefore undermine democracy (see Speth 1999, 321; and Weede 2000).

In addition to the economic arguments in favour of free trade and financial flows as leading to economic growth and to development (and thus reducing poverty), it should be emphasized that the persistence of poverty endangers global peace and security as well. The way in which the international system and society deal with poverty is likely to determine whether the coming decades will be relatively peaceful and stable, or relatively violent and dangerous (see Mansbach and Rhodes 2003; and Nel 2000).

Philosophers of economic development such as Thomas Pogge have recently worked on developing ideas that might bring together the normative and pragmatic approaches. That is, ideas such as bringing together private interests (of commercial firms and MNCs) and other social and political forces (such as NGOs and national governments) into establishing an international fund for eradicating some of the pernicious consequences of poverty; for example, the lack of access to medical prescriptions due to legal protection of pharmaceutical inventions. The idea here would be that it will be in the interest of private businesses to relinquish control over their inventions in order to be rewarded according to the results of their free provision of such medicines to the poorest populations of the world.[4]

The realities of poverty and inequality affected (or not) by globalization might be a serious cause for the growth of social violence, political and social instability, ethnic conflicts, and civil and international wars that shape the global system. For instance, poverty and inequality directly linked to over-population, resource scarcity, and environmental degradation as witnessed in West Africa have been a direct source of social conflicts, civil wars, and the generation of refugee flows in that region of the world (Hurrell 1999, 260).

As Robert Kaplan argued, 'Precisely because a large part of Africa is staring into the abyss, it gives a foretaste of how wars, frontiers, and ethnic politics will look a few decades from now' (quoted in Martin and Schumann 1997, 25). These are indeed gloomy and pessimistic arguments and statements that indicate the relevance, and even urgency, of the issues at stake.

---

[4] I would like to thank Luis Roniger for his comments on this point.

## The ethical dimension: human rights and distributive justice

### Poverty as a global moral problem

*In principle*, there seems to be enough room for a normative compatibility between the scope of globalization (universal and cosmopolitan, by definition) and that of moral and ethical issues, which are also inherently universal. Thus, if there are any truths of morality, then surely they are supposed to be universal, which is to say, *global* truths (Goodin 2003, 71). Yet, this cosmopolitan logic contradicts the realities of the Westphalian state system.

Thinking ethically about problems of world politics, including poverty and inequality, does not contradict the logic of globalization. Hence, our moral judgment on poverty and inequality does not necessarily condemn globalization of being unjust. To the contrary, globalization might be a morally good thing, at least in principle, since its universalizing and cosmopolitan tendencies coincide with the universalism of morality itself (Goodin 2003, 78). Thus, for instance, there seems to be a global moral obligation, in terms of human rights and of distributive justice, to help the developing countries to eradicate poverty, and there is even a moral consensus that 'there is no more commanding moral imperative for people in the West than to urge each other, and their governments, to bring relief to the world's poorest' (*Economist*, 13 March 2004, 13).

*In practice*, however, there are serious and practical obstacles in translating universal principles of social justice into policy measures at the global level, due to the stark contrast between the universal, cosmopolitan, transnational, and non-state logic of economic globalization and the political division of the world into an international system of states, characterized by political and economic hierarchy, inequality, and marginalization (see, for instance, Sen 2009, 388–415). Thus, we need to search for a sustainable *ethics of development* in the North–South relations, in which economic globalization should be subjected to moral and ethical considerations, while respecting international legal standards and principles of sovereignty (see Grinspun 2003, 17 and 83; Rawls 1999 and 2005; Robinson 2002, 5; and Sen 2009, 225–52).

We have to be aware that it is precisely the principles of sovereignty and non-intervention that stand both against globalization and the enforcement of universal moral norms. Moreover, given the premise that the Westphalian international system preceded what we call globalization, one can argue that processes of globalization are fundamentally embedded in the basic premises of the pre-existing international system, which by definition is not cosmopolitan.[5]

## Poverty and the logic of human rights

Human rights represent the basic normative common ground to fight poverty and to understand, in normative terms, our human and universal concern with the moral implications of globalization. Building an ethical and sustainable form of globalization is not exclusively a human rights matter, but it must include the recognition of a shared responsibility for the universal protection of basic human rights (Robinson 2002, 5). Basic considerations of sheer humanity, basic needs, and socio-economic human rights lead rich countries to help poor ones in extreme cases of humanitarian catastrophes and emergencies, such as relief of distress and famines. If extreme poverty is considered as a basic violation of social and economic human rights, then there is an inherent moral obligation to correct that violation.

Conversely, human rights abuses might in turn lead to poverty and to impoverishment. Violations of other rights of persons (other than their right not to be extremely poor) also cause poverty. Hence, there is an intrinsic link between poverty and (the lack of) human rights. Yet, it should be pointed out that this normative consensus limits itself only to cases of absolute deprivation. Thus, from this perspective, there is not much obligation to redistribute resources beyond a minimal guarantee of a basic human standard. In this sense, the distance from a human rights analysis of moral obligation and a prudential or rational justification to the eradication of poverty is very short indeed; the two might overlap in practice.

There is no necessary trade-off between economic development and human rights, if we think of economic development in broader, non-economic terms of human development, rather than narrowing our discussion just to issues of economic growth and personal income. Following Amartya Sen, we can think of economic development as a process of expanding the real freedoms that people enjoy; thus, prompting and fostering basic human rights, defined in terms of capabilities (Sen 1999, 3–4, and 2009, 366–71). Those freedoms depend on other determinants, including social and economic arrangements (access to health care and to education), as well as political and civil rights. In this sense, we can refer to poverty as deprivation of basic capabilities that are intrinsically important, rather than merely as low income (Sen 1999, 3–4 and 87–8).

---

[5]  I would like to thank Mor Mitrani and Daniel Schwartz for their insights on those issues.

According to this logic, a just international order would be one in which basic human rights were universally protected, or at least human capabilities would be assured, and in which actors in the international arena, corporations as well as states, would conduct themselves so as to avoid exploiting either individuals or other collective human groups.

It seems to me that the normative differentiation between human rights (as related to poverty) and distributive justice (as related to inequality) serves only analytical and heuristic purposes. In reality, it is difficult to disentangle those two. For instance, it is clear that the enormous and even grotesque disparities in wealth and income in the world might have damaging and disabling effects upon the development of human capabilities (Derber 1998, 148). In other words, inequality might lead to poverty, and the lack of some form of global justice might conduce to the violation of basic human rights. Moreover, one can argue that human rights are not always limited to justice. Thus, moral perspectives on human rights do not necessarily focus on justice.[6]

*Inequality and the logic of distributive justice*

The second normative theme, distributive justice, is often ignored in the arguments presented by mainstream economists of globalization, since it is directly related to social equality and inequality, rather than to poverty alleviation. Yet, issues of inequality and global (in)justice have become the major focus of the anti-globalization social movements around the world, as demonstrated recently in the 2011 worldwide protests calling for 'social justice', since they carry significant political implications.

Clearly, the globalization process creates both winners and losers, giving to the latter strong normative arguments to oppose the entire process. It is worth noting that the pressures from these penalized groups have led countries and international organizations alike to start thinking about the redistribution of wealth (addressing questions of equity and inequality), as important as redistribution of income (addressing questions of poverty).

For instance, former Brazilian President Fernando Henrique Cardoso used to say that Brazil is not an underdeveloped country, but rather an unjust country. Thus, the elimination of injustice as an ethical goal and as a preliminary and indispensable condition for economic development should be regarded, according to the critiques of neoliberalism, as the responsibility of all the countries in the world (quoted in Ferrer 1998, 204–5).

[6] I would like to thank Daniel Schwartz for his comments on this point.

Yet, distributive justice and the global eradication or reduction of poverty are more complicated and more difficult to reach and to apply in international relations in a cosmopolitan setting, in contrast to the eradication of poverty and the promotion of basic human rights within a domestic, national setting. To start with, there is no normative international consensus whatsoever for a moral case for reducing inequalities among states, or for reforming the global economic system, in the name of social and distributive justice beyond borders, rather than just promoting human rights.

Following the formulation of the late philosopher John Rawls, and according to Thomas Pogge and other Liberal Cosmopolitans, justice as fairness should be interpreted in terms of equal rights, reciprocity, global equity, and some form of redistribution of the global resources from the 'haves' to the 'have-nots'. As part of a hypothetical and ideal social contract, fairness implies that the poor should share in the gains of society as it grows, while the rich should share in the pains of society in times of crises. Social and economic inequalities are then admissible, but only in so far as they are to the greatest benefit of the least advantaged members of society.

Yet, Rawls himself never suggested that a scheme of global redistribution should be or could be put in practice easily at the global level, beyond the realm of the domestic society, or that it would be desirable to start with. Instead, Rawls offered a Liberal internationalist compromise to both respect and enhance human rights, but at the same time safeguarding the principles of sovereignty and non-intervention for all nations (see Dallmayr 2002; Nel 2000; Rawls 1971, 7, 12, 73, 83, and 1999; Sen 2009, 52–74; and Stiglitz 2002, 78).

Second, the logic of globalization might create an inherent tension between economic freedom and economic and social justice. Under conditions of globalization, the economic logic suggests that safeguarding the well-being of the least advantaged sectors of society might require at times policies that provide incentives to capital and highly skilled labour (the advantaged sectors of society), thus exacerbating levels of inequality within society, at least in the short term (this is the economic law known as the Kuznets' effect). This is why many political theorists think Rawls was not really so egalitarian.

From an egalitarian point of view, economic globalization can be normatively justified only if the less disadvantaged are compensated out of the benefits accruing to the gainers, a possibility that is difficult to implement, at both the domestic and especially the international levels. And yet, a more optimistic account of the advances in reducing poverty and inequality in the last twenty years might reach the conclusion that the global economic order is not fundamentally unjust, but instead, 'rather incompletely just' (see Dallmayr 2002, 137–44; *Economist*, 13 March 2004, 13; Koenig-Archibugi 2003, 6–7; and Risse 2005).

Third, our contemporary global economic system tends to ignore or shy away from issues of distribution as fairness, as demonstrated by the 'Washington Consensus' policies, that paid little attention to issues of destitution or fairness (Stiglitz 2002, 78), while following the logic of economic quasi-Darwinism through the forces of the market, according to the neoliberal credo of 'market fundamentalism'. Thus, the difficulties in trying to implement a scheme of global redistributive justice in international relations remains enormous, as long as we do not have in place a global polity that will guarantee maximum equal access to resources (or equal opportunity) to every member of the human community on a cosmopolitan, transnational basis. This is the new agenda of projecting global governance without a concomitant world government.

Cosmopolitan Liberals such as Charles Beitz and Thomas Pogge challenge these three qualifications against the case for cosmopolitan distributive justice. In their account, global poverty and global inequality are both ethical and global issues, which should be urgently tackled with. The rich countries cannot disown all interest in global poverty and inequality; to some extent, according to this cosmopolitan logic, the fate of every individual in the world affects us, or, even more importantly, we affect, in turn, the fate of each individual. Accordingly, distributional justice should be the same thing within and across nations (Milanovic 2007, 15).

In Pogge's account, the global poor have a compelling moral claim to some of the rich countries' affluence, based on a long history of colonial exploitation by the North and dependence of the South (see Pogge 2005a and 2005b). In his view, there is a compelling case for a *global justice* analysis that takes issue with Sen's explanations of poverty that focus on national and sub-national institutions and the policies of local and national governments. By contrast, Pogge brings to the fore the non-indigenous, external explanations for poverty that stem from the *global context*: the international rules of the game, the design of the world economic order, and the grand rules of the world economy; the dual identity of the elites of the developing countries, which act in relation with their own constituencies but also in a clientelistic fashion vis-à-vis foreign actors, such as the MNCs; the international recognition, international borrowing, and resources privileges, which guarantee that any successor democratizing governments inherit the debts of their previous authoritarian regimes (like in Latin America); and international resources privileges, that promote the illegal transfers of resources to the MNCs, as a kind of looting (see Pogge 2005a and 2005b).

This discussion about the normative arguments for global justice reveals the disagreement that still exists in this subject. The moral consensus refers only to the responsibility of the rich to help the poorest nations, in order to reduce or eliminate absolute standards of deprivation, such as famines, which are considered as basic violations of human rights. Yet, there is little evidence of any widespread moral consensus for the alleviation or reduction of inequalities within or between states, or for reforming the international economic system in the name of social and economic global redistributive justice (Woods 1999, 12, 16; see also Milanovic 2005, 158). Notwithstanding this normative debate, we should care about inequality (and not only about poverty), since growing inequalities might have powerful political consequences as well (Fischer 2003, 12).

## The prudential/pragmatic dimension: issues of security and political economy

As mentioned above, our concern regarding the implications of poverty and inequality is not only normative and moral, but also grounded on pragmatic, prudential, practical, and *realpolitik* terms of cost-benefit analysis. We should care about the mutual relationships between globalization and the distribution of wealth since there are at stake crucial issues of security (war and peace), and political economy (well-being and welfare). In this context, a central structural feature of our contemporary world is the emergence of a group of weak states and economies in the Third World that have not been able to benefit from economic globalization and from political democratization, thus posing increasing challenges to the stability of the international economic order, and even more, to global peace and security (see Callaghy 2001).

### Security arguments

In terms of security, the way in which the 'world' (meaning by that mainly the developed countries) copes with poverty and inequality is likely to determine whether the coming decades will be relatively peaceful and stable or violent and dangerous, and to what extent the current international order will not be disrupted. Moreover, according to human security approaches, humanitarian concerns are security problems per se.

In simplistic and dichotomy terms, we could think of our globalized world as composed of two different spheres of security. The first sphere of security exists in the North, in the advanced industrialized and democratic states, and it is characterized by relative peace, prosperity, and stability; it is a zone of peace. The second sphere of security is the realm of insecurity, a zone of war and conflict that prevails in and between many underdeveloped or developing countries of the South (the former Third World), and it is usually characterized by war, poverty, anarchy, and instability; it is punctuated by crises of migration, international terrorism, drug trafficking, AIDS epidemics, and environmental decay. In other words, global poverty and inequality might be a serious cause of global insecurity, not only with reference to the Third World, but to the international system as a whole (see Hillal Desouki 1993). In this sense, we can refer to poverty as both a cause and an effect of global insecurity.

As mentioned throughout the chapter, poverty produces frustration and anger, directed both at the governments of developing countries and at citizens of wealthy countries (Mansbach and Rhodes 2003). Moreover, the terrorist attacks on the United States in September 2001 resolved the discussion over whether poverty, marginalization, and the lack of development were only a humanitarian concern or a security problem as well. Resentment and rage against the United States and the West in general stemmed out of humiliation, not always as a result of inequality. Inequality gives rise to jealousy and envy, not necessarily to terrorism. Yet, the resentment is the fertile soil where terrorists might flourish, since they need the support of the civilian population. Thus, although the exact nature of the links between poverty, inequality, and global terrorism remains a matter of contention, it is clear that the renewed US interest in enlarging its aid and development to Third World countries stems from a clear anti-terrorist motivation, rather than just an altruistic drive (Mathews 2002, 9). Interestingly enough, the frustration and anger do not always come from the poor and underdeveloped, but at times from the rich and developed individuals and states, who claim to serve as their voice.

Furthermore, in cases of virulent domestic conflicts, the problem of poverty directly relates to international and civil wars, flows of illegal and legal migrations, refugees, environmental degradation, the spread of diseases, and threats to the existing international order emanating from demands of international and global justice, instrumented occasionally through terrorist and guerrilla activities. At the domestic level, there is also a clear relationship between urban poverty and criminality and violence. One of the common explanations for that is that economic inequality and the extreme vulnerability of the poor lead them to turn to crime as a means of survival, so that as poverty increases, violent crime rises accordingly. Regardless of the causes of increasing urban violence, its consequences are a growing matter of concern as an economic and social development issue, at the level of state–society relations (Moser 1998, 85).

To sum up, we should care about poverty and inequality since they have become part and parcel of the growing security agenda of the new millennium. Since the impact of globalization upon the developing states in the Third World is ambiguous and uneven, we should watch out for the disruptive effects of poverty and inequality back into the global system, as an unstable component and catalyst for wars, disasters, humanitarian emergencies, domestic and regional instability, environmental degradation, terrorism, refugees, and both legal and illegal migration flows.

### Political economy arguments

In terms of political economy, serious considerations of practicality and pragmatism should justify our concern with poverty and inequality, and their complex relationships with economic globalization. In our globalized world, there are different ways for the rich countries to help the poor ones: export capital to them, transfer technology from the North to the South, import products from them, or 'import' the global poor from the Third World through the easing of the political borders and the encouragement of migration flows, which are the source of remittances to their countries of origin (Gilpin quoted in Doyle 2000).

Due to the inherent, though asymmetrical, economic interdependence of the global economy, it makes perfect economic (and good common) sense to care about the economic growth and development of the developing world. As long as people live in poverty, their ability to contribute to economic growth, opportunity, and consumption is less than it could potentially be. In other words, poor people (and poor states) are also markets that we could sell to them, if they cease to be poor.[7] We should keep in mind that the developing countries are going to account in the next forty or so years for almost 90 per cent of the world's population and are going to be in the future the largest markets for the developed and the developing countries alike (De la Dehesa 2007, 9).

---

[7] I would like to thank David Pervin for his comments on this point.

Ours is a small world, after all. Nowadays, a considerable portion of the trade of the United States and Europe is geared towards several developing countries, where most of the world population lives. Moreover, those countries represent not only potential and emerging markets but also sources of indispensable raw materials. Thus, the costs of neglecting the rapidly growing international economic class divide, with its concomitant social and economic gaps, will be immense not just for the developing world, but also for the entire humankind, reaped in terms of environmental degradation, humanitarian disasters, and lack of economic growth and development. Hence, the West must have the foresight to act now regarding the South (Speth 1999, 17).

In this utilitarian and cost-benefit analysis about the economic fate of the developing countries, we can identify an interesting convergence between normative and practical arguments. Focusing resources and investing in policy and planning on poverty can be worthwhile simply on humanitarian grounds (the normative argument of promoting human rights and reducing inequality). And yet, the disadvantages of growing up in extreme poverty pose a challenge to a belief in the principle of equality of opportunity, both within and across nations (*Economist*, 16 June 2001, 11–12).

In times of economic crises, anger about inequality comes to the fore, having strong political and social consequences, since in good economic times even the poor feel better off. Therefore, helping the poor and the underclass to rejoin society is in the interests of all, at both the domestic and international levels. Thus, there is a strong *political economy* argument why we should be concerned about poverty and inequality, due to their economic *and* political implications (Väyrynen 2008, 5–7). Hence, normative (moral) and pragmatic (cost-benefit) arguments tend to converge and reinforce each other, rather than contradicting each other.

### Conclusions

In this brief chapter, I have presented two major normative and pragmatic arguments as to why we should be concerned with the economic, social, and political implications of poverty and inequality, as stemming from the potential effects of economic globalization. Even if globalization is not considered as a major cause of poverty and inequality, we should still care about the implications of this 'collective bad' (or global externalities), which might impinge back upon the local economic forces of globalization, affecting our political and normative interpretation of the pros and cons of the global economy.

48 Globalization and the Distribution of Wealth

As with many other political issues, the reading of the possible links between globalization, poverty, and inequality is first and foremost a matter of perception and of collective awareness. As the world becomes more integrated through processes of globalization, people across the globe are more aware of differences in their incomes and standards of living, so we might be coping with a kind of revolution of rising expectations that might challenge our conceptions and views of globalization and carry potent political implications both domestically and internationally. This process of increased mutual awareness is not confined to the poor world only, but also to the rich world as well (Milanovic 2005, 155–6).

At both the *domestic* and *global level*, I argued that issues of poverty and inequality should concern us in terms of violation of human rights, and of distributive justice. Moreover, they might become also a source of political resistance, social and political turmoil, violence, revolution, and political change. As a general proposition, one can argue that economic failure – a national economy stuck in a poverty trap, hyperinflation, or a debt default – often leads to state failure as well, and it is a certain source for political troubles (Sachs 2005, 332).

At the *international level*, inequality in particular is considered as a volatile political issue. Critiques of globalization in its neoliberal version argue that 'the international is an enactment of inequality' (Pasha and Murphy 2002, 2), and that 'the problem of inequality is already deeply inscribed in our modern account of the international, and thus of modern politics' (Walker 2002, 21). According to this critical view, the process of intensified global inequalities, exacerbated by the neoliberal path to economic development, is being challenged nowadays in an alternative form of global politics called 'the clash of globalizations', through the enactment of new forms of political agency, especially in the South, in the form of transnational social movements that stand against the neoliberal expression of globalization, while being part and parcel of the social fabric of a potential global civil society that promotes globalization from below, such as the Porto Alegre Forum (Gill 2002, 47; see also Falk 2009, 57–79; and Väyrynen 2008, 14). This 'clash of globalizations' might draw a more accurate picture of the world, rather than the fallacy of a 'clash of civilizations' in the form of a war of cultures.

Second, the importance attributed to the problems of poverty and inequality should not be framed exclusively in normative or prudential terms. It is not a question of morality versus interests, but rather, like the *problematique* of peaceful territorial change that I examined many years ago, a matter of finding a delicate equilibrium between considerations of morality and considerations of power (Kacowicz 1994, 239–40). Thus, in coping with poverty and inequality one should *be prudent and moral at the same time.* Poverty is associated with a variety of difficult problems and issues; for instance, 17 million people die each year in the developing world from curable diseases like malaria; 90 per cent of HIV carriers live in the poor countries (see Mansbach and Rhodes 2003). It is a matter of *both* moral and practical concern, both at the domestic and at the international levels.

# 3 The political dimension of the links between globalization and the distribution of wealth

One of the reasons that the debate about poverty and inequality has become a relevant issue in the study of international relations is that there are currently strong claims and counter-claims as to the effects globalization has had upon the distribution of wealth in economic, social, and political terms. It is becoming more and more evident, both rhetorically and in the actual practice of states and international institutions, that there are relevant and important links between globalization, poverty, and inequality. Yet, the evidence remains ambiguous, and there is an ideological debate among the different paradigms of international political economy (and by extension of international relations in general) with respect to the *significance* of these possible links.

For instance, the United Nations Development Programme (UNDP) recognizes, and even suggests, that countries should link their anti-poverty programmes not only to their national policies, but also to their foreign economic and financial policies, integrated into the world global economy, due to political and moral considerations. Moreover, since the debt crisis of 1982, which heavily affected the Latin American countries, it has become evident, at least in the Latin American context, that there is a direct relationship between external debt, poverty, and increasing inequality within the Latin American countries (see UNDP 2000, 10; see also Dollar and Kraay 2002 and 2004; Glenn 2007, 177; Mills 2009, 1; Nissanke and Thorbecke 2010; and Wade 2004).

What remains ambiguous in this debate is the character and direction of these links, ultimately interpreted according to the divergent paradigms of international political economy and the disparate normative (moral) views of international relations, such as the debate between Liberals, Radicals, and Realists (Keating 2008, 4). For instance, the Liberal view of global economic relations, which assumes the mechanism of 'mutual' (or 'complex') interdependence, regards international economic relations between developed and developing countries as mutually beneficial and benign, as a kind of win-win strategic game to the benefit of all humankind. According to this Liberal view, globalization stimulates

50

economic growth in developing nations, thus reducing and eventually eradicating poverty, by allowing the forces of the market to play out freely without any state intervention, leading to global economic integration.

By contrast, the Radical views sustain that the global economic relations between North and South are highly asymmetrical, and even approximate a type of zero-sum relationship, according to which the forces of economic globalization exacerbate poverty and inequality both within and between countries (Kim 2000, 1; and Mills 2009, 1). In essence, this discussion is also about the nature and substance of globalization itself.

Hence, the relationship between economic globalization, poverty, and inequality is inherently ambiguous, and the existing confusion in the literature is aggravated by the contradictory statistical gathering of evidence and by a tendency of both sides of the debate to claim an unreasonable degree of causation in one way or another (Aisbett 2007, 37). Furthermore, it is evident that economic globalization creates both winners and losers, since it does not necessarily homogenize the human condition; rather, at times it polarizes society, both at the local and global levels; hence, the tendency to increasing inequality. The divide here is not only between winners and losers but also between optimistic and pessimistic schools of thought about the consequences of globalization, alternating between benign and malign impacts. While the alleged benefits are deemed large, the potential damage is always viewed as even more dramatic (Berry 2003a, 15).

In addition to these two possible contradictory perspectives (Liberals vs Radicals), there are other, alternative explanations for the global scale of poverty and inequality that might not be necessarily related to economic globalization. For instance, Robert Wade focuses on a multicausal explanation that includes factors such as differential population growth; the debt trap; technological change; and the decline in the terms of trade against primary commodities in favour of secondary and tertiary products (see Wade 2004). Similarly, Nancy Birdsall emphasizes the internal (domestic) characteristics of countries as a better explanation for poverty and inequality than just economic globalization, including divergent economic policies; unequal land distribution; quality of governance; and level of democracy (quoted in Glenn 2007, 173; see also Wolf 2004, 140). Another compelling explanation refers to the importance of the economic structure within countries as a determinant of poverty and inequality. For instance, it is easier for a government to enact progressive social policies when the structure of the economy is based upon an export-led growth stemming from labour-intensive goods than in a country whose economic structure is based upon primary resources and raw materials.

In this chapter, I particularly emphasize the relevance of political factors in explaining the links between globalization and the distribution of wealth according to an *intermestic* model that considers the relevance of both domestic and international political variables. Moreover, there might be a two-way relationship between globalization, poverty, and inequality; for instance, poverty might substantially affect globalization as well. This is an important claim to make since in many ways it refutes the neoliberal perspective that focuses only on one possible direction; i.e., that globalization reduces poverty and inequality.

This claim could also be seen as the continuation of another important debate in political economy – the arguments between the neoclassic liberals and Keynesianism in the 1930s. Before the economic crises of the late 1920s, conservative (i.e., Liberal) economists viewed the national economy as relying almost solely upon economic market forces – i.e., perceiving them as forces of nature that cannot be tamed or controlled. Hence, policymakers could at best hope to adjust their policies to these natural forces. However, the negative externalities of those economic forces, such as the growing poverty and inequality, forced the paradigmatic shift to the Keynesian revolution in the 1930s and 1940s, which provided decision-makers with policy tools to moderate such externalities, giving birth to the modern welfare state and placing a renewed policy emphasis upon fiscal policy. After the recent global economic crisis of 2008–9, this might happen again.[1]

To sum up, it is very difficult to assess the consequences of economic globalization upon poverty and inequality, due to the contradictory accounts put forth by scholars, especially economists. In order to link globalization to poverty and inequality, it is necessary to examine the potential *causal mechanisms* between globalization and growing or decreasing poverty and inequality in the world, such as the Singer–Prebisch argument about the deteriorating terms of trade in the economic relationship between developed and developing countries, as a function of the unbalanced structure between the developed North and the developing or less-developed South.[2] In this book, I particularly pay attention to two potential avenues of such causal linkage: openness to trade (trade liberalization), and capital flows (financial liberalization) (see Harrison 2007, 20; Milanovic 2007, 12; and Prasad et al. 2007, 457).

In the following pages, I examine the links between globalization and the distribution of wealth, with an emphasis upon the political dimension of those links. Most of the discussion focuses upon the distribution of

---

[1] I would like to thank Orit Gal for her comments on this issue.
[2] I would like to thank Robert Gilpin for his comments on this point.

wealth *within* states, with important reverberations to the international political economy in general, and for North–South relations in particular. In logical terms, we can speculate about three such links: (a) globalization reduces and may even eradicate poverty and inequality, according to a Liberal logic; (b) globalization causes and deepens poverty and inequality, according to a Radical perspective; and (c) there is not necessarily a direct link between globalization, poverty, and inequality, according to a Realist or statist perspective that emphasizes the role of the state and other domestic and international political institutions, as crucial intermediaries (or active 'transmission belts') between economic globalization and its effects upon domestic societies. From this perspective, outcomes will depend on how globalization is ultimately managed and mediated by the relevant political and social institutions at the national, regional, and global levels, including first and foremost by the states themselves.

## The links between globalization and the distribution of wealth

### The Liberal argument

According to those Liberals who adopt the 'globalization thesis', a quantum leap in human affairs has taken place with the flow of large quantities of trade, investment financial capital, people, and technologies across borders expanding from a trickle to a flood in the international economic system. These globalization processes are bringing about a brave new world of increasing prosperity and international cooperation, ineluctably leading to a reduction of poverty, greater equality, and economic convergence in the performance of national economies across the world.

For Liberals, participation and integration in the world economy during the last three decades has been highly beneficial for several developing nations, including China, India, Brazil, Chile, and the newly industrialized countries (NICs) of East Asia and Southeast Asia. Hence, Liberals will bring considerable evidence that, on average, conditions have been improving in and for many developing countries (see Bhagwati 2000 and 2004; De la Dehesa 2007, 125; Dollar and Kraay 2002; Fischer 2003, 11; Gilpin 2000, 19, 293, 299–303; and Wolf 2004). Nonetheless, Liberals tend to ignore more contradictory facts, such as the sustained growth of Brazil during the Import Substitution Industrialization (ISI) period (from the 1930s to the 1970s), or the fast growth of India *before* it fully joined globalization and opened it up in the last fifteen years.

From a Liberal perspective, therefore, there seems to be a direct and inverse (positive) relationship between globalization and poverty (i.e., the greater the scope and intensity of globalization, the less poverty should prevail). The integration of global markets should contribute to faster and sustained economic growth, growth should lead to development, and development in itself has a substantial positive impact on poverty reduction, though in several cases, growth preceded the insertion into globalization and was not related to it. Liberals will argue that globalization is likely to spur faster growth through four complementary channels: trade, finance, people, and technology (Mandle 2003, 23). Liberals acknowledge that the acceleration of globalization tends to reduce the levels of poverty and inequality unevenly, despite its overall positive effects for worldwide development in the long run.

Overall, global poverty and inequality have been reduced because of the inclusion of China and India in the general statistics about the benefits of globalization; yet, many countries are still falling behind and there has been some increase in inequality within countries with a large number of poor people. In particular, conditions in most of sub-Saharan Africa, where per capita growth has been negative in nearly half the countries in the last quarter century, have been deteriorating, and Latin America has not done well in the 1990s, to say the least (see De la Dehesa 2007, 2; Fischer 2003, 11; and World Bank 2001, 1).

According to the Liberal approach, those countries that have become better integrated into the global economy grow faster and manage to reduce poverty. For example, outward-oriented (export-led) economic policies brought about dynamism and greater prosperity for much of East Asia and Southeast Asia, transforming it from one of the poorest areas of the world forty years ago into the most dynamic one nowadays. In contrast, where countries pursued inward-oriented economic policies, such as ISI, their economies stagnated or declined, as happened in much of Latin America and sub-Saharan Africa between the 1960s and the 1980s. Yet, Liberals tend to ignore 'inconvenient truths' such as the remarkable and steady annual growth of about 5 per cent in many Latin American countries, *before* the ISI economic policies hit stagnation in the late 1970s (see Chapter 4).

In sum, according to the Liberal proponents of globalization, by adopting and joining the process of global economic integration, states can reduce and resolve the problems of poverty and inequality, both within and between nations. Through the promotion of free trade sustaining high-quality growth, globalization holds the promise of improving living standards for all the peoples of the world. In this sense, economic opportunities in the Third World would be far greater, and poverty therefore vastly reduced, except for the barriers to free trade – that is, restrictions on economic freedom – which are erected by rich and poor countries alike (*Economist*, 23 September 2000, 17).

In addition to free trade, Liberals typically consider technology to be a key driver of globalization. Technology is essential in potentially alleviating and reducing poverty, if properly and effectively disseminated and adopted. Thus, the advances achieved in computing and telecommunications in the North offer enormous opportunities for raising living standards in the Third World. The adoption of liberal economic policies and the right technologies have already brought substantial benefits to all, both increasing the profits of multinational corporations, but also raising the productive employment and higher incomes for the world's poor. The key is to disseminate the appropriate technologies from the North to the developing nations, in order to foster growth, development, and prosperity.

As for the major argument suggested in this book, according to which greater governance (by strong states) might lead to a more optimal distribution of wealth in society, the Liberal paradigm is relatively moot. Liberals assume a separation between the economic and the political realms, so there is not much emphasis or role for an enhanced state, given their natural predilection for *laissez-faire*, free market, and minimal state intervention. At the same time, a *Liberal* variant of social democracy, which predicates some degree of state interventionism to foster equity and to reduce inequality, might overlap with the logic of strong states and greater governance (see Gilpin 1987, 26–9).

*The logic of economic convergence: trade, investment, growth, and the reduction of poverty and inequality* In a nutshell, the logic of *economic convergence* as posited by the Liberal approach includes a composite economic argument that focuses on economic growth, as follows: an increase in trade and foreign direct investments, together with a reduction in tariffs and other trade policies, will result in an increase of economic activities. The argument that trade and investment help to reduce poverty and inequality proceeds in two logical steps: first, trade and investment lead to growth; and second, growth reduces poverty and inequality.

According to the World Bank, there is enough empirical evidence to argue that increased openness to trade and investment has played an important role in accelerating growth and diminishing poverty in an increasing number of developing countries, reducing overall global inequality as well. Conversely, from this Liberal perspective, lack of openness increases poverty and inequality between countries since closed developing economies have performed much more poorly than more open ones (World Bank 2001, 5).

As a result of the larger volume of international trade, globalization makes it possible to allocate resources domestically and globally more efficiently, due to the fact that countries can specialize in producing what they are most competitive at, since they have comparative advantages in some products. Similarly, thanks to greater flows of foreign direct investment, globalization enables multinational corporations from the developed countries to set subsidiaries in developing countries, which can produce at a lower relative cost. Greater financial integration contributes to higher growth by expanding access to capital, enlarging access to new technology, stimulating domestic financial-sector development, reducing the cost of capital, and alleviating domestic credit constraints (De la Dehesa 2007, 7; Harrison 2007, 20; and Prasad et al. 2007, 458).

Similarly, trade and foreign investment lead to higher GDP per capita, resulting in a decrease in poverty when the poor can also benefit from the increase in their GDP per capita. Furthermore, technological advancement also helps the poor in obtaining access to basic services, such as modern medicine and public health. According to proponents of global economic liberalism, the empirical evidence strongly supports the conclusion that growth requires a policy framework oriented toward integration into the global economy. Accordingly, countries that have reduced poverty and income inequality most effectively are those that have grown the fastest over a sustained period of time, while poverty and inequality have expanded most in countries that have stagnated or fallen back economically. Thus, the prime engine of economic development remains substantial growth, which directly pulls people out of poverty and indirectly provides the resources to improve the health and education of the poor, while reducing inequality as well (Bhagwati 2008, 36–7; Fischer 2003, 3; Goldin and Reinert 2007, 214; and Neutel and Heshmati 2006, 31; see also Bhalla 2002, 183–4; and Friedman 2005, 204–11).

### The Radical argument

Most radical economists and sociologists would probably agree that globalization simply and unequivocally increases inequality between and within nations (Munck 2007, 599). In turn, inequality leads to poverty, in a vicious and self-reinforcing circle, mostly in relative terms. According to its critics, economic globalization leaves the poor behind; it actually causes and deepens poverty and inequality. This is due to several interrelated reasons.

First, without capital to invest, one cannot gain from economic integration. The poor have next to no capital, partly due to lack of entitlement rights and destitution.

Second, due to uneven development, globalization exacerbates social and economic gaps within and between states by reinforcing a process of 'creative destruction', leading to domestic, international, and global inequalities (Schumpeter quoted in Weede 2000, 9). Globalization requires economies and societies to adapt, and to do so fast. Since economies develop unevenly and some nations will grow faster than others, globalization will increase inequality both within and across nations.

Third, from a structural point of view, dependency theorists argue that the poverty of developing countries is caused by the affluence and exploitative practices of rich countries. According to this zero-sum logic, the very structure and processes of globalization perpetuate and reproduce the unequal relations and exchange between the core of the industrialized countries within the international economic system and its periphery (Gordon and Spicker 1999, 35; and Ramaswamy 2000, 4–9).

Finally, globalization has increased inequality, by having significant and uneven effects upon various types of social stratification, including class, the urban/rural divide, gender, and age, both between and especially within nations (Stewart and Berry 1999, 150). In this view, although processes of economic globalization have contributed to narrowing social hierarchies in certain respects, such as providing new opportunities for women to engage in waged employment, it has tended on the whole to widen gaps in life chances and social inequality. This is due to the uneven distribution of costs and benefits, which tend to favour the already privileged and to marginalize the already disadvantaged (Scholte 2000, 1–2). Overall, globalization exacerbates inequalities of resources, capabilities, and even of the power to make and break rules in the international arena (Hurrell and Woods 1999, 1).

How does economic globalization produce and reproduce poverty and inequality? From a dependency or Radical perspective, the adoption of the Liberal ideology of globalization and the restructuring of the world economy under the guidance of the Bretton Woods (Liberal) institutions increasingly deny developing countries the possibility of building their national economies in an independent or autonomous manner. Thus, the internationalization and globalization of macroeconomic policies transform poor countries into open economic territories, and their national economies into enclaves of cheap labour and natural resources. In this sense, globalization entails the end of economic independence, the erosion of political democracy, and a debilitating process of cultural homogenization (see Chossudovsky 1997, 37; and Gilpin 2000, 315).

In addition, the multinational corporations, as carriers of technology, capital, and skilled labour between states, have reinforced the negative effects of foreign capital penetration, further enlarging the gap between the rich and the poor (both within and between countries), thus exacerbating inequality. Such corporations have contributed to the development of so-called 'enclave economies' within the host countries, which are characterized by small regional pockets of economic development, surrounded by larger peripheral areas exhibiting extreme indexes of poverty and very little progress (Kim 2000, 1–2). In this sense, globalization is producing a new kind of hegemony that fuses economic power and wealth in a kind of *corpocracy* of financial markets and corporations that rule the world (Derber 1998, quoted in Dallmayr 2002, 145).

In sum, according to the Radicals, the processes of economic globalization have led to a ruthless capitalist system characterized by exploitation, domination, and growing inequalities both within and among national societies, composed of the rich core of developed economies and the exploited, impoverished periphery of the Third World countries. In the words of Joseph Stiglitz, a prominent Nobel Prize economist, 'globalization has not succeeded in reducing poverty, or in ensuring stability. If globalization continues to be conducted in the way it has been in the past, globalization will not only fail in promoting development, but will continue to create poverty and instability' (Stiglitz 2002, 214 and 248).

The Radical approach presents a compelling criticism of the neoliberal version of globalization. Globalization is envisioned as the triumph of a ruthless capitalist system characterized by exploitation, domination, and growing inequalities both within and among national societies. Capitalism is considered inherently unjust, since it privileges profit over human needs and because of its destructive effects upon individuals.

According to the Radicals, globalization seems to be leading a massive concentration of corporate power in the hands of the multinational corporations and its political allies, which is supported by the World Bank, the IMF, and the World Trade Organization (WTO), resulting in a kind of 'global apartheid' where the benefits of the global economy are reaped disproportionately by a handful of countries, political elites, and companies that set rules and shape the markets.

Hence, globalization is held responsible for stagnant real wages, increased wage inequality, job insecurity, and chronic unemployment, leading to deterioration in terms of working conditions and environmental degradation. Foreign direct investment (FDI) may relocate inferior, low-wage jobs from high-income countries to labour-abundant developing economies, forcing a competitive downward decline in wages all around the developing world, known as a *race to the bottom* (RTB). Certainly, cheaper labour in the developing world is one of the main factors for foreign direct investments, enabling companies to keep costs low and profits high (Glenn 2007, 183; and Mehmet 2006, 148).

Another pernicious result of capital flows is greater macroeconomic volatility, which has a significant negative causal impact upon poverty and inequality, particularly when the developing countries confront financial crises, for two main reasons. First, the poor have the least access to financial markets, making it difficult for them to diversify the risk associated with their income in difficult times. Second, since the poor rely heavily on the public services of the welfare state, any contraction in government spending as a result of pro-cyclical fiscal policies affect them badly (Prasad et al. 2007, 458; see also Harrison 2007, 20; and Soros 2002, 5).

Moreover, according to the Radicals, since the early 1980s, the macro-economic stabilization and structural adjustment programmes imposed by the IMF and the World Bank on developing countries have led to the impoverishment of hundreds of millions of people, and to social polarization with an extreme and atomized concentration of wealth (see Chossudovsky 1997; Gilpin 2000, 29, 293, 300; and Stiglitz 2002, 76, 214, 220–1).

For the Radicals, another dimension of economic globalization that has pernicious effects upon poverty and inequality is the argument about the deteriorating *terms of trade* of the developing nations, initially formulated by Singer and Prebisch several decades ago. It states that many countries that pursue liberalizing policies have experienced reductions in the value of trade in their primary products as a result of the overall decline in terms of trade of these commodities, alongside balance of payment difficulties that led those countries to contract their economies, and thus affect the vulnerable sectors of society – the poor and the disadvantaged. Hence, the Radicals would argue that trade is reinforcing global poverty and inequality because the international trading system is managed to produce these outcomes in the first place (Glenn 2007, 180).

Overall, according to the Radicals, economic globalization marginalizes large numbers of people by reducing public spending on social services and isolates economic reform from social policy. Globalization then pushes some groups, typically women (and minorities in more general terms), to the margins, further entrenching poverty. According to the Radical perspective, the widest effect of globalization on women has been their utilization as the cheapest and most exploited labour force that we have seen for the last fifty years. Moreover, it has also generated male unemployment, as well as child labour abuses.[3] In this way, the production of poverty is the result of interactions between globalization, marginalization, and gender, contrary to the view held by the Liberals (see Mittelman and Tambe 2000).

---

[3] I would like to thank Salomon Bergman for his comments on this point.

The ideological discontent with globalization arises from the principled opposition to what is considered as the neoliberal version of globalization, 'market fundamentalism' or 'unrestrained capitalism', as embodied in the 'Washington Consensus' policies of the late 1980s and the 1990s that advocated privatization, liberalization, and the fiscal contraction of the welfare state. Neoliberalism has embodied the extension of the economic rationale into the domain of politics, the triumph of capitalism over the state, and the fact that globalization has escaped the political regulations of the state, at least until the recent financial global crisis of 2008–9.

Since economic globalization is considered by the Radicals to be responsible for most of the social, economic, and political ills afflicting the world, neoliberalism is regarded as a manipulative 'wrong knowledge' of the overall society and economy, which has to be replaced by the right emancipatory project, whatever that means – revolutionary options; a world governance option; a different international system with new roles for new international institutions and for the state; and/or grassroots initiatives of globalization from below through the emergence of a vibrant and democratic global civil society (see Ish-Shalom 2008).

The Radical/Marxist approaches correctly focus on both the domestic and the international effects of a market economy upon the distribution of wealth. Yet, they might probably disagree with my argument about the direct linkage between an enhanced role for the state and the diminution of poverty and inequality. The main reason for their scepticism stems from their basic belief that the state is ultimately the servant of the dominant economic class, which is not necessarily the case (see Gilpin 1987, 43–53). Similarly to the Liberal paradigm, it is within the evolutionary (rather than revolutionary) *Marxist* strand of social democracy, associated with Edward Bernstein and Karl Kautsky, where we can find the roots for the argument for greater governance and a functioning welfare state. After all, the issue of the future of capitalist society in the era of the welfare state remains central to the question of the applicability of the core of Marx's general theory of historical developments for our times (see Gilpin 1987, 61).

### The Realist/statist argument

A third argument, neither Radical nor Liberal, but rather Realist or statist (in the sense of the international relations paradigm of political Realism that emphasizes the paramountcy of the nation-state), does not necessarily identify a clear or direct link between globalization and the distribution of wealth. For instance, Robert Gilpin (2000, 293–4) argues that many of the problems associated with globalization are linked to other factors, though related, which are not part and parcel of a more limited phenomenon of globalization. In his view, which I share and further develop below, globalization is a very important but rather limited phenomenon in international relations, whose domestic effects are largely determined by the way states and other political and social institutions respond to it and manage it (Gilpin 2000, 302–3). Paraphrasing Alexander Wendt, one could then argue that 'globalization is what states make of it', a kind of political regulation, if not social construction, of the international – and global – political economy, still determined, to a large extent, by nation-states themselves.

In other words, if we adopt a more minimalist definition of globalization only in economic terms (focusing for instance upon trade and financial flows), then technological changes per se, the third industrial revolution, the digital revolution, and the concomitant 'digital divide' should no longer be considered to be part of globalization itself. In this way, we cannot bless or blame globalization for having positive or pernicious effects upon poverty and inequality, since it is a much more limited phenomenon than we thought initially. Perhaps the relationship between globalization and the distribution of wealth might be merely a correlation rather than a consistent causal relationship, with the most salient causes of economic success (or failure) lying elsewhere, and being more complex than simply adopting (or rejecting) the premises of the 'Washington Consensus' (see Lazebnik 2005, 18).

According to this Realist approach, the relationship between globalization and the distribution of wealth is open-ended and undetermined. For instance, there might not be a direct or causal linkage between globalization and poverty, though the indirect links are countless. The impact of globalization is then mediated and channelled through the role of states and other political and social actors, who translate those effects into domestic social and economic policies.

For example, globalization might have a positive or negative impact on poverty through the encouragement (or discouragement) of the development of *social capital*, which is defined by the World Bank as 'the institutions, relationships, and norms that shape the quality of a society's social interactions' (see World Bank 2009). Yet, social capital development in itself is directly related, first and foremost, to the policy decisions adopted by the national governments in relation to their own societies. In other words, there are a myriad of factors, other than economic globalization, that might explain the occurrence and recurrence of poverty and inequality. They include, among others: the speed with which countries embrace technological changes, their level of education, their health policies, their social strata, their domestic economic structure, their domestic political structure, and the domestic conditions of war or peace in any given society (see Lazebnik 2005, 20; and Keating 2008, 6).

From this perspective, the direct impact of trade liberalization and of capital flows upon poverty and inequality is mediated by a series of political and socio-economic factors, such as the type and level of state intervention, the structure of the national economy, and the level of development and income of the country concerned (Glenn 2007, 180). Probably the most important singular factor in this context is the choice of economic and social policies in managing globalization that might have an overall impact upon levels of poverty and inequality. It is a country's domestic *political equilibrium*, largely governed and affected by domestic forces and institutions other than economic globalization, which determines whether the impact of globalization will be a positive or a negative one (see Glenn 2007, 185; Katzenstein 1978; and Robinson 2003, 72).

Moreover, this Realist and statist approach suggests that serious problems that have affected the fate of peoples and states, including poverty and environmental degradation, are first and foremost directly related to national governments and to national policies, as well as to domestic political institutions, rather than to the supra-national or supra-territorial forces of the global market. Thus, the principal culprits and saviours of increasing (or reducing) poverty, of abusing (or conserving) the environment, are the national governments themselves, through their decision-making procedures and implementation and their simultaneous interactions with the international system and with their respective societies.

From this perspective, in normative terms globalization should no longer be catalogued as 'good' or 'bad', while having the potential to do enormous good or tremendous harm. Rather, it is the management of globalization by the states themselves (and other political and social institutions), or, in other words, the way states cope with the processes of globalization, that should become the focus of our inquiry, as it is presented in the *intermestic* political model developed below (see Haass and Litan 1998; Stiglitz 2002, 20 and 215).

As for my argument about the causal link between greater governance and a better distribution of wealth within society, it might fit well within a Realist perspective, though it probably transcends it. In other words, Realists might agree that good governance might be an effective instrument to strengthen the state, and that dealing with poverty and inequality might be considered nowadays as a matter of national security. And yet, the focus upon an enhanced role for the state is outwardly oriented, with reference to constant competition with other states in international relations, rather than inwardly oriented, like in my own *intermestic* model.

## The causal mechanisms between globalization and the distribution of wealth: reconciling the three approaches?

Before we turn to a detailed examination of the *intermestic* political model, let us briefly summarize the contending arguments regarding the possible causal mechanisms that link economic globalization to poverty and inequality. There is a logical need to understand in clear terms the causal relationship between globalization and the distribution of wealth. There is an ongoing controversy regarding the causes of poverty and growing inequality in the world. For instance, some scholars argue that while global trade may have even helped to reduce poverty and global inequality, foreign direct investments and other forms of capital flows, by contrast, have tended to increase them.

According to a pure economic perspective, what are the transmission mechanisms through which processes of economic globalization might affect poverty and inequality, directly and indirectly? There are at least three such causal chains: (1) the globalization–growth–inequality–poverty channel; (2) the globalization–capital and labour mobility–poverty channel; and (3) the globalization–technology–poverty channel (see Nissanke and Thorbecke 2007, 5–7).

### *The globalization–growth–inequality–poverty causal chain*

Bhagwati (2000 and 2004, 54–5) argues that globalization affects poverty and inequality through its positive impact on growth. In other words, growth is considered to be the main (though not the only) economic strategy for raising the incomes, and hence the wealth, living standards, and consumption, of the poor. Some types of growth might help the poor more than others, depending on the presence of other variables such as policy distortions and government intervention that might reinforce or reduce the effects of growth upon the poor. From a very purist, fundamentalist Liberal perspective, growth is considered in itself as a sufficient condition for poverty reduction, without any further action beyond the economic domain (Bhalla 2002, 206).

In reality, the causal links between growth, inequality, and poverty are more complicated than what Bhalla and other fellow Liberals argue. Those links should be disaggregated, since there might be mixed and even contradictory effects of growth upon poverty (less) and inequality (more), at least in the short term. The first and main manifestation of economic globalization is through trade and capital movement liberalization, which are supposed to affect growth in a positive way through increased exports, imports, and capital flows (see Nissanke and Thorbecke 2007, 2).

Thus, Liberals assume, almost by definition, that an increase in international trade will increase growth and reduce poverty through job creation, expansion of markets, and increased competition, raising productivity, leading to improvements in education and health, and bringing about technological learning and diffusion, all of which have the potential for increasing the real incomes of poor people (Goldin and Reinert 2007, 10 and 47). Similarly, the influx of capital flows through foreign direct investment might contribute to poverty alleviation when it supports the generation of new employment, promotes competition, improves the education and training of host-country workers, and transfers new technology (Goldin and Reinert 2007, 12, 37, 79, and 81).

The second link in the causal chain from economic globalization to poverty is the more complicated and less evident connection between growth and inequality. It might certainly be the case that growth might lead to an increase in income inequality, so that the poor might either benefit slightly or even be hurt by the globalization processes, at least in the short term, in what is known in the economic literature as the Kuznets' effect (see Nissanke and Thorbecke 2007, 2). Thus, for instance, while trade liberalization is usually considered as good for growth, it requires complementary supply-side and social policies in order to reach equitable growth. Similarly, financial liberalization might lead to growth, though it might also raise the vulnerability of the poor population to cope with the financial crises. Those crises usually develop out of the inability of the developing economies to restructure their external debt, as was the case in Latin America in general, and in Argentina in particular (Serrano 2003, 85–6).

Finally, the third link in the causal chain captures the combined net effects of growth and a change in income inequality upon the phenomenon of poverty. Here, the focus should be on the structure of growth and economic development, rather than on the rate of growth itself. In other words, for globalization to lead to a reduction of poverty, there should be both a combination of higher growth and a deliberate social policy of pro-poor distribution of the gains from this growth.

Growth that results from processes of economic globalization, such as increased international trade and transnational financial flows, has to be accompanied by a deliberate intervention of the state in order for it to be translated into social and economic advantages for the most vulnerable sectors of society. Thus, many social and collective measures instrumented by the state and sectors of civil society should be in place in order for globalization to have a positive effect upon poverty and inequality. These measures should include: public investments in education and health; social institutions that can ensure adherence to basic norms of equity and fairness; and, finally, a social welfare network that might be able to protect and insure low-skill workers and other vulnerable and disadvantaged sectors of society from the economic and financial volatility that follows the integration of the national economy into the global market (Nissanke and Thorbecke 2007, 3 and 7).

In this context, one could ask whether globalization creates any incentives for governments to invest in such social policies. After all, it might be the case that under conditions of extreme global competition, governments cannot afford such policies, as we see in the current challenges to the welfare state in Europe and in the United States.[4]

### The globalization–capital and labour mobility–poverty causal chain

The link between economic globalization and labour market dynamics is very important, especially in the case of labour-abundant developing countries. In principle, and according to liberal economic theory, the impact of economic globalization upon developing countries that are endowed with available unskilled labour should lead to a reduction of income inequality due to an increased demand for unskilled labour.

In theory, following the 'upward convergence' view, a greater openness in global trade raises the burden of adjustment on a high-cost environment. Through labour-intensive production in developing countries there is a possibility of lowering costs for profit-seeking multinational firms, so that becomes a legitimate source of comparative advantage, whereas the North buys more labour-intensive cheap products and sells more of its more capital-intensive products, for the benefit of everybody (Mehmet 2006, 150; and Nissanke and Thorbecke 2007, 4).

Yet, in practice, as I demonstrate in the empirical chapters dealing with Latin America and Argentina, the reduction in income inequality has not happened; furthermore, the wage gap between skilled and unskilled labour has been increasing within many developing countries. Thus, the logic of global competition might generate pressures to lower wages and labour standards across the world, creating a 'race to the bottom' phenomenon, with pernicious implications in terms of poverty and inequality, by further reducing wages.

A second causal mechanism that implicates capital and labour mobility refers to the fact that globalization allows for larger migratory flows, leading to a convergence of income levels among countries. This is directly related to the remittances the migrant workers send to their (developing) home countries, together with the knowledge and experience they

---

[4] I would like to thank Galia Press-Bar-Nathan for her insights on this point.

acquire, as an effective way to reduce both poverty and inequality at the individual and state levels (De la Dehesa 2007, 8; and Goldin and Reinert 2007, 14). For instance, for several small developing economies, such as the Central American states, remittances of their migrant workers from the United States becomes an indispensable source of their national income.

### The globalization–technology–poverty causal chain

If we include technology in the definition of globalization, then the nature of technical progress and technological diffusion can be considered as another channel, or causal chain, through which globalization might affect poverty and income distribution, though its effects are contradictory and highly debated. Liberals argue, following the Solow–Ramsey theory of neoclassical growth, that all countries end up having access to the dominant technology, which is the major factor in improving social well-being, providing exogenous improvements to everybody, albeit with a considerable delay in many cases.

For instance, fast-growing economies like Brazil, China, and India are able to increase their economic growth, based on rapid technological upgrading financed by the rapid growth of their exports (Sachs 2008, 19–20; see also De la Dehesa 2007, 132–3). By contrast, Radicals argue that the diffusion of technology from the more-developed to the less-developed countries maintains and even intensifies the hierarchical structure of global inequality, keeps the worldwide distribution of income more or less stable, and determines how political, institutional, and economic differences are translated into differences in income per capita between and within countries (De la Dehesa 2007, 133).

As with other factors such as trade and capital flows, one can argue that, at least in the short and medium term, technology might reduce poverty while at the same time increasing inequality (Nissanke and Thorbecke 2007, 6; see also De la Dehesa 2007, 3–6, 30–1). It is evident that technological diffusion has accelerated with globalization since the 1980s, bringing greater absolute prosperity and welfare for nearly everyone compared with their situation previous to its development and implementation. But at the same time, technological development inexorably causes inequality in the short term since it tends to discriminate and benefit the countries or people and sectors that invent and discover it, usually the richer strata of society, giving them a huge advantage over the poor countries (and peoples). Thus, the wage gaps and the increase in inequality might be directly related to increases in the premium for skills generated by technological change.

Therefore, it is hard to disaggregate the effects of trade from those of technological diffusion and foreign investment. It is in fact the combination of these three factors, namely trade, technological diffusion, and foreign investment, that might raise the relative wages of skilled workers and widen the gap in the income distribution (World Bank 2007, 81).

The analysis of these three possible causal links between globalization, poverty, and inequality clearly demonstrates the complexity, and sometimes even contradictory nature, of these links, as well as the need for a crucial role for the state to cope with globalization. Furthermore, it makes evident the futility of embarking in pure ideological discussions about who is right in the debate (Liberals vs Radicals), or in bringing contested statistical evidence to prove or disprove the claim that capital flows, trade, and technology transfer might bring about more (or less) poverty, and more (or less) inequality. Hence, the logical conclusion to reach at this stage is that in the real world of *political* economy, neither Liberals nor Radicals can be completely right (or completely wrong), since it is in the domain of politics – both international and domestic – where we can find perhaps a better model of explanation, albeit not elegant or parsimonious, about how processes of economic globalization might affect domestic societies, in terms of their impact upon poverty and inequality. I turn now to the depiction of that political, *intermestic* model.

## The *intermestic* model: bringing politics back to the fore

The main argument of this book is that politics plays a crucial role in our effort to discern and to make sense of the problematic effects of globalization upon domestic societies, as well as a vital part of the effort to tame globalization and find proper solutions to its potential externalities, including poverty and inequality. Even if the effects of economic globalization along several social dimensions are deemed benign, on balance, rather than malign, we need *political institutions* to monitor and to balance globalization, in order to improve upon the positive potential outcomes that globalization might achieve. In other words, the model focuses on the *political agents* (or actors) that manage globalization: the state and the institutions linked to their own society, and regional and international institutions that might serve as well as 'transmission belts' between globalization and the state.

In this sense, political institutions, first and foremost national governments and state institutions themselves, should play an essential role not only in mitigating market failures, but also in ensuring social justice. Thus, the choice for national governments is not how to confront globalization, but rather how to manage it and channel it for positive results within their own societies (Haass and Litan 1998; and Stiglitz 2002, 218). National governments act as 'transmission belts', mediating the impact of globalization on their citizens and upon society as a whole. Consequently, variations in the effects of globalization upon poverty and inequality are best understood by examining the interplay of domestic politics and international affairs. The argument here fits the concept of a 'post-Washington Consensus', by emphasizing the role of governance in determining the effects of globalization for developing and liberalizing states.

The *intermestic* model assumes the need for a pragmatic and eclectic approach, following Katzenstein's plea for 'analytical eclecticism' (Sil and Katzenstein 2005). The argument then synthesizes and transcends the ideal types or paradigms that we are familiar with (Realism, Liberalism, and Marxism), by emphasizing the relevance of politics, and by analysing the political mechanisms that act between the external forces of globalization and the domestic reverberations within society, such as the economic and social policies adopted by national governments. The model stems from the Realist approach as presented above, but it adds to it by specifically referring to the interactions between the external and the domestic domains, following also the logic of the 'second image reversed' posed by Peter Gourevitch back in 1978, according to which the international system might be an important determinant of the logic of domestic politics.

The *external* domain focuses upon the position of the state in the regional and international structures, and especially its relations with regional and global institutions. The predominant factor here is the degree of autonomy or insertion of a given state in the global economy, as shaped by the external forces of economic globalization. The *domestic* domain refers to the social and economic stratification within societies, as well as the political divisions within the different states, alongside state–society relations that are characterized by the level of strength (or weakness) of the state in relation to its own society (see Holsti 1996; and Kacowicz 1998).

Contrary to the widespread assumption that globalization undermines the role of the state both in international relations and vis-à-vis domestic societies, I tend to agree with Clark (1999) that globalization might open to the state (and to other political institutions) new spaces to manoeuvre, to act, and to react, by taking initiatives within the international political economy. Thus, the relationship between globalization and the state is not zero-sum, but rather mixed-motive and symbiotic, if not completely positive-sum or win-win. In terms that remind us of the structurational

Constructivist emphasis on the mutual constituency of structures and agents, Clark (1999, 55) argues that 'globalization shapes the state and is, at the same time, what states make of it'. In other words, the state occupies a *middle position* between the internal (societal) and the external (international) realms, so it is itself both shaped by, and formative of, the processes of globalization (Clark 1999, 9–10).

My model is reminiscent also of the 'statist approach' developed by Stephen Krasner in his seminal work on raw material investments and US foreign policy more than thirty years ago (Krasner 1978). In that book, Krasner referred to the state as an autonomous actor, yet constrained by domestic as well as international structures. Thus, a state chooses a certain socio-economic model as a result of structural constraints (the effects of globalization), alongside its own choices and its ideological preferences. The model also reflects the importance of the domestic structure of the state, as a critical intervening variable without which we cannot understand the relationship between economic globalization and the policies adopted by states (see Katzenstein 1978).

In a similar vein, my approach also recreates the 'Realist theory of state action' formulated by Mastanduno, Lake, and Ikenberry twenty-three years ago, in which they made two major claims. First, the ability of governments to pursue domestic policies effectively is influenced and constrained by developments in the international system, which provide the state with the general setting, constraints, and menu for choice. Second, and conversely, the realization of international goals depends meaningfully on domestic politics and economics (Mastanduno et al. 1989, 457).

Similarly, I argue here that in order to make sense of the links between globalization, poverty, and inequality we should focus upon the role of the state and other political actors and social institutions, as framing the national (economic, social) policies that act as critical variables to reap the benefits of globalization and to cope with its adverse effects within domestic society. This truism has to be spelled out by referring to the state and other political actors as kind of active *transmission belts*, or intermediary actors, between the structural forces of economic globalization and the structural domestic characteristics of any given society, plagued sometimes by poverty and by social and economic inequalities.

This is a two-way street, where the mutual impact and relationship between the external and the domestic (which together make the *intermestic* model) is a matter of degree and sequencing. As we will examine in detail in Chapter 5, different trajectories of failure (in the 1980s) and success (in the 2000s) of the 'ABC countries' (Argentina, Brazil, and Chile) can be attributed to the paramount effects and the systemic conditions of the international context (the debt crisis in the 1980s and the economic bonanza in the 2000s). By contrast, in the 1990s, we can register some variance between the three countries, as a function of divergent economic and social policies adopted by their respective governments.[5]

This is inherently an *intermestic* (international + domestic) model of politics that attempts to answer the question about the links between globalization and the distribution of wealth by referring to the critical role that political and social actors might play within those structures. For instance, as the cases of Latin America in general and of Argentina in particular demonstrate, the vulnerability of developing countries to the risk factors associated with financial globalization is intrinsically related to the quality of macroeconomic policies and of domestic governance – such as their level of political corruption, within the constraints of the relevant regional and international structures (see Prasad et al. 2007, 464–5; and Chapters 4–5 in this book).

The processes of economic globalization can be considered as an exogenous, external, and structural constraint (outside of the box of the state and the domestic political and social institutions), and at the same time as an endogenous force that is internalized, managed, mediated, and manipulated by the state and other political and social institutions (inside the domestic box), through the formulation of domestic (political, social, and economic) policies about how to cope with globalization and its impact. Thus, the domestic political and institutional equilibrium is itself influenced (from the outside) by globalization, which can affect the political and bargaining power of domestic political actors, which in turn can use globalization in order to increase their own domestic power, from the inside (Robinson 2003, 72).

As mentioned above, the domestic (internal) dimension of the model is mostly determined by the nature of state–society relations within a given polity. Moreover, the nature of state–society relations is a function of the level of strength (or weakness) of a state vis-à-vis its own society.

A *strong state* is a state that enjoys a high level of political legitimacy, authority, and recognition by its citizens and its civil society, as epitomized by the state's ability to collect taxes and to mobilize its population, in times of both peace and war. Strong states tend to be full-fledged nation-states, usually without irredentist claims; they also tend to occupy a preponderant position vis-à-vis their own societies.

Conversely, a *weak state* is a state with low levels of political legitimacy and of political institutionalization, lack of authority to mobilize

---

[5] I would like to thank Leonardo Gasparini for his brilliant insights on this point.

its population's resources, and lack of capacity to do so; it is usually not a consolidated nation-state. According to Holsti (1996), weak and non-democratic states have tended to be the loci of civil wars since 1945, especially in the post-colonial Third World. Moreover, a weak state is usually marred by internal (ethnic) conflicts, due to the disjunction between the state and the nation, so it parallels a weak position in international relations, in terms of power and status (see Miller 2007).

In this book, I suggest that the external forces of globalization tend not to exacerbate poverty and inequality in strong states that manage to institute progressive domestic economic and social public policies. By contrast, globalization might tend to aggravate poverty and inequality in weak states because they are less likely to institute such policies. In other words, a strong state is a necessary, but not sufficient, condition for progressive public policies to be enacted by national governments coping with poverty and inequality. We should now disaggregate the concept of 'strong' and 'weak' states in order to clarify this point further.

*Strong and weak states within the* intermestic *model*

According to Centeno (2002, 2), a state is defined as the permanent institutional core of political authority on which regimes rest and depend. The institutionalization refers to a certain degree of autonomy from any social sector, where its authority is accepted within society beyond the political debates over specific policies. This definition actually fits the characterization of a *strong state*, according to which the state has domestic legitimacy and can command loyalty (exercise the right to rule) in order to penetrate society, regulate social relationships, extract the resources necessary to provide services, maintain sovereignty and a certain monopoly over the legitimate use of force (at least formally), and to operate within the context of a consensus-based political community (Holsti 1996, 82–3 and 97; and Migdal 1988, 4–5). Thus, the most effective states are those whose societies are sufficiently homogeneous and egalitarian to set the ground for the creation of a common sense of citizenship and political community. This, in turn, allows states to develop effective power to mobilize resources and to promote development, enjoying a high degree of political legitimacy (Mann 2004, 198).

In practical terms, we should look for strength (or, alternatively, weakness) of states in different issue-areas, and along a continuum. The proponents of *strong states* tend to underline the capabilities involving the state's penetration of society and the extraction of resources, through economic and social policies of regulation and taxation, income transfer, and wealth redistribution, reflecting sound macroeconomic policies and good (or decent) domestic governance. In a nutshell, a strong state is a state capable of mobilizing its population through mechanisms of social control that include compliance, participation, and legitimation (by which the population accepts the state's rules of the game). Moreover; a strong state can also carry on and implement its own decisions, in different issue-areas such as security and welfare.

By contrast, *weak states* lack the capabilities involving regulation of social relationships and the appropriation of resources in determined ways, as well as the failure and inability actually to implement decisions, partly due to the weakness in the institutional structure of the state (Migdal 1988, 8, 21–2; see also Centeno 2002, 10; and Prasad et al. 2007, 464).

According to my *intermestic* model, the impact of globalization upon poverty and inequality is mediated, mitigated, and transformed by the response of the state and other political and social institutions. These political actors might formulate sound (or incompetent) social and economic policies, as a function of the degree and quality of domestic governance and the nature of state–society relations. Conversely, their degrees of freedom and choice are also restrained by the structural context of globalization and by the power position and status the state enjoys in the regional and international hierarchy of power. Although globalization does not *cause* poverty and inequality, it nevertheless directly affects the actions of states (and other political and social actors in the domestic scene) by constraining and restraining their menu of options, setting the external parameters within which states and other actors can cope with poverty and inequality and formulate relevant policies and responses.

While globalization and poverty are both processes that have transcended nationalism; i.e., they affect people transnationally, our ways to cope with them are still nation-based. The political institutions might perform at three different levels of analysis: local (domestic, national); regional; and international/global. Figure 3.1 briefly summarizes the *intermestic* model.

According to this model, there is a *double feed-back* from poverty and inequality within societies, which impinge upon the state and other political domestic institutions, and might also affect the external context, including the structural forces of globalization, as represented by external shocks and impacts, trade, capital flows and FDI flows, and technological diffusion. Furthermore, since the state is supposed to be an active 'transmission belt', the domestic consequences affect the functioning of the state, which in principle could adopt an active role in coping with the external context. In other words, the state occupies a *double middle*

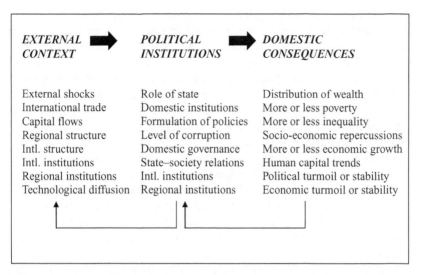

Figure 3.1 The *intermestic* model

*position* between the external context and the domestic consequences, acting as an intermediary *in both directions*.[6]

### *Levels of analysis of the* intermestic *model*

The *intermestic* model can be applied at three different and complementary levels of analysis – domestic (national), regional, and international – in terms of the relevant institutions that mediate between globalization and its domestic social effects. At stake, we have here a kind of 'three-level game' among the international, the regional, and the domestic, with a feedback among all three levels.

At the *domestic/national level*, we examine the political and institutional endogenous factors and structures that make it possible (or impossible) for many states to emerge from marginalization and poverty, as mentioned above: the type of political regime; the nature of state–society relations; the presence or absence of a strong and vital civil society; the level of corruption; the quality of domestic governance; and the policies and institutions that developing countries have adopted as independent, sovereign states, or that they have inherited from the colonial period (De la Dehesa 2007, 6 and 70; see also Risse-Kappen 1995). At this level of analysis, although the focus remains on the *state*, we should bring

[6] I would like to thank Carlos Acuña for his comments on this point.

also into consideration the relevance of other, non-state actors and social institutions from within society, or from without (such as transnational actors who might act at the domestic/national level, like multinational corporations).

At the *regional level*, states might act collectively and in cooperation and unison, through the promotion of regional frameworks of integration and the institutionalization of international organizations, in order to cope simultaneously with the challenges of globalization and the reduction of poverty and inequality. For instance, in the Latin American context several regional organizations – the Organization of American States (at the Pan-American level), the Rio Group (at the Latin American level), the recently created Union of South American Nations (UNASUR) (at the South American level), and Mercosur (at the sub-regional level) – all include in their rhetorical and policy mandates specific references to the promotion of growth and the reduction of poverty and inequality (see Chapter 4).

Regional institutions might then act as collective active intermediaries between the structural forces of the global economy and the domestic societal repercussions. At the same time, these regional institutions play an *intermestic* role, since they both affect the economic foreign policies of the member-states that compose the regional integration frameworks, and their policies are internalized by the national governments, affecting their domestic social and economic policies as well. It should be noticed that despite the obvious intra-regional variance (take, for instance, the enormous disparity between Brazil and Haiti in Latin America), we might trace common regional features, and policies, in the way states and societies in a given region address common social and economic problems (see Chapter 4).

At the *international level*, the focus turns to the role of the so-called international or global institutions – the United Nations, the World Bank, the International Monetary Fund, and the World Trade Organization – that are considered harbingers of globalization but also international institutions that can be manipulated and used by states in order to promote their own interests, to cope with and to tame globalization, and to implement comprehensive programmes that address problems of poverty and inequality.

Even in a more striking fashion than their regional counterparts, these global/international institutions have played a paramount role in affecting and even designing the foreign and domestic policies of specific states. As Claudia Kedar argues in her brilliant historical examination of the Argentine–IMF relations from 1944 to 1977, there has been a pattern of asymmetrical interdependence that led to a kind of 'routine of dependency' of successive Argentine governments in obtaining loans from the IMF, and, even more important, in obtaining the IMF seal of approval (in the form of standby agreements) to allow loans to be raised from private, commercial sources (see Kedar 2009). Thus, the IMF, and to a lesser extent the World Bank and the World Trade Organization, also played a crucial *intermestic* role, as both external forces, and also by being internalized in the decision-making processes that led to domestic social and economic policies, stemming from the intervention of these international institutions.

Another example of the multi-faceted role of these global institutions has been the formulation of the so-called Millennium Development Goals, a decade ago, as an attempt to reconcile globalization with the interests of the poor, and the inherent interdependence between growth, poverty reduction, and sustainable development. Although the implementation has been only partial, those development goals set a kind of road map at the international and global levels, to create a global compact of rich and poor countries in order to reduce poverty, disease, and environmental degradation. This can still be deemed *intermestic*, since there is international and global cooperation to deal with an inherent domestic problem with international repercussions.

In addition to these international organizations, one should also mention the role of multinational corporations in shaping the contours of the global economy, pursuing (private) wealth, while at the same time affecting the economic and social fate of millions of people worldwide. Furthermore, at the global level of analysis, we should include, in addition to international institutions and multinational corporations, a series of non-state actors and networks, including coalitions of citizen activists that rival international governmental organizations (IGOs) and MNCs and shape what is known as an incipient *global civil society*, as an expression of globalization from below (see Falk 2009).[7] All these actors actually work at the three different levels of analysis as mechanisms of global governance.

*The state as 'transmission belt' in practical terms: economic and social public policies to deal with poverty and inequality* States act as 'transmission belts' through the formulation of effective (or less effective) public policies designed to deal with poverty and inequality, resulting in progressive or regressive effects. How much countries have focused, attempted, and succeeded on reducing poverty and promoting equity, along with the strategies they have adopted, varies widely. For instance,

---

[7] I would like to thank Roee Kibric for his comments on this point.

some countries have actively promoted the use of public resources to improve the situation of the bottom tier of the income distribution, while others have focused on the top percentiles through highly progressive taxes (International Monetary Fund 1998, 6).

In general, the goals of governments have been to manage distributional conflicts in order to ensure social stability and domestic peace, finding a delicate equilibrium between the needs for redistribution of wealth and the logic of the market (see Rudra 2008, 7). In other words, well-designed domestic policies are likely to be the most powerful instruments to reduce both inequality and poverty in any specific country. In theoretical terms, such policies need not interfere with sustainable long-term growth, by formulating equity-enhancing policies that are also efficient (see World Bank 2001, 10, and 2007, 91). In reality, some of those policies fall short of their progressive stated goals.

A series of economic and social policies, which sometimes are very difficult to disentangle, are formulated in order to cope with poverty and inequality in appropriate ways. *Economic policies* include: (a) public finance (such as expenditures on programmes targeted to specific individuals and groups); (b) macroeconomic policies, among others, fiscal policies, monetary policies such as exchange rate strategies, public debt management, and privatization (or appropriation) of public enterprises. In progressive terms, adoption of a macroeconomic policy framework that heightens growth is supposed to open the way for policies that enhance human capabilities, improve income distribution, and hence reduce poverty. Moreover, those policies refer to the industrial domain (emphasis upon innovation); technology (the creation and diffusion of knowledge); and support for small and medium firms.

Conversely, *social policies* are considered as a system of redistribution of wealth, as a function of the legal and fiscal power of the state. Fiscal policies for redistribution of wealth should include recovering the state's capacity to support and promote the creation and expansion of the infrastructure needed for development, including the growing provision of quality public goods (health, education, and social and human security), as well as social protection for the destitute and poverty reduction (see Bárcena 2010, 3; Fajnzylber 1990, 76; and Lo Vuolo et al. 1999, 76).

Among key social policies designed to deal with poverty and inequality we can mention: fiscal policy, from the standpoint of income; wage policy; employment policy (in urban, marginal, and rural sectors); conditional transfer programmes, which pay households that engage in socially useful behaviour such as keeping children at school; unemployment insurance; recruitment subsidies; job creation programmes; training programmes;

reducing inequality in the labour market; redistribution through transferences and income transfers (through the pension system); the establishment of collective equipment for popular housing; social welfare systems; support for urban and rural small industries; health policies; policies intended to favour social organizations (unions, parties, cooperatives, and associations); and first and foremost education services (see Bárcena 2010, 2011; and Fajnzylber 1990, 76).

Fiscal policy – through taxation and spending – remains the government's most direct tool for redistributing income and wealth, though its effects have remained relatively small. By contrast, the expenditure side of the budget might be more relevant to affect poverty and inequality. In other words, the link between income distribution and social spending, especially in the case of health and education, might lead to the strengthening and distribution of human capital, reducing income inequality, and by extension poverty, over the long run.

*Hypotheses of the* intermestic *model*

On the basis of the model depicted in Figure 3.1 and the three levels of analysis discussed above, we can formulate one general working assumption (considered as a truism or parameter) and four working hypotheses, which will be tested in the empirical chapters, as follows:

General Assumption 1: State actions regarding the implementation of social and economic policies of their national governments are constrained by the international structure (both at the regional and international/global levels and through globalization processes). In turn, these structural constraints are mediated, moderated, and negotiated by the actions of the state.

Hypothesis 1 (H1): The stronger a state is (in relation to its own society), the better it will function as an effective actor in coping with poverty and inequality. Conversely, the weaker a state is (in relation to its own society), the worst it will perform as an active actor in coping with poverty and inequality, thus being exposed and vulnerable to the external shocks of the global economy.

Hypothesis 2 (H2): To the extent that a state can enact better socio-economic policies (in terms of their quality and effectiveness, such as a low level of corruption), and enjoy high levels of 'good governance', the better it will be prepared to cope with poverty and inequality.

Hypothesis 3 (H3): The more institutionalized the regional institutions of any given region are, the more positive effects they might have in helping states in the region to cope with poverty and inequality.

Hypothesis 4 (H4): The more intrusive and assertive global institutions are, the larger the effect they might have upon the policies adopted by states in coping with poverty and inequality. In turn, the effects of those global institutions might be a function of: (a) the power and status of any given state in the regional and international hierarchy; (b) the level of strength of any given state (in relation to its own society); and (c) the level of consent and ideological convergence of the (domestic) political leaders who choose voluntarily to accept the policy recommendations and agenda of the global institutions.

*Explaining the rationale of the hypotheses*

Since the state, or more precisely its national government and bureaucracy, plays a crucial intermediary role in the causal chain between the international structure and the distribution of wealth by mediating and channelling the effects of globalization, one should ask what role the state does play in alleviating and reducing poverty and inequality. Alternatively, is the state itself part of the problem or the solution? There are several answers to these important questions.

First, according to a Liberal logic, states open up their economies to trade, capital, and (to some extent) labour because they deem it as part of their interests and in the interests of their citizens, strengthening both wealth and legitimacy, as is usually the case with *prosperous, market-oriented democracies*. Similarly, Amartya Sen (1999 and 2009) considers that all countries that are liberal democracies provide an intrinsic and excellent foundation for the possibilities of growth and development, and thus for poverty reduction (De la Dehesa 2007, 91; and Wolf 2004, 251). Unfortunately, many developing countries are neither entirely liberal nor democratic.

Second, if globalization is to be fair, there is an *enhanced*, rather than a reduced, *role for governments to assist the potential victims of globalization and liberalization*, and to strike a balance between openness (to trade and to capital flows) and domestic needs, in terms of welfare and social security. In this sense, the state is not only the source of authoritative action but it also acts as the framework that both facilitates the spontaneous economic and political competition of the market, but also it is ready to step in and to tame or harness them toward the provision of social goals, including the alleviation of poverty and inequality, that cannot be addressed only by the magic of the Liberal 'invisible hand' (Lowi 2002, 60–1; and Mandle 2003, 27).

Third, the role of the state is partially determined by its *relative strength vis-à-vis its own society*, as specified and operationalized in the previous section. Similarly to the claim in international security that a strong state (vis-à-vis its society) is a pre-condition for reaching and maintaining domestic and international peace, one can make a similar argument in terms of welfare that a strong state (vis-à-vis its society) is essential to reduce poverty and to enhance social equality.[8] In other words, how governments and societies organize themselves and how they absorb ideas and allow their citizens and economic firms to operate is a key determinant of growth and poverty reduction (Goldin and Reinert 2007, 209).

Fourth, in practical terms, the role of the state as an active 'transmission belt' between globalization and the distribution of wealth is operationalized through the *different and diverging economic and social public policies adopted by the state and other political actors and social institutions*, in the issue-areas of trade, capital flows, migration, fiscal guidelines, monetary issues, social spending, labour, and welfare. Policies at the national level remain crucial for poverty and inequality reduction even in a globalized context. Well-designed domestic policies are likely to remain the most powerful instruments to reduce both inequality and poverty in any specific country. Of all the policies that have been correlated with the level of per capita income, the most important are those related to education and health care.

Yet, since the state adopts a Janus-faced stance in this *intermestic* model, those public policies might be influenced as well by decisions and stances taken by other countries, in regional contexts and by regional organizations, and by international institutions such as the International Monetary Fund, the World Bank, and the World Trade Organization. Henceforth, the impact of the regional and global institutions upon the national policies of the states is a function of: (a) the strength of the state vis-à-vis its society; and (b) the position of the state in the regional and/or international hierarchy, in terms of power and status. Thus, paraphrasing Gourevitch (1978), it is the international structure that plays also an important role in structuring domestic politics (see Berry 2007a, 216; De la Dehesa 2007, 83–6; Glenn 2007, 176; and World Bank 2007, 91).

Fifth, a major determinant of a successful (or failed) role of any state in addressing poverty and inequality in the context of globalization is likely

---

[8] I am indebted to Carlos Escudé for drawing this parallel in the context of the Argentine case, in juxtaposition to my own explanation of the long South American peace in Kacowicz (1998).

to be the *quality of governance*; that is, the quality of the public and private institutions within the polity and the society as a whole. It is the quality of governance, rather than the type of political regime, which becomes a crucial political factor leading countries out of poverty. In this sense, low quality implies a high level of corruption, government incapacity, and political and economic instability. By contrast, high quality implies lack of corruption, a liberal system that protects property rights and guarantees equal treatment before the law, the absence of bureaucratic harassment, and protection from any form of organized crime (Bhagwati 2008, 38; Goldin and Renert 2007, 219; and Stiglitz 2007, 55).

According to the World Bank doctrine, *good governance* has emerged as one of the most important pre-requisites for economic development, because of the role of governments as builders and providers of institutions. Furthermore, economic globalization has put a premium on good governance, due to the demands of an increasingly competitive global marketplace, the requirements of transparency and accountability, and the higher costs of mismanagement (World Bank 2001, 9). In this context, we should be aware that the term 'good governance' is usually used as an ideologically neutral euphemism for market-oriented policies. That is, in many cases, the 'Washington Consensus' assumes that any type of state intervention in developing countries is 'bad governance' due to the weaknesses of domestic institutions and bureaucracies.

The *policy implications* of the several elements described above in relation to the role of states – the relative advantage of prosperous, market-oriented democracies; an enhanced role for governments to assist the potential victims of globalization; the relative strength of the state vis-à-vis its own society; the adequacy of social and economic policies; the quality of governance; and the international position and status of the state vis-à-vis regional and international institutions – all point in the direction of adopting a model of social democracy in order to cope successfully with the challenges and opportunities of globalization. In my assessment, social democracies are the best prepared to cope with the challenges of economic globalization by effectively cushioning the domestic socio-economic implications of globalization (see Sandbrook 2003a, 2–9; Sandbrook et al. 2007; and Stiglitz 2007, 44).

### Conclusions

In this chapter, I assessed the different and alternative relationships between economic globalization and the distribution of wealth as a political problem in international relations, by suggesting three logical and causal links. First, from a Liberal perspective, as epitomized by the tenets

of the 'Washington Consensus' of the late 1980s, the forces of globalization are considered to be the potential solution to the global problems of
poverty and inequality, by reducing and eventually eradicating poverty,
at least in absolute levels. From this perspective, the reduction and eradication of poverty can be achieved eventually by promoting free trade,
expanding capital flows, improving the efficiency of markets, and dis-
seminating in a wiser way the technological benefits of the information
revolution. Second, from a Radical perspective, one can argue that globalization causes and deepens poverty and inequality both within and
among nations, due mainly to structural reasons. Third, a Realist, or
statist, view suggests that there may be no necessary and clear causal
direct linkage between globalization and the distribution of wealth. The
argument here, based on a minimalist version of globalization, points
to national governments and states, as well as other political and social
institutions, as being ultimately capable of perpetuating, exacerbating, or
alleviating poverty and inequality in a globalized international context.

The examination of the possible causal links between globalization,
growth, poverty, and inequality also leads us to a kind of analytical limbo.
Although there are several alternative causal mechanisms and channels
by which trade and financial openness might enhance economic growth
and then reduce poverty (but not necessarily inequality), the convoluted
economic logic suggests that it is very difficult to establish clear-cut causal
relationships between growth, capital, labour mobility, trade, financial
flows, and technology, on the one hand, and poverty and inequality, on
the other. In several cases, the causal links bring about contradictory
results, such as in the case of the effects of technology diffusion: less
poverty, but more inequality, at least in the short term (Harrison 2007,
24; and Prasad et al. 2007, 458).

All in all, the links between globalization and the distribution of wealth
remain complex and ambiguous; globalization might have both detrimental and positive effects simultaneously. It all depends essentially on
how globalization is managed by the relevant political and social institutions at the national, regional, and global levels, first and foremost
the state itself. That is, states can (or might) use globalization to reduce
poverty and inequality within their own societies. When globalization
is properly managed, it can deliver enormous benefits in terms of both
growth and social equity; conversely, when globalization is mismanaged,
it might have adverse effects in terms of poverty and inequality (Prasad
et al. 2007, 458; and Stiglitz 2008, 71).

If states are the key to how globalization might impinge upon poverty
and inequality, they might channel the positive effects as predicted by the
Liberals, and at the same time mitigate the negative effects as predicted

by the Radicals. As a matter of fact, this is a Herculean job for states to perform, and it should take into consideration the complex *intermestic* realities where states' choices are restricted, embedded, and conditioned by the global structure itself, including globalization processes and the hierarchical distribution of power within the region and the international system, alongside the political and social pressures within their own societies.

# 4    The Latin American experience, 1982–2008

At the turn of the twenty-first century, much of the economic debate in Latin America has revolved around the ambiguous and contradictory effects of economic globalization upon the distribution of wealth and especially the income distribution in the region. For example, several international institutions, such as the IMF and especially the World Bank, have tended to emphasize the potential benign effects of globalization, especially of trade liberalization. Other institutions, such as the Economic Commission for Latin America and the Caribbean (ECLAC) at the United Nations (or, in Spanish, CEPAL), are less sanguine about the positive effects of globalization, especially of financial liberalization, regarding poverty and income distribution.[1]

With the exception of the Latin American version of the *dependency* theory, which has been a substantial theoretical contribution to the study of international politics, the region has occupied only a marginal place in theorizing about international relations in general and about globalization and the distribution of wealth in particular. Yet, my focal argument in this chapter is that the Latin American experience can serve as a useful and fascinating laboratory for testing theories of social sciences, not only on issues of war and peace (see Kacowicz 1998 and 2005), but also with reference to international political economy and relevant issues such as poverty and social inequality (Filgueira 2008, 41).

This theoretical and empirical lacuna is even more striking when contrasted to the strong tradition of the radical Latin American critique of imperialism, neocolonialism, and nowadays of globalization, as developed by a vast literature on economic development, including the *dependencia* (dependency) approach of the late 1960s and 1970s, which emphasized the nefarious role of international and structural factors, such as the US influence, the international financial institutions (IFIs), economic imperialism, and the transnational presence of multinational

---

[1]  I would like to thank Albert Berry for his comments on this point.

corporations for the region's economics and politics (López-Alves and Johnson 2007, 11; see also Cardoso and Faletto 1979).

According to this argument, which might still be relevant nowadays, the processes of economic globalization have led to the incorporation of the countries of the region into the world economy, even allowing for some form of 'dependent development', though domestically the bulk of the population, the poor and disadvantaged, have not benefited from growth or from economic development. In this context, it is interesting to point out that for many Latin Americans economic globalization has served as a paramount political pretext for the enactment of domestic policies, either as an incentive to develop specific policies (such as the adoption of neoliberalism *à outrance* in the early 1990s in countries like Argentina and Peru), or as a political manipulation not to perform reforms at all.[2]

In this chapter, I address these convoluted issues, by looking at the complex and ambiguous relationships between the phenomena of economic globalization and the distribution of wealth in the regional context of Latin America from 1982 until 2008. Based on the *intermestic* model depicted in Chapter 3, I argue that in order to understand the links between globalization, poverty, and inequality in Latin America we should focus upon the role of the state and its national policies as critical to cope with globalization and reap the potential benefits of a deeper integration into the global economy, while addressing its potential hazards (Bouzas and Ffrench Davis 2004, 1).

The Liberal premise, according to which globalization should bring about growth and by extension a reduction of poverty and inequality, has been questioned in the region since the neoliberal experience of the 1980s. Neoliberalism has been the dominant ideology of the international financial system, which includes the commercial banks and the network of official banks, including multilateral lending institutions such as the IMF, the World Bank, and the various regional banks (the international financial institutions, or IFIs). The IFIs have argued that deeper economic integration into the world economy would raise the potential for economic growth and for development in the region. In effect, the IFIs constitute the broader international context, which partly define the contours of the economic policy choices available for the countries of the region. Yet, the Latin American experience since 1982, as demonstrated empirically, among others, by ECLAC, has suggested otherwise: growth has not led to a reduction of inequality or even to the diminution of poverty, but rather to pernicious negative effects in terms of social welfare, especially the widening of the socio-economic gap between the

[2] I would like to thank Bruno Ayllón Pino for his comments on this point.

few rich and the many poor (see Burki and Perry 1997, 91; Korzeniewicz and Smith 2000, 8; Stiglitz 2002, 79; and Teichman 2001, 44).

For instance, during the 1990s, poverty and inequality had actually worsened in many countries of the region that experienced economic growth, breeding discontent and political opposition as to the social and economic effects of globalization and economic reform (Bouzas and Ffrench Davis 2004, 1; and Stiglitz 2002, 79). High inequality in Latin America meant that, whatever the rate of growth, the positive or benign growth effects on reducing poverty were less than might have been expected with a more equal distribution of income to start with, and a better distribution of its potential gains (Birdsall and Sezkely 2003, 51–2). Whether the exacerbation of poverty and inequality should be causally linked to the forces of globalization or to the (ir)responsibility of the national governments remains an open question to be addressed in the bulk of this chapter.

Latin America is a relatively rich region, compared to other developing regions of the world. Its average per capita GDP of $10,497 (as of 2007) is larger than that of East Asia, South Asia, and sub-Saharan Africa. The region does not have a significant problem in terms of lack of resources or lack of natural wealth, but rather a striking maldistribution of wealth (resources, assets, and income). For instance, data from 2006 shows an appalling reality according to which about 120 million out of 566 million Latin Americans lived on less than $2 a day, while 47 million lived on less than $1 a day (Helwege and Birch 2007, 5). Widespread poverty in Latin America represents a moral outrage, a serious obstacle to sustainable growth, a political and social threat to the consolidation of democracy, and a major impediment to long-term social and political stability (Burki and Perry 1997, 87).

Moreover, income distribution in Latin America remains probably the most unequal in the world, even surpassing the Gini coefficients of sub-Saharan Africa, posing a striking degree of extreme inequality between the privileged elites and the impoverished majorities in the Latin American societies. Between 2002 and 2008 for the first time there has been a significant decline in inequality in the region, with the exception of the Dominican Republic and Guatemala. Yet, the Gini coefficients of the major Latin American economies are still very skewed, particularly in the largest and most developed economies of the region: Brazil (0.55 in 2007); Mexico (0.481 in 2006); Argentina (0.487 in 2006); and Chile (0.52 in 2006) (see *Economist*, 3 December 2011, 51; Rapoport 2006, 40; and Table 4.8). The disparity of the income distribution in Latin America remains very high, with the average per capita income of households in the tenth decile as approximately seventeen times greater than that of the poorest 40 per cent of households (see Bouzas and Ffrench Davis 2004, 3; ECLAC 2009, 5; Helwege and Birch 2007, 5; Hilton 2001; Hoffman and Centeno 2003, 365; and Meyer 2000).

Poverty and inequality remain the two major socio-economic problems of Latin America, with pernicious political and social implications and connotations. Why is that the case? To what extent can we blame globalization for the persistence of poverty and the exacerbation of inequality in the region? In general terms, one can argue that from Christopher Columbus to our days, Latin America has been strongly influenced by external and international processes, including that of economic globalization, though the region as a whole (with some particular successful exceptions, such as Chile, Costa Rica, Panama, and most recently Brazil) had failed to take full advantage of the opportunities and challenges offered by globalization, and had not been able to moderate the negative impact of these external factors (Ferrer 1999, 9–10). What, then, are the explanations for this relative failure?

Structural and *dependencista* arguments might point out to the effects of global capitalism in general, and to the financial and commercial vulnerability of the Latin American economies in particular, as a possible culprit for the exacerbation of poverty, the deepening of inequality, the domestic social violence, and the chronic deficit of political legitimacy of the political systems in the region (see Filgueira 2008, 16; Harris and Nef 2008b, 273–4; and Romero 2002). Conversely, an alternative domestic politics argument might suggest that the causes of poverty and inequality in Latin America are not necessarily related to economic globalization, but rather stem from the structural domestic characteristics of the Latin American societies and polities, first and foremost the relative weakness of their political institutions (see for instance Hoffman and Centeno 2003).

In the following pages, I briefly describe the historical and contemporary context of the subject matter. Then I address the so-called 'Latin American puzzle' of poverty and especially of high and persistent inequality and outline the links between globalization and the distribution of wealth. Finally, I apply my *intermestic* political model to the region to make sense of these intricate links.

### The historical record: Latin America and globalization

*The period up to 1982*

Latin America's economic integration into the world economy is not a new phenomenon. Following Aldo Ferrer (1999), one might argue that after the 'discovery' of the Americas in 1492, the region was incorporated as a colonial domain into the world economy. Thus, the early insertion of Latin America into the global economy started when the Spanish and Portuguese colonizers exploited the region's vast natural resources and developed cash crops for export to the European markets (Ferrer 1999; and Hecht Oppenheim 2000, 1).

*The golden (first) age of globalization, 1880s–1914* After the independence of the Latin American countries at the beginning of the nineteenth century from Spain and Portugal, followed by a long period of independence wars and civil wars (except for the peaceful transition to independence by Brazil in 1822), it was only in the second half of the nineteenth century that the Latin American countries became integrated into the world economy. The last part of the nineteenth century was regarded as the golden age of Liberalism, the liberal order defined as the first age of globalization that took place between the 1880s and World War I. In this period, many Latin American countries, first and foremost Argentina and Brazil, prospered by exporting commodities under the economic hegemony and international political stability provided by the United Kingdom.

Towards the end of the nineteenth century, economic globalization had a profound impact upon the major economies of the region. The development of railways and steamboat navigation lowered the prices of transportation, thus facilitating the incorporation of the Southern Cone of South America into the world trade. The diversification and growth of trade also put in motion enormous migratory flows from Southern Europe to South America, as well as important foreign investments. By 1914, about 40 per cent of foreign investments and 30 per cent of world trade were focused in Latin America only. During the period between 1900 and 1913, Latin America maintained a faster pace of GDP growth than most of the advanced economies of the world. For instance, per capita exports from Latin America averaged $25 in 1913 compared with less than $4 a head for Asia (Maddison 1989, 43; see also Ferrer 1999, 61–2).

During the last two decades of the nineteenth century and the early twentieth century, the economic development of the Latin American countries centred around the export of coffee, bananas, minerals, sugar, cereals, and meat. The fiscal and monetary regimes, the favourable balance of payments, the macroeconomic stability, the accumulation of capital, the rates of employment and of income distribution, all were decisively affected by the insertion of Latin America into what today is usually referred to as the global economy. This was the period of export-led growth (*crecimiento hacia afuera*) in which Argentina ranked among the ten richest economies of the world. In the three biggest Latin American economies, Brazil, Argentina, and Mexico, foreign investment per head averaged $202, compared with less than $8 in the biggest Asian countries at that time (Maddison 1989, 43).

After World War I and following the Great Depression of the 1930s, Latin America drifted away from the liberal economic order towards state intervention in the economy and the adoption of the Import Substitution Industrialization (ISI) model of development. Only in the late 1970s and early 1980s, in the second and contemporary age of globalization, would Latin America return to be fully integrated into the world economy.

*The ISI interregnum, 1930s–70s* By the early 1950s, most of the Latin American countries implemented an ISI economic strategy, following the economic doctrines of structuralism (industrialization and developmentalism) prompted by the Argentine economist Raúl Prebisch and ECLAC. The intellectual work of ECLAC, based on the assumption of a secular decline in the external terms of trade for primary products of the developing countries, provided the theoretical justification for the policies Latin American governments had already begun to adopt, including raising tariffs and striving for regional integration (see Bulmer-Thomas et al. 2006, 5–6).

This strategy seemed the most suitable to adopt, against the background of the Great Depression of the 1930s and World War II. The Latin American countries veered sharply towards ISI with the help of debt default, exchange controls, quantitative restrictions, tariff barriers, and discriminatory practices. As a result, the state intervened massively in the economy. At least between 1931 and 1950, Latin America had done better than any other part of the world economy (Maddison 1995, 68; see also Iglesias 1992, 25).

Between the late 1940s and 1980, the Latin American countries experienced sustained high rates of growth. When World War II ended in 1945, rapid worldwide growth and the active 'developmentalist' (*desarrollismo*) policies adopted by the national governments throughout the region maintained high rates of growth that averaged about 5.2 per cent a year between 1945 and 1981. As a result of this growth, poverty incidence in the region fell from about 65 per cent in 1950 to about only 25 per cent in 1980. Interestingly enough, over this period, inequality remained virtually unchanged from its extremely high initial level for the region as a whole and there were widespread incidences of inflation (Berry 2007a, 213–14; Kuczynski 2003a, 21; and Maddison 1989,

68–70). Hence, while the ISI-growth strategy had its flaws regarding the preponderant role of the state in the economy, the strategy proved to be quite successful in terms of rapid growth and poverty decline, alongside high levels of inequality (Berry 2007b, 40).

The ISI economic strategy became increasingly unsustainable by the 1970s, leading to a series of political and economic crises and the adoption of neoliberal reforms, especially in the Southern Cone of South America. The shortcomings and the disillusionment with the application of ISI in the region created the economic and political background to search and implement reforms aimed at modernizing the Latin American economies. The alternative chosen, neoliberalism, embraced free-market policies, liberalization, and economic globalization.

By the late 1970s, the ISI model was doomed since its inner economic logic exhausted itself. The poor performance of the exports was partly due to the capital inflow that put upward pressure on the exchange rates, which would in the 1980s catapult into a huge debt crisis. There was a widespread misperception in Latin America that the region could successfully accommodate itself to high levels of inflation, prompting irresponsible populist policies, much less cautious than in Europe.

For instance, for Argentina and Brazil, the fiscal cost of ISI led to high inflation even before the debt crisis of 1982. By 1981, both countries already had annual inflation over 75 per cent. Whether indebtedness had been used in the late 1970s to keep the steam of development going in spite of severe trade shocks occasioned to an oil importer (Brazil), or to finance the euphoria of consumption, football, and an inconceivable war against Britain (Argentina), the consequences in both cases were catastrophic. As a result of expansionist macroeconomic policies, many countries in the region experienced recurring deficits in their balance of payments and escalating inflationary processes that exhausted the feasibility of the ISI economic model (see Gerchunoff and Llach 2009, 17; Maddison 1989, 37; and Sznajder 2011, 19).

The factors that accounted for the transformation of the Latin American economies away from the ISI economic strategy back into embracing economic globalization included the perceived stagnation of ISI in the 1960s and especially in the late 1970s, the economic crises that led to political impasses, crises, and military coups, the debt crisis of the 1980s, the adoption of the neoliberal ideology that advocated the primacy of the markets over the states, and the influence of the United States, alongside international institutions such as the IMF and the World Bank, in favour of free-market policies (Hecht Oppenheim 2000, 2; see also Iglesias 1992, 30; Kaufman 2003, 100; and Sáinz 2007, 243).

*The 1982–2008 period: Latin America's reinsertion into the global economy*

The economic and political history of the shift towards economic globalization started in the early 1980s, against the background of the debt crisis. This was arguably a globalization-related crisis, and it was the precursor of all subsequent financial crises. Throughout the last three decades, most of Latin America has left the state-centric model of economic development behind. Since the early 1980s, globalization in Latin America involved a dramatic shift away from import substitution to export promotion, as part of structural adjustment programmes that followed the 1982 debt crisis.

Many Latin American countries experienced a thorough restructuring and integration into the global economy, under the aegis of the neoliberal model, both through expanding trade in goods and services and through the liberalization of capital accounts, as well as with the privatization of state-owned enterprises and the deregulation of economic interactions, as enacted in the 'Washington Consensus' guidelines of the late 1980s (Hecht Oppenheim 2000, 1; and Kaufman 2003, 98).

During the 1980s and 1990s, most of the Latin American countries experienced profound economic changes, caused mainly by external influences. While the 1990s was the decade of the fulfilment of the so-called 'Washington Consensus', from 1994 to 2002, the Latin American economies, like many other emerging market economies in the developing world, experienced a series of financial and currency crises, as part of their insertion into financial globalization: the 1995 Mexican peso crisis (the *Tequila effect*) was followed by the 1997 East Asian crisis, the 1999 Brazilian crisis, the 2001–2 Argentine crisis, and most recently the 2008–9 global financial crisis (see De la Escosura 2007a, 17; Filgueira 2008, 15; Morley 2003, 63; Robinson 2004, 159; and Sáinz 2007, 242).

Paradoxically, during the years 2003–8, most of the Latin American economies underwent a benign period of strong economic growth, as a result of the global macroeconomic bonanza of the new millennium – buoyant commodity prices, favourable terms of trade, cheap capital, and plentiful foreign investment, as well as the consequence of sound management and effective policy frameworks (OECD 2008, 11). Since most of the Latin American nations continued to adhere to market solutions, rejected protectionism, controlled spending, contained inflation, and kept their economies open to foreign trade and investment, it seems that the Latin American countries in the last few years were finally making their way through the wreckage of the global economy (Noriega 2009, 4).

The Latin American countries have generally embraced globalization since 1982, as the following indexes of globalization clearly show: the

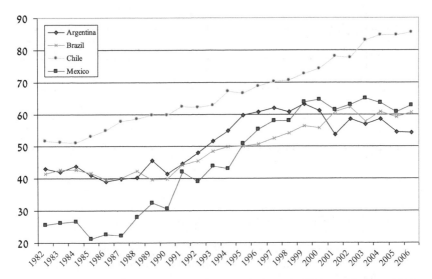

Figure 4.1 Economic globalization index of ABC + Mexico, 1982–2006
*Source:* http://globalization.kof.ethz.ch/; Dreher 2006, updated in Dreher et al. 2008.

improvement in the ranking of the economic globalization index; the steady and increasing growth in the GDP per capita based on purchasing-power parity (PPP); the percentage of real GDP growth rate, despite its frequent fluctuations that reflect economic and financial crises; trade as a percentage of the GDP; and FDI net flows as a percentage of the GDP. In Figures 4.1–4.5, I register these globalization economic indicators for the four most important economies in the region (Brazil, Mexico, Argentina, and Chile in that order, or, in short, ABC + Mexico).

Several preliminary conclusions can be drawn from the reading of these figures, which illustrate in graphic terms the economic trajectories of the four most important economies in the region:

(1) As for the economic globalization index, which is ranked in a scale between 1 and 100, there has been a steady increase for these four Latin American countries since 1982. By far, Chile is the most global-ized country in Latin America, with a 2010 ranking of 17 and a score of 87.14 (for the sake of comparison, 1 is Singapore with a score of 97.48, 109 is Venezuela with a score of 49.32, and 155 is Cuba with no score registered). After Chile and far below down in the list, Mexico ranks 81 in the global ranking (with a score of 61.28); Brazil ranks 91 with a score of 58.18; and Argentina ranks 107 with a score of 51.59. There are other, small Central American and Caribbean

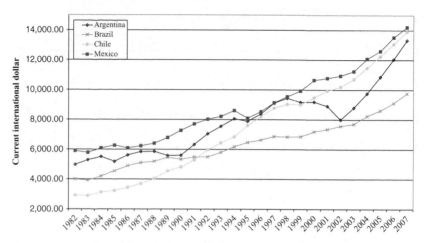

Figure 4.2 GDP per capita, ABC + Mexico, 1982–2007
*Source:* International Monetary Fund, *World Economic Outlook Database,*
April 2009.

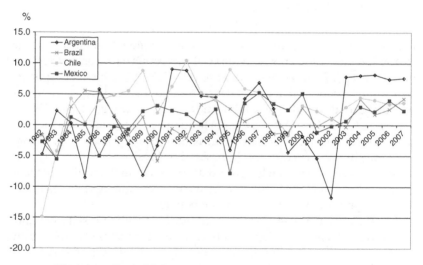

Figure 4.3 Real GDP growth rate (percentage) of ABC + Mexico,
1982–2007
*Source:* International Monetary Fund, *World Economic Outlook Database,*
April 2009.

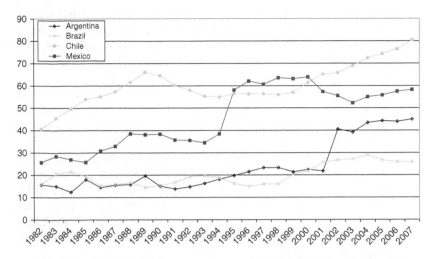

Figure 4.4 Trade (as a percentage of GDP) of ABC + Mexico, 1982–2007
*Source:* World Development Indicators, 2009.

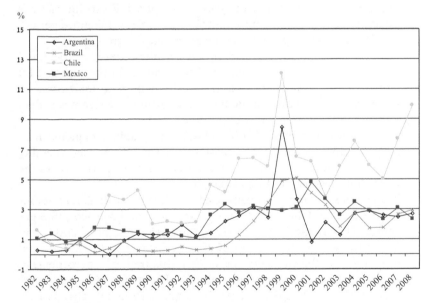

Figure 4.5 FDI net flows (as a percentage of GDP) of ABC + Mexico, 1982–2008
*Source:* UNCTAD – United Nations Conference on Trade and Development.

countries that rank relatively high in terms of economic globalization, such as: Panama (29 with a score of 81.09); Trinidad and Tobago (39 with a score of 76.47); Costa Rica (42 with a score of 75.44); Honduras (47 with a score of 74.54); and El Salvador (52 with a score of 71.28).

(2) We also learn from Figure 4.1, as well as from Figures 4.3 and 4.5, about the fluctuations in terms of growth and investments associated with economic and financial crises that affected the region in 1995, 1999, 2001, and in recent years. In this sense, Table 4.3 complements the analysis by showing the data regarding positive and negative growth, which clearly overlaps with periods of recession and crises (for instance, negative growth rates for Argentina in 1982, 1985, 1988, 1989, 1990, 1995, 1999, 2000, 2001, and especially 2002; for Brazil in 1983, 1990, 1992, and 1999; for Chile especially in 1982 and 1983, and in 1999; and for Mexico in 1982, 1983, 1986, and 1995).

(3) There is an interesting discrepancy between Figures 4.2 and 4.3. While there has been a steady growth in the GDP per capita based on PPP (except for the Mexican and Argentine cases in 1995–6 and 2001–3 respectively), the percentage of GDP growth rate has fluctuated between the four countries throughout the entire period, oscillating between positive and negative rates of growth.

(4) There is a significant correlation between the indexes of trade and FDI net flows, though the financial fluctuations in the case of FDI (Figure 4.5) are far more volatile and dramatic than the figures on trade. At the same time, trade flows have been more significant than FDI net inflows, as a percentage of the GDP.

(5) When examining Figures 4.3 and 4.5, the graphics depicted here resemble an economic roller coaster, in terms of financial volatility and economic fluctuations. That seems a fair characterization of the Latin American economies in general.

(6) Trade as a substantial percentage of the GDP is particularly relevant for the cases of Chile (80.4 per cent in 2007) and Mexico (58.2 per cent in 2007), and less so for Argentina (45 per cent in 2007) and Brazil (only 25.8 per cent in 2007, due in part to the continental dimensions of the country). It is evident that trade as a percentage of GDP is crucial for the smallest countries, like those in Central America (i.e., Costa Rica, Honduras, Nicaragua, Panama). By contrast, the volume of FDI's inflows as a percentage of the GDP is much smaller than the volume of trade.

These figures are further corroborated by Tables 4.1–4.5, which refer to eighteen significant Latin American countries (out of thirty-three):

Table 4.1 *Economic globalization index of Latin American countries, 1982–2006*

| | Argentina | Bolivia | Brazil | Chile | Colombia | Costa Rica | Dominican Republic | Ecuador | El Salvador | Guatemala | Honduras | Mexico | Nicaragua | Panama | Paraguay | Peru | Uruguay | Venezuela |
|---|---|---|---|---|---|---|---|---|---|---|---|---|---|---|---|---|---|---|
| 1982 | 42.97 | 48.42 | 41.45 | 51.62 | 31.13 | 47.05 | 20.62 | 30.31 | 31.30 | 53.18 | 48.50 | 25.63 | 71.63 | 33.53 | 31.36 | 31.88 | 46.77 | 38.04 |
| 1983 | 42.05 | 46.21 | 42.69 | 51.32 | 32.68 | 45.18 | 22.95 | 31.07 | 29.10 | 53.76 | 49.18 | 26.16 | 66.44 | 36.17 | 30.64 | 33.09 | 52.65 | 34.90 |
| 1984 | 43.88 | 47.12 | 42.58 | 51.16 | 33.37 | 43.92 | 25.02 | 31.93 | 30.68 | 53.28 | 49.00 | 26.67 | 60.96 | 35.99 | 32.29 | 33.00 | 53.21 | 37.42 |
| 1985 | 41.10 | 47.82 | 41.75 | 53.17 | 36.19 | 43.99 | 28.42 | 31.97 | 30.46 | 52.83 | 48.73 | 21.30 | 65.02 | 36.62 | 34.02 | 32.91 | 52.93 | 35.98 |
| 1986 | 39.12 | 48.65 | 39.64 | 54.81 | 36.79 | 44.14 | 27.69 | 34.09 | 35.15 | 57.38 | 54.27 | 22.56 | 62.70 | 36.34 | 36.20 | 33.44 | 53.89 | 37.27 |
| 1987 | 39.95 | 48.15 | 40.05 | 57.65 | 36.31 | 46.22 | 30.66 | 36.73 | 38.20 | 61.00 | 55.37 | 22.12 | 60.07 | 34.67 | 38.32 | 32.38 | 51.52 | 37.14 |
| 1988 | 40.29 | 42.61 | 42.32 | 58.46 | 34.56 | 48.96 | 32.05 | 37.97 | 40.65 | 63.19 | 56.63 | 28.03 | 59.57 | 38.71 | 39.30 | 31.50 | 51.44 | 37.66 |
| 1989 | 45.76 | 43.49 | 39.64 | 59.67 | 38.33 | 50.45 | 32.13 | 38.76 | 37.70 | 64.83 | 57.79 | 32.40 | 64.04 | 37.45 | 41.53 | 31.66 | 52.47 | 43.72 |
| 1990 | 41.56 | 47.15 | 39.93 | 59.73 | 38.36 | 51.51 | 31.77 | 38.47 | 38.87 | 66.37 | 59.25 | 30.71 | 65.85 | 40.84 | 43.01 | 34.17 | 52.61 | 52.86 |
| 1991 | 44.62 | 50.69 | 44.30 | 62.32 | 42.35 | 53.63 | 29.73 | 41.21 | 40.32 | 67.59 | 58.70 | 42.11 | 67.09 | 43.37 | 43.76 | 36.01 | 50.71 | 54.21 |
| 1992 | 48.09 | 51.50 | 45.56 | 62.21 | 44.82 | 55.14 | 30.76 | 43.00 | 40.70 | 67.84 | 58.15 | 39.11 | 68.07 | 45.30 | 46.53 | 35.95 | 50.11 | 52.27 |
| 1993 | 51.64 | 53.52 | 48.50 | 62.66 | 46.47 | 56.48 | 34.33 | 43.31 | 41.64 | 67.59 | 58.50 | 43.83 | 69.26 | 49.02 | 48.33 | 37.55 | 51.84 | 54.65 |
| 1994 | 54.95 | 54.70 | 49.84 | 67.10 | 47.46 | 56.87 | 34.34 | 46.91 | 40.45 | 67.89 | 59.24 | 42.97 | 71.74 | 53.06 | 51.75 | 38.56 | 53.62 | 57.08 |
| 1995 | 59.79 | 58.81 | 50.07 | 66.44 | 49.40 | 53.10 | 35.89 | 54.47 | 42.77 | 67.77 | 66.11 | 50.96 | 71.16 | 55.91 | 52.45 | 39.57 | 56.91 | 55.88 |
| 1996 | 60.72 | 60.40 | 50.59 | 68.67 | 55.70 | 58.66 | 34.21 | 55.63 | 45.35 | 68.63 | 65.52 | 55.24 | 73.18 | 57.81 | 52.50 | 44.82 | 56.72 | 61.06 |
| 1997 | 61.88 | 62.09 | 52.50 | 70.13 | 58.88 | 60.69 | 39.43 | 56.13 | 46.78 | 68.95 | 63.89 | 57.83 | 76.10 | 58.87 | 54.08 | 55.57 | 56.35 | 64.54 |
| 1998 | 60.72 | 64.35 | 54.05 | 70.54 | 56.23 | 65.55 | 42.01 | 57.62 | 48.20 | 68.73 | 64.20 | 57.85 | 76.56 | 58.00 | 57.00 | 60.19 | 57.06 | 61.67 |
| 1999 | 63.16 | 65.55 | 56.23 | 72.48 | 54.08 | 70.87 | 46.02 | 61.83 | 50.21 | 69.47 | 63.06 | 63.77 | 76.78 | 60.38 | 51.35 | 59.54 | 58.82 | 59.44 |
| 2000 | 61.08 | 65.92 | 55.74 | 74.22 | 57.02 | 70.39 | 48.83 | 63.72 | 53.27 | 69.50 | 63.01 | 64.60 | 77.48 | 61.55 | 52.00 | 60.16 | 60.56 | 61.33 |
| 2001 | 53.66 | 63.70 | 60.80 | 77.99 | 58.37 | 67.62 | 55.22 | 61.90 | 51.74 | 72.21 | 60.86 | 61.41 | 78.76 | 58.91 | 53.30 | 61.77 | 60.15 | 58.14 |
| 2002 | 58.46 | 65.74 | 62.13 | 77.47 | 58.79 | 68.12 | 58.30 | 59.65 | 48.39 | 71.95 | 59.07 | 62.97 | 73.33 | 58.71 | 49.96 | 65.27 | 59.10 | 55.21 |
| 2003 | 56.82 | 62.62 | 57.76 | 82.88 | 61.02 | 71.20 | 60.55 | 59.32 | 48.10 | 71.56 | 59.01 | 64.98 | 78.77 | 60.21 | 52.93 | 63.57 | 64.73 | 61.10 |
| 2004 | 58.48 | 60.92 | 60.80 | 84.60 | 60.55 | 64.64 | 58.67 | 59.23 | 49.94 | 69.44 | 60.53 | 63.51 | 80.25 | 62.47 | 56.20 | 67.68 | 65.44 | 61.32 |
| 2005 | 54.45 | 58.23 | 59.12 | 84.51 | 63.19 | 66.39 | 58.36 | 60.15 | 54.49 | 69.57 | 64.09 | 60.63 | 79.42 | 64.46 | 57.02 | 69.21 | 68.77 | 61.70 |
| 2006 | 54.26 | 64.48 | 60.48 | 85.48 | 59.15 | 69.64 | 62.29 | 59.76 | 55.48 | 68.88 | 61.85 | 62.71 | 81.65 | 66.12 | 58.71 | 65.86 | 69.93 | 56.59 |

Table 4.2 GDP per capita based on purchasing-power parity (PPP) of Latin American countries, 1982–2007

| | Argentina | Bolivia | Brazil | Chile | Colombia | Costa Rica | Dominican Republic | Ecuador | El Salvador | Guatemala | Honduras | Mexico | Nicaragua | Panama | Paraguay | Peru | Uruguay | Venezuela |
|---|---|---|---|---|---|---|---|---|---|---|---|---|---|---|---|---|---|---|
| 1982 | 4,981 | 1,955 | 3,988 | 2,899 | 2,686 | 2,957 | 2,266 | 3,073 | 2,135 | 2,420 | 1,804 | 5,897 | 1,922 | 3,511 | 2,259 | 3,446 | 3,701 | 6,056 |
| 1983 | 5,297 | 1,910 | 3,914 | 2,884 | 2,776 | 3,111 | 2,407 | 3,022 | 2,240 | 2,391 | 1,800 | 5,788 | 2,021 | 3,411 | 2,211 | 3,172 | 3,698 | 5,785 |
| 1984 | 5,511 | 1,938 | 4,180 | 3,119 | 2,915 | 3,389 | 2,469 | 3,183 | 2,341 | 2,431 | 1,889 | 6,080 | 1,995 | 3,557 | 2,290 | 3,337 | 3,770 | 5,906 |
| 1985 | 5,195 | 1,923 | 4,545 | 3,225 | 3,033 | 3,414 | 2,431 | 3,337 | 2,408 | 2,427 | 1,966 | 6,270 | 1,907 | 3,765 | 2,379 | 3,431 | 3,917 | 5,932 |
| 1986 | 5,617 | 1,876 | 4,892 | 3,424 | 3,215 | 3,575 | 2,511 | 3,429 | 2,441 | 2,421 | 1,962 | 6,086 | 1,865 | 3,901 | 2,363 | 3,843 | 4,334 | 6,380 |
| 1987 | 5,850 | 1,934 | 5,103 | 3,687 | 3,410 | 3,741 | 2,772 | 3,232 | 2,540 | 2,512 | 2,073 | 6,234 | 1,839 | 3,854 | 2,449 | 4,159 | 4,779 | 6,622 |
| 1988 | 5,860 | 2,016 | 5,189 | 4,022 | 3,595 | 3,896 | 2,860 | 3,605 | 2,639 | 2,632 | 2,176 | 6,398 | 1,610 | 3,382 | 2,599 | 3,812 | 4,985 | 7,070 |
| 1989 | 5,586 | 2,127 | 5,454 | 4,540 | 3,784 | 4,163 | 3,032 | 3,664 | 2,722 | 2,771 | 2,286 | 6,787 | 1,588 | 3,522 | 2,766 | 3,353 | 5,201 | 6,548 |
| 1990 | 5,606 | 2,264 | 5,332 | 4,806 | 4,021 | 4,371 | 2,919 | 3,830 | 2,913 | 2,896 | 2,306 | 7,268 | 1,599 | 3,881 | 2,956 | 3,239 | 5,388 | 7,007 |
| 1991 | 6,326 | 2,417 | 5,482 | 5,282 | 4,175 | 4,521 | 2,998 | 4,073 | 3,101 | 3,017 | 2,393 | 7,695 | 1,603 | 4,308 | 2,945 | 3,357 | 5,741 | 7,771 |
| 1992 | 7,042 | 2,462 | 5,487 | 5,966 | 4,369 | 4,938 | 3,338 | 4,221 | 3,388 | 3,149 | 2,511 | 8,008 | 1,594 | 4,681 | 3,042 | 3,356 | 6,301 | 8,238 |
| 1993 | 7,542 | 2,553 | 5,797 | 6,423 | 4,633 | 5,288 | 3,611 | 4,308 | 3,696 | 3,247 | 2,651 | 8,203 | 1,572 | 4,957 | 3,158 | 3,533 | 6,578 | 8,261 |
| 1994 | 8,049 | 2,653 | 6,169 | 6,824 | 4,880 | 5,492 | 3,722 | 4,508 | 3,976 | 3,342 | 2,596 | 8,591 | 1,632 | 5,111 | 3,268 | 4,074 | 7,140 | 8,057 |
| 1995 | 7,882 | 2,755 | 6,460 | 7,587 | 5,145 | 5,661 | 3,953 | 4,583 | 4,287 | 3,467 | 2,681 | 8,082 | 1,752 | 5,209 | 3,438 | 4,446 | 7,136 | 8,363 |
| 1996 | 8,375 | 2,849 | 6,622 | 8,183 | 5,248 | 5,665 | 4,255 | 4,685 | 4,412 | 3,537 | 2,752 | 8,526 | 1,847 | 5,607 | 3,442 | 4,574 | 7,629 | 8,326 |
| 1997 | 9,099 | 2,955 | 6,855 | 8,754 | 5,412 | 5,927 | 4,606 | 4,857 | 4,644 | 3,647 | 2,858 | 9,122 | 1,903 | 5,970 | 3,528 | 4,893 | 8,073 | 8,822 |
| 1998 | 9,448 | 3,051 | 6,830 | 9,017 | 5,401 | 6,340 | 4,912 | 4,917 | 4,839 | 3,756 | 2,895 | 9,541 | 1,941 | 6,371 | 3,514 | 4,840 | 8,442 | 8,765 |
| 1999 | 9,160 | 3,035 | 6,844 | 8,995 | 5,152 | 6,796 | 5,242 | 4,585 | 5,043 | 3,848 | 2,808 | 9,915 | 2,048 | 6,604 | 3,441 | 4,880 | 8,272 | 8,199 |
| 2000 | 9,189 | 3,105 | 7,187 | 9,479 | 5,325 | 7,120 | 5,578 | 4,726 | 5,228 | 3,926 | 2,959 | 10,647 | 2,122 | 6,611 | 3,331 | 5,055 | 8,282 | 8,517 |
| 2001 | 8,904 | 3,160 | 7,346 | 9,924 | 5,475 | 7,187 | 5,733 | 5,303 | 5,407 | 3,814 | 3,038 | 10,773 | 2,173 | 6,681 | 3,413 | 5,108 | 8,112 | 8,929 |
| 2002 | 7,995 | 3,220 | 7,562 | 10,192 | 5,608 | 7,353 | 6,083 | 5,401 | 5,592 | 3,932 | 3,133 | 10,940 | 2,171 | 6,822 | 3,403 | 5,375 | 7,574 | 8,118 |
| 2003 | 8,804 | 3,303 | 7,698 | 10,713 | 5,890 | 7,813 | 6,108 | 5,632 | 5,802 | 4,017 | 3,270 | 11,246 | 2,214 | 7,129 | 3,540 | 5,624 | 7,752 | 7,500 |
| 2004 | 9,759 | 3,454 | 8,231 | 11,455 | 6,265 | 8,182 | 6,001 | 6,151 | 6,013 | 4,112 | 3,421 | 12,069 | 2,312 | 7,728 | 3,735 | 5,998 | 8,510 | 8,925 |
| 2005 | 10,872 | 3,664 | 8,603 | 12,240 | 6,745 | 8,739 | 6,563 | 6,667 | 6,367 | 4,185 | 3,555 | 12,594 | 2,410 | 8,354 | 3,972 | 6,475 | 10,015 | 9,992 |
| 2006 | 12,054 | 3,881 | 9,105 | 13,062 | 7,329 | 9,615 | 7,391 | 6,978 | 6,800 | 4,437 | 3,834 | 13,517 | 2,525 | 9,200 | 4,195 | 7,091 | 10,813 | 11,157 |
| 2007 | 13,318 | 4,083 | 9,747 | 13,898 | 7,967 | 10,430 | 8,116 | 7,242 | 7,257 | 4,724 | 4,101 | 14,202 | 2,613 | 10,351 | 4,509 | 7,764 | 11,948 | 12,176 |

Table 4.3 *Real GDP growth rate (percentage) of Latin American countries, 1982–2007*

| | Argentina | Bolivia | Brazil | Chile | Colombia | Costa Rica | Dominican Republic | Ecuador | El Salvador | Guatemala | Honduras | Mexico | Nicaragua | Panama | Paraguay | Peru | Uruguay | Venezuela |
|---|---|---|---|---|---|---|---|---|---|---|---|---|---|---|---|---|---|---|
| 1982 | -4.76 | -5.90 | -1.73 | -14.90 | -1.22 | -9.98 | -0.62 | 0.63 | -7.04 | -5.93 | -4.51 | -2.76 | -4.06 | 3.08 | -4.26 | -2.72 | -9.92 | -2.20 |
| 1983 | 2.28 | -6.00 | -5.60 | -4.29 | -0.57 | 1.20 | 2.20 | -5.37 | 0.93 | -4.96 | -4.01 | -5.58 | 1.15 | -6.55 | -5.86 | -11.46 | -3.90 | -8.10 |
| 1984 | 0.29 | -2.24 | 2.93 | 4.22 | 1.20 | 4.97 | -1.13 | 1.49 | 0.71 | -2.00 | 1.13 | 1.23 | -4.85 | 0.51 | -0.17 | 1.41 | -1.72 | -1.61 |
| 1985 | -8.51 | -3.69 | 5.53 | 0.34 | 0.98 | -2.23 | -4.44 | 1.75 | -0.18 | -3.09 | 1.00 | 0.08 | -7.27 | 2.71 | 0.85 | -0.22 | 0.83 | -2.53 |
| 1986 | 5.79 | -4.57 | 5.32 | 3.88 | 3.71 | 2.45 | 1.04 | 0.54 | -0.82 | -2.40 | -2.34 | -5.03 | -4.30 | 1.39 | -2.82 | 9.60 | 8.24 | 5.23 |
| 1987 | 1.37 | 0.37 | 1.53 | 4.82 | 3.26 | 1.88 | 7.47 | -8.25 | 1.29 | 1.00 | 2.84 | -0.28 | -4.02 | -3.84 | 0.87 | 5.35 | 7.33 | 1.03 |
| 1988 | -3.14 | 0.81 | -1.67 | 5.49 | 1.95 | 0.69 | -0.22 | 7.86 | 0.47 | 1.33 | 1.49 | -0.76 | -15.31 | -15.16 | 2.62 | -11.38 | 0.87 | 3.25 |
| 1989 | -8.15 | 1.67 | 1.28 | 8.75 | 1.40 | 2.97 | 2.14 | -2.06 | -0.61 | 1.41 | 1.24 | 2.22 | -4.97 | 0.37 | 2.56 | -15.24 | 0.55 | -10.77 |
| 1990 | -3.37 | 2.50 | -5.87 | 1.93 | 2.33 | 1.10 | -7.30 | 0.64 | 3.04 | 0.63 | -2.85 | 3.10 | -3.04 | 6.08 | 2.89 | -7.00 | -0.25 | 3.04 |
| 1991 | 9.02 | 3.11 | -0.66 | 6.18 | 0.32 | -0.07 | -0.79 | 2.74 | 2.87 | 0.66 | 0.24 | 2.30 | -3.17 | 7.26 | -3.74 | 0.14 | 2.94 | 7.16 |
| 1992 | 8.81 | -0.43 | -2.15 | 10.41 | 2.29 | 6.77 | 8.84 | 1.31 | 6.80 | 2.03 | 2.57 | 1.74 | -2.81 | 6.21 | 0.94 | -2.27 | 7.29 | 3.61 |
| 1993 | 4.69 | 1.37 | 3.26 | 5.24 | 3.66 | 4.67 | 5.74 | -0.23 | 6.64 | 0.79 | 3.19 | 0.11 | -3.58 | 3.51 | 1.48 | 2.89 | 2.05 | -1.98 |
| 1994 | 4.49 | 1.76 | 4.20 | 4.03 | 3.14 | 1.70 | 0.94 | 2.46 | 5.32 | 0.80 | -4.09 | 2.56 | 1.66 | 0.95 | 1.35 | 12.92 | 6.28 | -4.50 |
| 1995 | -4.04 | 1.77 | 2.62 | 8.95 | 3.31 | 1.01 | 4.06 | -0.37 | 5.67 | 1.66 | 1.19 | -7.81 | 5.18 | -0.12 | 3.09 | 6.95 | -2.06 | 1.72 |
| 1996 | 4.28 | 1.46 | 0.60 | 5.85 | 0.10 | -1.80 | 5.64 | 0.32 | 1.01 | 0.11 | 0.74 | 3.53 | 3.50 | 5.63 | -1.76 | 0.96 | 4.93 | -2.30 |
| 1997 | 6.87 | 2.04 | 1.82 | 5.22 | 1.45 | 2.93 | 6.48 | 1.97 | 3.53 | 1.43 | 2.16 | 5.23 | 1.33 | 4.73 | 0.82 | 5.24 | 4.08 | 4.22 |
| 1998 | 2.69 | 2.11 | -1.45 | 1.88 | -1.31 | 5.78 | 5.48 | 0.12 | 3.04 | 1.86 | 0.19 | 3.45 | 0.89 | 5.55 | -1.49 | -2.17 | 3.42 | -1.73 |
| 1999 | -4.43 | -1.94 | -1.23 | -1.67 | -5.96 | 5.67 | 5.19 | -8.09 | 2.74 | 0.98 | -4.40 | 2.44 | 3.97 | 2.18 | -3.47 | -0.62 | -3.40 | -7.79 |
| 2000 | -1.83 | 0.14 | 2.77 | 3.13 | 1.14 | 2.53 | 4.15 | 0.89 | 1.45 | -0.15 | 3.13 | 5.10 | 1.43 | -2.02 | -5.26 | 1.38 | -2.01 | 1.67 |
| 2001 | -5.37 | -0.63 | -0.17 | 2.25 | 0.40 | -1.42 | 0.36 | 9.58 | 1.01 | -5.14 | 0.26 | -1.19 | 0.00 | -1.30 | 0.04 | -1.31 | -4.36 | 2.38 |
| 2002 | -11.75 | 0.17 | 1.16 | 0.93 | 0.67 | 0.56 | 4.28 | 0.09 | 1.64 | 1.33 | 1.35 | -0.19 | -1.83 | 0.36 | -1.99 | 3.42 | -8.23 | -10.65 |
| 2003 | 7.82 | 0.42 | -0.32 | 2.92 | 2.85 | 4.04 | -1.67 | 2.11 | 1.60 | 0.02 | 2.19 | 0.66 | -0.11 | 2.33 | 1.86 | 2.45 | 0.22 | -9.53 |
| 2004 | 8.01 | 1.90 | 4.20 | 4.43 | 2.95 | 2.01 | -0.13 | 6.47 | 1.15 | 0.63 | 3.89 | 2.95 | 2.61 | 5.62 | 2.83 | 3.38 | 4.41 | 15.96 |
| 2005 | 8.14 | 2.20 | 1.71 | 4.03 | 4.08 | 3.72 | 7.71 | 4.49 | 2.38 | 0.83 | 3.75 | 2.17 | 1.68 | 5.34 | 1.14 | 5.20 | 14.20 | 8.15 |
| 2006 | 7.41 | 2.62 | 2.53 | 3.38 | 5.27 | 6.59 | 9.10 | 1.40 | 3.47 | 2.71 | 4.47 | 3.99 | 1.49 | 6.68 | 2.29 | 6.10 | 4.60 | 8.18 |
| 2007 | 7.59 | 2.43 | 4.24 | 3.61 | 5.86 | 5.63 | 6.93 | 1.07 | 3.93 | 3.67 | 4.16 | 2.31 | 0.78 | 9.57 | 4.67 | 6.62 | 7.60 | 6.27 |

Table 4.4 Trade (percentage of GDP) of Latin American countries, 1980–2007

| | Argentina | Bolivia | Brazil | Chile | Colombia | Costa Rica | Dominican Republic | Ecuador | El Salvador | Guatemala | Honduras | Mexico | Nicaragua | Panama | Paraguay | Peru | Uruguay | Venezuela |
|---|---|---|---|---|---|---|---|---|---|---|---|---|---|---|---|---|---|---|
| 1980 | 11.55 | 46.81 | 20.36 | 49.80 | 31.79 | 63.30 | 48.11 | 52.05 | 67.41 | 47.11 | 81.29 | 23.68 | 67.50 | 186.94 | 44.01 | 41.82 | 35.66 | 50.60 |
| 1982 | 15.6 | 58.5 | 15.9 | 40.6 | 26.1 | 87.2 | 33.6 | 48.6 | 51.2 | 33.5 | 54.7 | 25.6 | 42.0 | 159.2 | 31.9 | 36.1 | 31.6 | 46.9 |
| 1983 | 15.0 | 52.4 | 20.4 | 45.3 | 23.7 | 60.8 | 32.7 | 47.3 | 54.4 | 27.5 | 55.4 | 28.4 | 49.4 | 127.5 | 26.6 | 39.2 | 49.3 | 30.7 |
| 1984 | 12.3 | 49.5 | 21.5 | 49.6 | 24.3 | 58.0 | 61.1 | 49.1 | 50.3 | 28.2 | 57.7 | 26.9 | 45.9 | 125.2 | 38.0 | 34.8 | 48.0 | 45.6 |
| 1985 | 18.0 | 41.9 | 19.3 | 53.9 | 26.3 | 55.8 | 65.3 | 51.7 | 52.2 | 24.9 | 55.0 | 25.7 | 36.6 | 128.2 | 48.4 | 39.4 | 47.9 | 42.2 |
| 1986 | 14.5 | 47.1 | 15.2 | 55.1 | 30.8 | 54.0 | 57.8 | 48.4 | 53.7 | 30.6 | 54.9 | 30.8 | 33.6 | 132.6 | 58.5 | 29.3 | 46.5 | 40.1 |
| 1987 | 15.4 | 44.4 | 15.7 | 57.3 | 29.9 | 57.4 | 63.0 | 57.7 | 45.1 | 38.1 | 48.8 | 32.9 | 25.5 | 134.2 | 61.3 | 23.7 | 40.9 | 44.8 |
| 1988 | 15.7 | 41.9 | 16.6 | 61.5 | 30.2 | 60.9 | 74.8 | 59.3 | 38.1 | 38.0 | 55.2 | 38.5 | 76.3 | 133.8 | 71.3 | 41.4 | 39.8 | 47.8 |
| 1989 | 19.6 | 45.7 | 14.4 | 66.0 | 31.8 | 64.4 | 78.0 | 65.0 | 36.9 | 39.8 | 65.3 | 38.1 | 97.7 | 149.1 | 67.7 | 24.6 | 41.2 | 55.2 |
| 1990 | 15.0 | 46.7 | 15.2 | 64.5 | 35.4 | 66.5 | 77.5 | 65.0 | 49.8 | 45.9 | 77.1 | 38.3 | 71.3 | 165.4 | 72.7 | 29.6 | 41.6 | 59.6 |
| 1991 | 13.8 | 48.4 | 16.6 | 60.2 | 35.3 | 70.7 | 83.2 | 67.4 | 47.7 | 39.5 | 72.1 | 35.6 | 74.3 | 189.7 | 68.4 | 27.1 | 38.6 | 57.6 |
| 1992 | 14.7 | 49.1 | 19.3 | 58.0 | 33.5 | 75.1 | 81.1 | 67.2 | 48.5 | 45.4 | 68.4 | 35.5 | 70.5 | 196.2 | 66.7 | 28.4 | 40.1 | 55.3 |
| 1993 | 16.2 | 47.5 | 19.6 | 55.2 | 35.2 | 78.0 | 78.8 | 51.8 | 53.5 | 43.8 | 78.4 | 34.4 | 68.3 | 189.7 | 84.8 | 28.2 | 38.7 | 54.1 |
| 1994 | 18.1 | 48.9 | 18.7 | 54.8 | 35.9 | 76.7 | 78.3 | 51.0 | 55.2 | 42.4 | 89.7 | 38.4 | 47.8 | 194.8 | 121.4 | 27.9 | 40.1 | 53.2 |
| 1995 | 19.7 | 49.7 | 16.0 | 56.4 | 35.5 | 77.9 | 75.1 | 54.0 | 59.4 | 44.7 | 91.8 | 58.1 | 53.8 | 198.8 | 130.7 | 30.8 | 38.1 | 48.9 |
| 1996 | 21.5 | 49.9 | 14.9 | 56.2 | 36.0 | 82.1 | 73.4 | 50.5 | 55.0 | 40.4 | 98.8 | 62.1 | 59.3 | 165.6 | 112.6 | 31.5 | 39.5 | 57.8 |
| 1997 | 23.3 | 50.5 | 15.8 | 56.3 | 35.6 | 85.3 | 76.4 | 51.3 | 63.4 | 41.6 | 98.0 | 60.6 | 70.9 | 175.8 | 102.9 | 32.9 | 37.7 | 51.2 |
| 1998 | 23.3 | 52.3 | 15.9 | 56.9 | 35.9 | 97.6 | 79.4 | 49.8 | 61.9 | 44.4 | 100.5 | 63.5 | 69.7 | 160.3 | 110.0 | 31.7 | 35.6 | 43.6 |
| 1999 | 21.3 | 44.2 | 20.2 | 56.9 | 36.1 | 97.7 | 79.9 | 56.5 | 62.2 | 46.4 | 97.0 | 63.1 | 76.6 | 134.3 | 83.4 | 32.5 | 33.4 | 42.1 |
| 2000 | 22.4 | 45.6 | 21.7 | 61.3 | 36.3 | 94.4 | 82.9 | 68.1 | 69.8 | 49.1 | 120.4 | 63.9 | 75.0 | 142.4 | 87.2 | 34.2 | 36.7 | 47.9 |
| 2001 | 21.7 | 45.2 | 25.7 | 65.1 | 37.1 | 86.0 | 74.7 | 57.9 | 67.5 | 69.5 | 115.9 | 57.3 | 70.9 | 138.6 | 79.2 | 33.5 | 36.3 | 42.1 |
| 2002 | 40.5 | 49.4 | 26.7 | 65.7 | 36.7 | 90.0 | 72.8 | 55.8 | 67.4 | 66.0 | 118.0 | 55.5 | 71.1 | 129.7 | 92.6 | 33.4 | 40.0 | 48.6 |
| 2003 | 39.2 | 52.0 | 27.1 | 68.9 | 39.5 | 95.7 | 86.5 | 53.5 | 70.0 | 66.0 | 122.2 | 52.2 | 76.0 | 122.1 | 98.8 | 35.5 | 50.6 | 50.6 |
| 2004 | 43.4 | 57.5 | 29.0 | 72.3 | 38.7 | 95.7 | 83.9 | 57.1 | 72.9 | 69.1 | 135.5 | 55.0 | 82.2 | 131.5 | 96.0 | 39.3 | 51.8 | 55.4 |
| 2005 | 44.3 | 66.6 | 26.6 | 74.1 | 38.3 | 102.5 | 65.5 | 62.7 | 71.7 | 66.0 | 136.5 | 55.8 | 87.8 | 144.5 | 106.8 | 44.3 | 61.5 | 55.4 |
| 2006 | 43.9 | 70.7 | 25.8 | 76.3 | 39.8 | 104.4 | 68.0 | 66.9 | 74.0 | 66.8 | 131.5 | 57.5 | 92.1 | 146.2 | 111.9 | 48.4 | 58.9 | 60.1 |
| 2007 | 45.0 | 76.1 | 25.8 | 80.4 | 37.9 | 102.4 | 69.0 | 66.1 | 76.2 | 67.1 | 129.9 | 58.2 | 100.4 | 155.0 | 104.8 | 51.3 | 56.9 | 55.7 |

Table 4.5 *FDI flows (net) as a percentage of GDP of Latin American countries, 1982–2007*

| | Argentina | Bolivia | Brazil | Chile | Colombia | Costa Rica | Dominican Republic | Ecuador | El Salvador | Guatemala | Honduras | Mexico | Nicaragua | Panama | Paraguay | Peru | Uruguay | Venezuela |
|---|---|---|---|---|---|---|---|---|---|---|---|---|---|---|---|---|---|---|
| 1982 | 0.28 | 1.03 | 1.10 | 1.59 | 0.79 | 0.87 | -0.01 | 0.27 | -0.03 | 0.99 | 0.40 | 1.03 | 0.39 | 7.58 | 0.71 | 0.23 | -0.16 | 0.32 |
| 1983 | 0.21 | 0.23 | 0.65 | 0.65 | 1.35 | 1.52 | 0.45 | 0.37 | 0.65 | 0.56 | 0.48 | 1.38 | 0.00 | 1.56 | 0.09 | 0.24 | 0.11 | 0.26 |
| 1984 | 0.29 | 0.23 | 0.72 | 0.38 | 1.29 | 1.20 | 0.54 | 0.37 | 0.25 | 0.45 | 0.52 | 0.82 | 0.27 | -2.52 | 0.02 | -0.53 | 0.07 | -1.34 |
| 1985 | 1.04 | 0.26 | 0.64 | 0.79 | 2.47 | 1.40 | 0.65 | 0.37 | 0.20 | 0.62 | 0.63 | 1.01 | 0.00 | 1.18 | 0.20 | 0.01 | -0.17 | 0.17 |
| 1986 | 0.54 | 0.34 | 0.12 | 1.61 | 1.63 | 1.09 | 0.75 | 0.68 | 0.58 | 0.91 | 0.66 | 1.74 | 0.00 | 0.34 | 0.65 | 0.10 | 0.63 | -0.39 |
| 1987 | -0.02 | 0.93 | 0.40 | 3.89 | 0.74 | 1.63 | 1.42 | 1.11 | 0.37 | 2.38 | 0.78 | 1.76 | 0.08 | -8.92 | 0.21 | 0.09 | 0.68 | 1.03 |
| 1988 | 0.90 | 0.73 | 0.85 | 3.63 | 0.44 | 2.10 | 1.85 | 1.47 | 0.29 | 4.72 | 0.88 | 1.57 | 0.00 | -10.67 | 0.12 | 0.08 | 0.62 | 1.24 |
| 1989 | 1.34 | 0.76 | 0.25 | 4.22 | 1.23 | 1.52 | 1.33 | 1.54 | 0.21 | 1.02 | 0.83 | 1.42 | 0.11 | 0.92 | 0.33 | 0.17 | 0.48 | 1.38 |
| 1990 | 1.30 | 1.38 | 0.21 | 1.97 | 1.05 | 2.24 | 1.42 | 1.12 | 0.04 | 0.87 | 1.20 | 1.00 | 0.02 | 2.23 | 1.53 | 0.14 | 0.50 | 1.65 |
| 1991 | 1.29 | 1.79 | 0.25 | 2.15 | 0.93 | 2.49 | 1.49 | 1.29 | 0.47 | 1.08 | 1.42 | 1.51 | 1.49 | 1.62 | 1.47 | -0.02 | 0.32 | 0.45 |
| 1992 | 1.94 | 2.16 | 0.48 | 2.02 | 1.39 | 2.64 | 1.59 | 1.34 | 0.26 | 1.01 | 1.17 | 1.21 | 1.40 | 1.90 | 2.06 | -0.22 | 0.09 | 3.31 |
| 1993 | 1.18 | 2.16 | 0.27 | 2.10 | 1.58 | 2.56 | 1.48 | 3.15 | 0.24 | 1.40 | 1.25 | 1.09 | 1.25 | 2.04 | 1.15 | 2.18 | 0.68 | 0.72 |
| 1994 | 1.41 | 2.18 | 0.36 | 4.59 | 1.81 | 2.82 | 1.49 | 3.10 | 0.03 | 0.56 | 1.01 | 2.61 | 1.34 | 4.54 | 1.77 | 7.32 | 0.88 | 1.44 |
| 1995 | 2.17 | 5.57 | 0.57 | 4.10 | 1.05 | 2.88 | 2.67 | 2.24 | 0.40 | 0.58 | 1.47 | 3.33 | 2.37 | 2.47 | 1.28 | 4.77 | 0.81 | 1.32 |
| 1996 | 2.55 | 5.80 | 1.29 | 6.35 | 3.20 | 3.61 | 0.57 | 2.35 | -0.05 | 0.55 | 1.85 | 2.76 | 2.92 | 4.46 | 1.71 | 6.21 | 0.67 | 3.20 |
| 1997 | 3.13 | 10.78 | 2.18 | 6.37 | 5.21 | 3.17 | 2.19 | 3.06 | 0.53 | 0.53 | 2.27 | 3.20 | 5.09 | 12.88 | 2.66 | 3.62 | 0.58 | 7.23 |
| 1998 | 2.44 | 12.07 | 3.42 | 5.83 | 2.87 | 4.34 | 3.43 | 3.74 | 9.19 | 3.89 | 1.58 | 3.01 | 5.45 | 11.00 | 4.32 | 2.90 | 0.73 | 5.46 |
| 1999 | 8.46 | 12.20 | 4.87 | 12.00 | 1.75 | 3.92 | 6.24 | 3.89 | 1.73 | 0.95 | 3.67 | 2.86 | 8.02 | 7.55 | 1.29 | 3.76 | 1.12 | 2.95 |
| 2000 | 3.66 | 8.77 | 5.08 | 6.46 | 2.91 | 2.56 | 4.03 | 4.52 | 1.32 | 1.34 | 5.31 | 3.10 | 6.77 | 6.03 | 1.47 | 1.52 | 1.36 | 4.01 |
| 2001 | 0.81 | 8.67 | 4.05 | 6.12 | 3.10 | 2.81 | 4.40 | 6.26 | 2.02 | 2.67 | 3.98 | 4.79 | 3.64 | 3.43 | 1.31 | 2.12 | 1.60 | 3.00 |
| 2002 | 2.11 | 8.56 | 3.28 | 3.79 | 2.63 | 3.91 | 3.68 | 3.15 | 3.29 | 0.99 | 3.50 | 3.66 | 5.06 | 0.63 | 0.20 | 3.80 | 1.58 | 0.84 |
| 2003 | 1.27 | 2.44 | 1.84 | 5.82 | 2.17 | 3.28 | 3.06 | 3.04 | 0.94 | 1.20 | 4.89 | 2.58 | 4.91 | 5.96 | 0.49 | 2.18 | 3.72 | 2.44 |
| 2004 | 2.69 | 0.97 | 2.73 | 7.50 | 3.08 | 4.27 | 4.21 | 2.56 | 2.30 | 1.24 | 6.16 | 3.46 | 5.60 | 7.08 | 0.54 | 2.29 | 2.52 | 1.32 |
| 2005 | 2.87 | -3.01 | 1.71 | 5.91 | 8.34 | 4.31 | 3.35 | 1.33 | 2.99 | 1.87 | 6.15 | 2.86 | 4.97 | 6.22 | 0.72 | 3.25 | 5.10 | 1.78 |
| 2006 | 2.58 | 2.45 | 1.76 | 4.98 | 4.89 | 6.61 | 4.29 | 0.65 | 1.29 | 1.96 | 6.18 | 2.30 | 5.41 | 14.58 | 1.87 | 3.75 | 7.73 | -0.32 |
| 2007 | 2.47 | 2.79 | 2.63 | 7.67 | 5.37 | 7.32 | 3.85 | 0.44 | 7.40 | 2.23 | 6.62 | 3.05 | 6.73 | 9.66 | 1.54 | 5.07 | 5.58 | 0.27 |

Argentina, Bolivia, Brazil, Chile, Colombia, Costa Rica, Dominican Republic, Ecuador, El Salvador, Guatemala, Honduras, Mexico, Nicaragua, Panama, Paraguay, Peru, Uruguay, and Venezuela.

To sum up, about thirty years into the current, second, wave of globalization, Latin American countries have gone through difficult and at times traumatic political, social, and economic experiences. During these three decades, the region left behind the last phase of state industrialization to experience indebtedness and a serious external debt crisis in 1982. After that, Latin America suffered a painful period of adjustment and structural reform in the late 1980s and the 1990s that reversed decades of state interventionism and developmentalism in favour of private initiatives and free-market reforms.

This process was extremely painful, since it involved tremendous social costs in terms of deterioration of living standards, such as employment conditions, poverty levels, access and quality of education, and health coverage (Margheritis 2003, 4). Thus, the cost of insertion into globalization included a number of troublesome features: low average economic growth; high inflation relative to other parts of the world; high volatility in terms of trade, capital flows, and overall economic performance; fluctuating exchange rates; balance of payment crises; high unemployment; and widespread poverty and income inequality (see López-Alves and Johnson 2007, 4; and Loser 2008, 27). Let me turn now to a detailed analysis of the last thirty years of the Latin American political economy.


*The 1980s: the debt crisis and the 'lost decade'* From 1975 to 1981 Latin America became heavily indebted while funds were in some cases misused, leading to the economic crisis known as the debt crisis of 1982, in which relatively big economies like Mexico, Brazil, and Argentina defaulted on their loans. During those years, the outstanding debt of Argentina, Brazil, Chile, Mexico, Colombia, and Peru combined rose from $35 billion to $248 billion, a much bigger growth than in any earlier period and faster than in other parts of the world. Cheap money was available from the 'petrodollars' invested in European and US banks, international commodity prices were favourable for the Latin American countries, and interest rates were low. Hence, countries could borrow at low rates with reasonable prospects of repayment (see Maddison 1989, 91–2; and Salvucci 1996, 166).

However, these rosy parameters changed suddenly by the early 1980s. The change to restrictive monetary policy initiated by the US Federal Reserve induced recession and pushed up interest rates suddenly and sharply. Thus, the average real interest cost of floating rate debt rose to nearly 16 per cent in 1982–3 compared with −8.7 per cent in 1977–80. As a result, in the early 1980s, Latin America entered its longest and most severe economic crisis since the Great Depression of the 1930s.

The crisis was caused by a number of factors, both external and internal, including the inadequacies and excesses of the national economic policies. The sudden rise in interest rates, the drying up of foreign capital flows, and the long-term decline in the terms of trade all together precipitated the region into a profound financial and debt crisis, reminiscent of the contemporary financial crisis this time initiated in and by the United States in 2008 (see Maddison 1989, 92).

The fundamental problem was that the Latin American countries had been forced to carry the burden of interest rate volatility, a structural external factor that they did not and could not have control over (Stiglitz 2008, 75). The Latin American countries were then compelled to insert themselves into the neoliberal model of globalization, and had no way out but to cope with the consequences of the debt crisis within the framework of their structural constraints.

As a result, the rest of the decade of the 1980s, known in Latin America as the *década perdida* ('lost decade'), was (literally) spent by a succession of both unilateral and multilateral efforts to manage the debt problem. The phrase itself refers to the substantial reduction in growth that occurred with the onset of the debt crisis in 1982. For example, while the growth of per capita income in Latin America averaged 3.3 per cent per year in the 1970s, in the 1980s, it fell 1.1 per cent yearly as production shrank. The debt crisis transformed many Latin American countries into net exporters of capital, with an astronomic amount of 219 billion dollars between 1982 and 1990, much more than the amount Germany had to pay after World War I (Robinson 2004, 162).

In addition, the debt crisis started a long and socially painful process of structural *stabilization adjustment*, in which the Latin American countries had to cope with their fiscal deficits and their balance of payments, while addressing pressing problems of inflation and even hyperinflation. The measures implemented included the curbing of imports, the expansion of exports, and achieving the necessary financial requirements to service their astronomic debt (see Iglesias 1992, 50; Loser 2008, 29; Robinson 2004, 160; and Salvucci 1996, 165).

The effects of the debt crisis, in itself a symptom of economic globalization, and the ensuing economic stagnation in the 1980s were devastating, leading to a worsening of poverty and inequality. The sudden interruption of growth, aggravated by inflationary pressures and the application of drastic adjustment policies, led to growing unemployment, decreasing real wages, and a dramatic curtailment of social welfare (Rosenthal 1989, 64–5). As fallout from the debt crisis imposed hardships throughout the region, the rates of poverty and indigence increased, and per capita income fell at an average annual rate of −1.1 per cent, leading to negative rates of GDP growth in several key Latin American countries in the early 1980s (see Table 4.3).

The majority of the Latin American countries underwent an acute negative redistribution of income in the 1980s, with regressive net outcomes by the end of the decade. Stagnation swelled the ranks of the so-called informal sectors of the region's economies, with the proportion of poor people rising from 41 per cent to 44 per cent of the population. The social crisis that hit hard in the early 1980s has continued well into the twenty-first century (see Altimir 1996, 50; Berry 1997, 121; Helwege 1995, 101; Iglesias 1997, 235; Korzeniewicz and Smith 2000, 13; and Teichman 2001–2, 2).

*The 1990s: neoliberalism and the 'Washington Consensus'* If the 1980s were considered as a 'lost decade' for Latin America, Liberal advocates refer to the 1990s as the decade of economic recovery and Latin America's definitive embracement of globalization. By the mid-1990s, most countries in the region had initiated substantial domestic economic and political reforms to encourage free trade and capital flows. Tariffs on imports dropped dramatically from 42 per cent to 14 per cent between 1986 and 1995. The devaluation and free-float of exchange rates became an integral part of the liberalization process for most countries. Foreign investment – both foreign direct investment, and portfolio investment – also expanded in the 1990s after a critical stagnation during the 1980s, focusing especially upon the largest and richest economies of the region – Mexico, Brazil, Argentina, Venezuela, and Chile (Meyer 2000, 1; see also Table 4.5).

Yet, as it turned out, the growth that ensued was ephemeral and lasted only for a few years. It could not be sustained over the long term, since it was based on heavy borrowing from abroad and on privatization of state infrastructures that were sold off to foreigners. There was indeed a consumption boom; GDP per capita increased notably, but the overall national wealth did not expand substantially. Moreover, the liberalization reforms led, on the one hand, to a retreat of the state towards the market, and, on the other hand, to deepening patterns of poverty and inequality, and to the reintroduction of populism in a political atmosphere characterized by increasing de-politicization (Stiglitz 2007, 36; see also Tables 4.2 and 4.3).

The 1990s was the decade of the fulfilment of the so-called 'Washington Consensus', promulgated in the late 1980s as an international political economy programme that promised economic reform and economic development for the region, under the auspices of the IMF, the World Bank, the Inter-American Bank for Development (IDB), the US government, the US-based transnational corporations, and neoliberalism in general as the hegemonic ideological discourse for economic development (Harris and Nef 2008a, 8). As high inflation, and even hyperinflation, broke out in many of the Latin American countries, the 'Washington Consensus'' focus on fighting inflation made sense in the short term, and it succeeded in that particular realm. The premises were those of free trade, free flow of transnational capital, fiscal discipline and reform of the state, privatization, and deregulation of economic activities, leading to a drastic reduction of government services, public subsidies, and public employment (Harris and Nef 2008a, 14; and Stiglitz 2007, 36).

The crystallization of the 'Washington Consensus' sparked intense debates over the likely social impact of macroeconomic stabilization and structural adjustments that took place in the region in the late 1980s and early 1990s. Academic critics and political opponents argued that the economic reforms lacked a coherent theory of economic growth and were bound to bring about negative trends in terms of social inequality and deterioration of popular welfare. Conversely, the advocates of the neoliberal credo were confident that in the long run these reforms would lead to sustainable growth and greater equality, and would enhance social welfare in Latin America (Korzeniewicz and Smith 2000, 7). As expected, both advocates and critics were proven partially right (and wrong).

On the bright and optimistic side, after the 'lost decade' of the 1980s, the early 1990s witnessed a distinct improvement for Latin America with steady annual growth rates of about 3.2 per cent to 4 per cent (see Table 4.3). Poverty levels declined significantly as well. The region's exports burgeoned; capital flew again into the region in response to a new climate of confidence, with a net transfer of funds of nearly 7 billion dollars in 1991. This marked a reversal of the tendency to transfer savings abroad during the 1980s, when resources of some 220 billion dollars were diverted from the region (Altimir 1996, 54; Aninat 2000; and Iglesias 1997, 233–4).

Total trade and foreign investment levels in the region were up considerably in the early 1990s, with a special emphasis upon the impressive growth of foreign investment (Hecht Oppenheim 2000, 6). Other achievements in this period included the establishment of successful stabilization programmes that killed hyperinflation, as well as the promotion of greater efficiency of the state. Perhaps the most favourable economic consequence in this context was the fact that inflation declined to levels well in line with the rest of the world, monetary policies became more effective, the financial system became liberalized, and fiscal imbalances were reduced (Loser 2008, 38–9).

On the dark and negative side, the rosy picture of the early 1990s as depicted by the IMF, the World Bank, and the IDB was somehow misleading. While there was a certain resumption of growth in the 1990s, that economic recovery was accompanied by high levels of poverty and increased inequality. Moreover, when population growth is factored in, then the regional per capita annual income in the region had increased only by a paltry 1.1 per cent, not enough to make a significant dent on poverty (Sanchez 2003, 1). Although the resumption of moderate economic growth in the early 1990s resulted in the reduction of poverty in urban areas, poverty and inequality remained distinctively high, even above the levels reached prior to the debt crisis of 1982. The ranks of the poor in the mid-1990s numbered about 210 million people, even some 50 million more than the figures for the previous 'lost decade'. Furthermore, there has been a rise in the unemployment rate by three percentage points, and a further deterioration in the income distribution and income gaps within the different countries of the region. Thus, paradoxically, while the overall macroeconomic situation of countries such as Argentina and Peru had steadily improved, the fate of many of its citizens, especially the poor and disadvantaged, had steadily deteriorated (Korzeniewicz and Smith 2000, 15; Sáinz 2007, 242; and Stewart and Berry 1999, 168).

*The globalization crises of the late 1990s and early 2000s* From 1994 to 2002, the Latin American economies, like many other emerging markets, experienced a series of financial and currency crises, as part of their insertion into financial globalization and their exposure to the 'contagion effect', with serious negative impacts on growth, poverty, and inequality (Berry 2007a, 217; and Nudelsman 2006, 15). Financial crises, as the most outstanding symptoms of financial globalization, took place in Mexico (1994–5), Brazil (1999), and Argentina (2001–2). These crises were partly a result of ripple effects and spillover consequences of the financial crises of East Asia (1997) and Russia (1998), and partly a reaction to continuing difficulties in coordinating the finances of national governments and implementing a thorough fiscal adjustment. Although both Mexico and Brazil survived their financial crises with relative success, the bulk of their population endured severe recessions in order to keep the macroeconomic stability and the respectability vis-à-vis the international financial markets in place (Kaufman 2003, 105; and Meyer 2000, 2).

The vulnerability of Latin American economies to external economic fluctuations was caused, among other factors, by the lack of regulation of foreign capital, coupled with continued reliance on resource-based exports. In addition, due to the lack of sufficient resources for saving and investment, the Latin American economies depended heavily on the fluctuations of these international capital markets, which were inherently volatile and subjected to virulent financial crises. Hence, external financial liberalization generated fundamentally unsustainable external liabilities for the Latin American economies, due to their overwhelming reliance on external capital flows (Hecht Oppenheim 2000, 7; and Serrano 2003, 87–8).

At the domestic level, a fragile banking sector invited an attack on the local currency, where a sharp depreciation frequently created bank failures. High inflation and currency crises, like in Argentina in 2001–2, were associated with weak fiscal, financial, and monetary institutions (see Hecht Oppenheim 2000, 7; Iglesias 2000, 3; Nudelsman 2006, 10; and Chapter 5 in this book).

From 1998 to 2003, the Latin American region suffered from stagnation, as net capital inflows became negative again. The economic crises of the late 1990s had profound negative consequences for the social policies of the Latin American countries, bringing about a reduction in welfare expenditures, the deterioration of public services, and deep fiscal imbalances in the systems of social security. Consequentially, the percentage of the poor Latin American population was higher in 2003 (44 per cent) than in 1980 (40.5 per cent) (see Sáinz 2007, 243 and 257).

*After the 'Washington Consensus': disillusion and economic recovery, 2003–8* As Latin America entered the new millennium, the region experienced the erosion of the 'Washington Consensus' of the 1990s, as far as the promises of growth and poverty reduction were concerned. The failure of market reforms to deliver equitable prosperity was reflected in a growing disillusionment on the part of Latin Americans with market reforms and the neoliberal ideology that advocated a 'market fundamentalist' version of globalization. The combination of persistent poverty and inequality, together with the political consolidation of democracies, tended to cause a movement to the so-called political 'new left' in the region, with a few exceptions (notably in Mexico and Colombia). As a result, the Latin American left gained presidential elections and formed governments in many Latin American (especially South American) countries, in different shades and colours – social democratic, populist, and otherwise.

By the early 2000s the neoliberal project was partly modified, and at least in rhetorical terms strongly criticized. The development discourse had changed significantly, as it adopted themes such as poverty eradication, inequality reduction, redistribution, and national sovereignty over natural resources as paramount subjects. The (North) American dream of neoliberalism had become an inconclusive Latin American project, a lingering work in progress. The freeing of markets in the region, a result of the insertion of Latin America into globalization, was expected to bring about growth and prosperity; yet, it has failed to deliver on its promises (Teichman 2001–2, 14). This paved the way for the ideological condemnation of the neoliberal hegemony and for the election of leftist political leaders who professed antineoliberal views and offered alternative policies within the so-called Latin American 'new left' (Castañeda 2008, 231; and Harris 2008, 90).

This 'pink tide' was an upsurge of popular will; a spontaneous expression of discontent by disenchanted segments of Latin American society. It was the politically logical result of the combination of secular poverty and inequality with full-fledged representative democracy that would bring to power governments seeking to rule on behalf of the poor and the dispossessed (Castañeda 2008, 233; and Smith 2008, 342). By the end of 2007, nine countries have elected or re-elected parties that identified with the left or the centre-left in Chile, Venezuela, Brazil, Argentina, Uruguay, Bolivia, Peru, Nicaragua, and Ecuador (see Teichman 2002, 3; and Castañeda and Morales 2008).

A kind of post-Liberal, or *post-Washington* consensus did emerge in the region, stressing the renewed role of the state to cope with social exclusion, the promotion of norms of social justice and economic development, the critique of extreme neoliberalism, and the adoption of prudential fiscal management. This revised consensus represented a shift in focus from the previous single-minded concern with growth and efficiency towards a more nuanced approach, which also emphasizes policy measures to reduce poverty and inequality (Harris and Nef 2008b, 289).

Yet, in many cases, there was a significant continuity in the enactment of economic policies by the new regimes and there were only middling policy reversals. In other words, despite the disillusion about the 'Washington Consensus' and the left-wing ideological claims to the contrary, there were no significant policy changes in coping with economic globalization and its consequences. Thus, many of the leftist governments remained comfortable for the most part with market economics (see Morales 2008, 38). At the same time, there was some improvement in the socio-economic indicators in several countries of the region, regarding poverty and inequality. As a matter of fact, the countries in Latin America that have the highest levels of Human Development Index (HDI) have leftist governments and/or social democracies (Uruguay, Argentina, Chile until 2010, Costa Rica, and Cuba). Moreover, the social-democratic regimes in the region (Chile, Brazil, and Uruguay) seemed to cope better with poverty and inequality (see Lustig 2009).

In sum, most of the 'new left' regimes of the region have remained linked to economic globalization, which makes pragmatists of even the most populist politicians. Thus, ironically, the political backlash that led to the rise of the left by rejecting the premises of the 'Washington Consensus' is nowadays balanced by the economic interactions with the rest of the world, including the new globalized economic powerhouses, China and India (Price and Haar 2008, 3–4).

The 2003–8 period witnessed a strong economic recovery in Latin America. Compared to the 'lost decade' of the 1980s and the low growth rates of the early 1990s, the economic performance in the first decade of the twenty-first century was particularly strong. The region as a whole grew 5.6 per cent in 2007, the fourth consecutive year of growth of more than 4 per cent (O'Neill 2008, 13; see also Table 4.3). The growth was not only related to the wiser national economic policies adopted in comparison to the recent past, but rather to external *positive* shocks to the region, this time in the form of the growth in demand and price of commodities, including copper, soy, iron, ore, petroleum, timber, gold, silver, meat, coffee, sugar, ethanol, and cotton. Foreign direct investments also poured back, posting substantial gains before the recent economic crisis of 2008–9 (Noriega 2009, 1; and Price and Haar 2008, 3).

During those boom times, poverty rates in the region fell by ten percentage points, from 44 per cent to 34 per cent of the population, continuing a steady fall from a peak of 48.4 per cent in 1990. Moreover, indigence – the level below which people cannot satisfy their food needs – also declined significantly, from about 19 per cent in 2002 to less than 13 per cent in 2008 (Bárcena 2011, 20). An outstanding feature of this period was the fact that, in most of the countries, policymakers placed high priority in maintaining macroeconomic balances, which helped in generating surpluses in both their external and fiscal accounts (Maira 2008, 500–1; and United Nations Economic and Social Council 2009, 3). However, despite this growth and the reduction of poverty, Latin America's income gap remained very high in absolute terms in many countries of the region, and in comparison to other emerging market economies at similar levels of social and economic development (Rojas-Suarez 2009, 1).

*The effects of the recent economic crisis upon poverty and inequality in Latin America*  In the beginning, it was a problem in the subprime mortgage market in the United States in late 2007. Just over a year later, it became a systemic financial crisis that crippled the credit markets of the developed countries and had an extreme negative impact upon the world economy as a whole. Although the Latin American region has been better prepared to face this contemporary crisis than the previous ones, there were a number of channels through which the economies of the region were negatively affected.

First, the slowdown in the world economy lowered the volume and prices of the region's exports, bringing down remittances and cutting foreign direct investment and demand for tourism services. Thus, the countries of the region were also faced with more difficult access to external credit, the cost of which did increase (United Nations Economic and Social Council 2009, 1).

Second, the decrease in merchandise exports had a greater impact on growth in the more open economies, in those that trade more with developed countries, and, in particular, in those that sell a larger proportion of manufactured goods to developed markets as it became more difficult quickly to find alternative markets for such goods. This was the case of Venezuela, Chile, Costa Rica, Ecuador, Honduras, and Mexico (see United Nations Economic and Social Council 2009, 7).

Third, Mexico, Central America, and the Caribbean (especially El Salvador and Jamaica) were hit hardest by a significant drop in remittances sent home by immigrant workers in the United States (Noriega 2009, 1; UNDP 2009, 1).

Fourth, to sum up, four recessionary forces have affected the Latin American region in the past few years: first, the collapse of manufacturing and the plunging of trade – total exports fell by one third, fewer goods were sold, and the price of commodities fell; second, the flow of capital dried up; third, remittances have begun to contract; and fourth, fewer tourists visited the region (*Economist*, 2 May 2009, 47–9).

*The bad news*  There is no doubt that the recent global economic crisis has left a trail of negative side effects in Latin America. One of the most serious effects is the increased poverty in the region. The economic downturn abruptly ended six years of uninterrupted growth in the region, which enabled several million people to lift out of poverty.

According to ECLAC statistical assessment, the crisis caused the number of poor people in the region to rise by 9 million to 189 million by the end of 2009, while the ranks of the destitute (living in extreme poverty) increased to 76 million. The most optimistic forecast from ECLAC predicted only 1.9 per cent growth for the following years; a significant decline compared to previous growth rates of 5.5 per cent in 2006, 4.6 per cent in 2007, and 4.6 per cent in 2008 (UNDP 2009, 1). The 9 million people added to the ranks of the poor is equivalent to almost one fourth of the 41 million people who had climbed out of poverty in the region between 2002 and 2008, thanks to higher economic growth, an increase in social spending, the demographic dividend, and better income distribution (*Latin American Herald Tribune* 2009, 1).

Some countries, such as Mexico, were expected to experience higher-than-average increases in poverty and extreme poverty due to a sharp decline in the country's gross domestic product and to deteriorating salaries (partly related to its high level of economic interdependence with the United States). In the several years ahead, each country in the region will have to contend with resurgent poverty brought on by the current slowdown and tame inflation that might stem from stimulus spending and growing debt. As unemployment rises and the economy contracts dramatically, poverty could jump about 10 per cent (Noriega 2009, 3). Moreover, in terms of social policies, the recession has halted some of the significant social progress of the previous five years.

. . . *and the good news* Paradoxically, it can be argued that against the background of previous globalization crises in the 1990s and the early 2000s this most contemporary crisis has had less of an impact on regional poverty than previous downturns, such as the Mexican *Tequila crisis* of 1994–5, the Asian crisis of 1997–2000, and Argentina's 2001–2 default crisis. This is due to several reasons, as follows.

First, one can track a veritable process of learning through the previous crises, and a remarkable improvement in the way the Latin American governments prepared themselves to cope with the economic crisis this time. Fiscal and monetary anchoring had made Latin American economies more resilient to external shocks, compared to previous times. Above all, the region has diversified its external sources of growth through international trade and FDIs away from reliance exclusively upon the United States, by strengthening its economic ties with Europe and Asia (particularly with China and India) in recent decades (OECD 2008, 11). In this sense, Mexico and Central America suffered the most negative consequences of this crisis, as compared to the South American countries.

Second, most Latin American governments had taken positive steps toward putting their fiscal houses in order before the crisis imploded in 2008. They improved public debt management, lowered fiscal deficits, adopted fiscal responsibility laws, and created stabilization funds in the form of savings in foreign currency assets, among other measures. One of the most important elements of increasing prudence in this regard has been the build-up of foreign exchanges as an effective guard against external shocks. Consequently, the overwhelming majority of the countries of the region did not have to seek external support for its balance of payments. It is for this reason that the use of funds from multilateral financial institutions was very limited.

As it was mentioned above, much of Latin America's strong growth during 2003–8 was the result of the global macroeconomic bonanza of the new millennium – buoyant commodity prices, favourable terms of trade, cheap capital, and plentiful foreign investment – but it was also the consequence of sound management and effective policy frameworks (OECD 2008, 11).

Third, in terms of social policy, the region was also better placed to deal with this global crisis than previously. This was due to the fact that governments had invested more in social policies during the bonanza years, with public social expenditures per capita rising between 1990 and 2007 from 43 per cent to 60 per cent of the average total public expenditures in the region (*Latin American Herald Tribune* 2009, 1). In this context, we can point out better-targeted social policies, especially cash-transfer schemes for the poor, in the cases of Brazil, Mexico, and Argentina.

Fourth, the Latin American countries did adopt a variety of wise measures in response to the deepening international financial crisis. They were all aware that, although most of them had macroeconomic foundations that were significantly stronger than in the past, the region would not escape the impact of instability in world financial markets and the expected recession in the developed economies (United Nations Economic and Social Council 2009, 17). The larger economies of the region in particular, especially Brazil and Chile, did enter the crisis better able to cope with it than during previous economic shocks. The grounds for limited optimism included:

- A major reduction in debt, especially denominated in foreign currencies.
- Some commodity exporting countries, like Chile, Peru, Mexico, and Brazil, had built up 'rainy days' stabilization funds during the commodity boom years.
- Governments had reduced their deficits, or even run surpluses.

Thus, the negative social impacts and repercussions of the contemporary global economic crisis upon the Latin American countries have been relatively minor in comparison to previous globalization crises. Therefore, there is both bad news and good news to report from the implications of this global economic crisis in terms of poverty and inequality in the region. The major variable that seems to explain the variance, in contrast to previous crises, is the more effective role the national governments have played in several countries of the region, such as Chile and Brazil.

Still, this brief history of the political economy of Latin America displays a troubling pattern that has remained more or less constant through the recent economic history of the region – although there has been some significant reduction in the high levels of poverty since 1990, inequality remains very high. In an attempt to explain this puzzling reality, I turn in the next section to a detailed analysis of those two inter-related subjects.

### The Latin American puzzle: poverty, low growth, and the persistence of high inequality

While Latin America shares many features with the rest of the developing world, and countries within the region differ significantly among themselves, there is a common characteristic that makes this region unique and most of its countries similar: Latin America is the most socially unequal of the world's developing regions, even surpassing the income inequality of sub-Saharan Africa.

Just to illustrate this claim from data gathered for 2000, on average the highest earning 5 per cent of the Latin American population received 25 per cent of the national income; the top 10 per cent earned about 40 per cent of the income, while the poorest 30 per cent of the population received only 7.5 per cent of the national income (Meyer 2000, 3–4). Latin America displayed a Gini coefficient of about .537 (as of 2005), which is fifteen points above the average for the rest of the world and the highest regional Gini in the world (see Franko 2007, 398; O'Neil 2008, 15; and Sanchez 2003, 13).

In a comparative perspective vis-à-vis other regions of the world, Latin America is characterized by high levels of poverty and exorbitant indexes of inequality, given the prevailing levels of per capita income, containing the most unequal income distribution in the world (see Chapter 6). This has been referred to in the literature as 'excess' poverty and inequality that characterizes a 'lopsided continent', a particular Latin American puzzle that demands pertinent explanations.

Across the region, social inequality is a result of deep structural realities, such as unequal land distribution; discrimination on the basis of gender, ethnicity, and geography; the distorted allocation of endowments; and the skewed distribution of natural resources and of human capital in society. The systematic and historical denial of equal opportunities to women, to people of mixed race, and to ethnic minorities (mainly indigenous people) partly explains this puzzle. Other analysts suggest that the reasons are rather external, directly related to the role of economic globalization in keeping the minimum wages low (see Bouzas and Ffrench Davis 2004, 3; De Janvry and Sadoulet 2001, 20; Franko 2007, 385 and 400–2; Hoffman and Centeno 2003; and O'Neil 2008, 15).

The Latin American income inequality is striking and puzzling, since Latin America is not a particularly poor region. Latin America boasts seventeen of the 200 richest people in the world, and only Haiti is ranked among the world's forty-eight poorest countries, so the plight of the world's poorest relative to the world's richest leaves most of the region somewhere in the middle range (Meyer 2000, 3–4).

If we sum up the long-term trends of poverty in Latin America, we can argue that there was a relatively rapid decline from 1950 to 1980 (during the ISI period), a sharp increase from 1980 until the mid-1990s, and a steady, albeit slow, progress in the reduction of poverty, as economic conditions in the region have significantly improved over the recent decade. Poverty has declined by almost 16 per cent in the last sixteen years, and indigence, or extreme poverty, by 25 per cent (Loser 2008, 30–1). Yet, this relative prosperity, and the fact that most Latin American countries are middle-income countries, should not mask the fact that there are still large numbers of poor people in the region (OECD 2008, 42; and Rojas-Suarez 2009, 1).

As I argued throughout this book, income inequality and poverty are separate, though related, subject matters. They are related since extreme income inequality makes it likely that a substantial proportion of the population in the region will fall below any conventionally drawn poverty line. Thus, one can argue that poverty is related to inequality (in other words, inequality leads to poverty), so the best way to reduce poverty would be to tackle social inequality (Berry 2001, 17). However, these are two separate subject matters, because an increase in inequality does not necessarily mean a corresponding increase in poverty or, alternatively, a decrease in poverty does not necessarily imply a reduction of inequality (see Reynolds 1996, 39).

For instance, it might be the case that the advanced sectors of the domestic economy are growing faster and more unequally with respect to the rest of the population, while at the same time the bulk of the poor and marginalized population is still gaining in absolute wealth. Hence, we might have *less* poverty but *more* inequality as a result of economic liberalization. Furthermore, poverty and inequality might contribute to low growth, which in turn perpetuates poverty, particularly given the condition of high inequality, into a vicious circle. Thus, despite a positive trend of economic growth in the region in the early 1990s, this was not translated into significant reductions in the indexes of poverty and inequality (Rojas-Suarez 2009, 2; Sanchez 2003, 15; and Stiglitz 2002, 79). Thus, we might witness in Latin America the peculiar phenomenon of *growth without development*; that is, slow economic growth that might be compatible with a worsening income distribution, stagnant high levels of poverty, and higher levels of inequality.

Despite these broad generalizations about the region, poverty and inequality vary widely across countries, implying, among other things, that over the long run growth has been differentially successful in affecting poverty and inequality. There is not a clear discernible regional trend in terms of poverty reduction over time, in contrast to the constant and high indexes of inequality that have persisted in the last thirty years (Helwege and Birch 2007, 1–3).

For instance, poverty rates are higher for countries with low per capita incomes, such as Guyana and Haiti. While significant progress has been achieved in a few large countries, such as Brazil and Mexico, the poorest countries are still very poor, and some significant countries (Argentina, Colombia, Peru, and Venezuela) have even seen increases in their poverty rates despite some economic growth until the recent decade (De Janvry and Sadoulet 2001, 21–2; Gafar 1998, 601; Helwege and Birch 2007, 1–3; and Sachs 2005, 71).

Tables 4.6, 4.7, and 4.8 provide some basic data regarding the percentage of poor people (relative poverty), the percentage of indigent people (extreme poverty), and the Gini coefficient of income inequality between 1982 and 2008 for eighteen Latin American countries.

From the reading of these tables, we can derive the following conclusions:

1. There is an important variance in the percentage of poor persons (Table 4.6), indigent persons (Table 4.7), and Gini coefficient (Table 4.8) across countries.
2. The incidence of *relative poverty* – that is, the number of people living below a poverty line that is some fixed proportion of the median income – has been considerably high in the region, as we can learn from Table 4.6. Even using the more conservative criterion of *extreme poverty*, which is the same across countries after controlling for differences in the prices of basic commodities, there are many indigent people in the region (see Table 4.7). For instance, the World Bank estimated that, in 2003, 9 per cent of the Latin American population lived on the equivalent or less of $1 a day. This corresponds approximately to 50 million Latin Americans (OECD 2008, 43).
3. The fluctuations in the percentage of poor people from 1980 to 2007 do not show a coherent pattern. While in some cases that

Table 4.6 *Percentage of poor persons in Latin American countries, 1980–2007 (relative poverty)*

| | Argentina | Bolivia | Brazil | Chile | Colombia | Costa Rica | Dominican Republic | Ecuador | El Salvador | Guatemala | Honduras | Mexico | Nicaragua | Panama | Paraguay | Peru | Uruguay | Venezuela |
|---|---|---|---|---|---|---|---|---|---|---|---|---|---|---|---|---|---|---|
| 1980 | 10.4 | – | – | – | 42.3 | – | – | – | – | 71.1 | – | – | – | – | – | – | – | – |
| 1981 | – | – | – | – | – | 23.6 | – | – | – | – | – | – | – | – | – | – | 14.6 | 25.0 |
| 1984 | – | – | – | – | – | – | – | – | – | – | – | 42.5 | – | – | – | – | – | – |
| 1986 | – | – | – | – | – | – | – | – | – | – | – | – | – | 41.0 | – | 59.9 | 20.4 | 32.2 |
| 1987 | – | – | – | 45.1 | – | – | – | – | – | – | – | – | – | – | – | – | – | – |
| 1988 | – | – | – | – | – | – | – | – | – | – | 76.1 | – | – | – | – | – | – | – |
| 1989 | – | 52.6 | – | – | – | – | – | – | – | 69.4 | – | 47.7 | – | 40.9 | – | – | – | – |
| 1990 | – | – | 48.0 | 38.6 | – | 26.3 | – | 62.1 | – | – | 80.8 | – | – | – | – | – | 17.9 | 39.8 |
| 1991 | – | – | – | – | 56.1 | – | – | – | – | – | – | – | – | 32.7 | – | – | – | – |
| 1992 | – | – | – | – | – | – | – | – | – | – | – | – | – | – | – | – | 12.0 | 37.0 |
| 1993 | – | – | 45.3 | – | – | – | – | – | – | – | – | – | 73.6 | – | – | – | – | – |
| 1994 | 16.1 | 51.6 | – | 27.6 | 52.5 | 23.1 | – | 57.9 | – | – | 77.9 | 45.1 | – | 25.3 | 49.9 | – | 9.7 | 48.7 |
| 1995 | – | – | 35.8 | 23.2 | – | – | – | – | 54.2 | – | – | – | – | – | – | – | – | – |
| 1996 | – | – | – | – | – | – | – | – | – | – | – | 52.9 | – | – | 46.3 | – | – | – |
| 1997 | – | 62.1 | – | 21.7 | 50.9 | 22.5 | – | 56.2 | 55.5 | – | 79.1 | – | – | 24.7 | – | 47.6 | 9.5 | 48.0 |
| 1998 | 23.7 | – | 37.5 | – | – | – | – | – | – | 61.1 | – | 46.9 | 69.9 | – | – | – | – | – |
| 1999 | – | 60.6 | – | – | 54.9 | 20.3 | – | 63.5 | 49.8 | – | 79.7 | – | – | 20.8 | 60.6 | 48.6 | 9.4 | 49.4 |
| 2000 | – | – | – | 20.2 | – | – | 46.9 | – | – | – | – | 41.1 | – | – | – | – | – | – |
| 2001 | – | – | 37.5 | – | – | – | – | – | 48.9 | – | – | – | 69.3 | – | – | 54.8 | – | – |
| 2002 | 45.4 | 62.4 | 38.7 | – | 51.1 | 20.3 | 47.1 | 49.0 | – | 60.2 | 77.3 | 39.4 | – | 34.0 | 61.0 | – | 15.4 | 48.6 |
| 2003 | – | 63.9 | 37.7 | 18.7 | – | – | – | – | – | – | 74.8 | – | – | – | – | 54.7 | – | – |
| 2004 | 29.4 | 63.9 | – | – | 51.1 | 20.5 | 54.4 | 51.2 | 47.5 | – | – | 37.0 | – | 31.8 | 65.9 | 48.6 | 20.9 | 45.4 |
| 2005 | – | – | 36.3 | – | 46.8 | 21.1 | 47.5 | 48.3 | – | – | – | 35.5 | 61.9 | 21.7 | 60.5 | 48.7 | 18.8 | 37.1 |
| 2006 | – | – | 33.3 | 13.7 | – | – | 44.5 | 39.9 | – | 54.8 | 71.5 | 31.7 | – | 29.9 | – | 44.5 | – | 30.2 |
| 2007 | – | 42.4 | 26.9 | – | – | 18.6 | 44.5 | 42.6 | – | – | 68.9 | – | – | 18.7 | 60.5 | 39.3 | 17.7 | 28.5 |

Table 4.7 Percentage of indigent persons in Latin American countries, 1980–2007 (extreme poverty)

| | Argentina | Bolivia | Brazil | Chile | Colombia | Costa Rica | Dominican Republic | Ecuador | El Salvador | Guatemala | Honduras | Mexico | Nicaragua | Panama | Paraguay | Peru | Uruguay | Venezuela |
|---|---|---|---|---|---|---|---|---|---|---|---|---|---|---|---|---|---|---|
| 1980 | – | – | – | – | – | – | – | – | – | – | – | – | – | – | – | – | 4.0 | 8.6 |
| 1981 | – | – | – | – | – | – | – | – | – | – | – | – | – | – | – | – | 5.2 | 11.1 |
| 1986 | – | – | – | – | – | – | – | – | – | – | – | – | – | 19.7 | – | 29.5 | – | – |
| 1989 | – | 23.0 | – | – | – | – | – | – | – | 42.0 | – | 18.7 | – | 18.6 | – | – | – | – |
| 1990 | – | – | 23.4 | 13.0 | – | 9.9 | – | 26.2 | – | – | 60.9 | – | – | 11.5 | – | – | 3.4 | 14.4 |
| 1991 | – | – | – | – | 26.1 | – | – | – | – | – | – | – | – | 11.5 | – | – | – | – |
| 1993 | – | – | 20.2 | – | – | – | – | – | – | – | – | – | 48.4 | – | – | – | – | – |
| 1994 | 3.4 | 19.8 | – | 7.6 | 28.5 | 8.0 | – | 25.5 | – | – | 53.9 | 16.8 | – | 7.8 | 18.8 | – | 1.9 | 19.2 |
| 1995 | – | – | – | – | – | – | – | – | 21.7 | – | – | – | – | – | – | – | – | – |
| 1996 | – | – | 13.9 | 5.7 | – | – | – | – | – | – | – | 22.0 | – | – | 16.3 | – | – | – |
| 1997 | – | 37.2 | – | – | 23.5 | 7.8 | – | 22.2 | 23.3 | – | 54.4 | – | – | 8.0 | – | 25.1 | 1.7 | 20.5 |
| 1998 | – | – | – | 5.6 | – | – | – | – | – | 31.6 | – | 18.5 | 44.6 | – | – | – | – | – |
| 1999 | 6.7 | 36.4 | 12.9 | – | 26.8 | 7.8 | – | 31.3 | 21.9 | – | 56.8 | – | – | 5.9 | 33.9 | 22.4 | 1.8 | 21.7 |
| 2000 | – | – | – | 5.6 | – | – | 22.1 | – | – | – | – | 15.2 | – | – | – | – | – | – |
| 2001 | – | – | 13.2 | – | – | – | – | – | 22.1 | – | – | – | 42.4 | – | 33.2 | 24.4 | – | – |
| 2002 | 20.9 | 37.1 | – | – | 24.6 | 8.2 | 20.7 | 19.4 | – | 30.9 | 54.4 | 12.6 | – | 17.4 | – | – | 2.5 | 22.2 |
| 2003 | – | 34.7 | 13.9 | 4.7 | – | – | – | – | – | – | 53.9 | – | – | – | – | 21.6 | – | – |
| 2004 | 11.1 | 34.7 | 12.1 | – | 24.2 | 8.0 | 29.0 | 22.3 | 19.0 | – | – | 11.7 | – | 14.8 | 36.9 | 17.1 | 4.7 | 19.0 |
| 2005 | 9.1 | – | 10.6 | – | 20.2 | 5.6 | 24.6 | 21.2 | – | – | – | 11.7 | 31.9 | 14.1 | 32.1 | 17.4 | 4.1 | 15.9 |
| 2006 | 7.2 | – | 6.7 | 3.2 | – | 7.2 | 18.5 | 16.1 | – | 29.1 | 49.3 | 8.7 | – | 14.3 | – | 16.1 | – | 9.9 |
| 2007 | – | 31.2 | 8.5 | – | – | 5.3 | – | 12.4 | – | – | 45.6 | – | – | – | 31.6 | 13.7 | 3.1 | 8.5 |

Table 4.8 Gini index of inequality within Latin American countries, 1982–2007

| | Argentina | Bolivia | Brazil | Chile | Colombia | Costa Rica | Dominican Republic | Ecuador | El Salvador | Guatemala | Honduras | Mexico | Nicaragua | Panama | Paraguay | Peru | Uruguay | Venezuela |
|---|---|---|---|---|---|---|---|---|---|---|---|---|---|---|---|---|---|---|
| 1982 | – | – | 58.15 | – | – | – | – | – | – | – | – | – | – | – | – | – | – | – |
| 1983 | – | – | 58.40 | – | – | – | – | – | – | – | – | – | – | – | – | – | – | – |
| 1984 | – | – | 58.43 | – | – | – | – | – | – | – | – | 46.26 | – | – | – | – | – | – |
| 1985 | – | – | 58.96 | – | – | – | – | – | – | – | – | – | – | – | – | – | – | – |
| 1986 | 44.51 | – | 58.13 | – | – | 34.48 | 47.78 | – | – | – | – | – | – | – | – | 45.72 | – | – |
| 1987 | – | – | 59.25 | 56.43 | – | – | – | 50.49 | – | 58.26 | – | – | – | – | – | – | – | 53.45 |
| 1988 | – | – | 60.97 | – | – | – | – | – | – | – | – | – | – | – | – | – | – | – |
| 1989 | – | – | 62.99 | – | – | 45.66 | 50.46 | – | 48.96 | 59.60 | – | 55.14 | – | – | – | – | – | 44.08 |
| 1990 | – | – | 60.59 | 55.52 | – | – | – | – | – | – | 57.36 | – | – | 56.82 | 39.74 | 43.87 | – | – |
| 1991 | – | 42.04 | – | – | – | – | – | – | – | – | – | – | – | – | – | – | – | – |
| 1992 | 45.35 | – | 57.37 | – | – | 46.28 | 51.36 | – | – | – | 54.51 | 51.06 | 56.38 | – | – | – | 42.16 | – |
| 1993 | – | – | 59.70 | – | – | – | – | – | – | – | 55.22 | 51.89 | – | – | – | – | – | 41.68 |
| 1994 | – | – | – | 55.19 | – | – | – | 52.00 | – | – | – | – | – | – | – | 44.87 | – | – |
| 1995 | – | – | 59.24 | – | 57.22 | – | – | – | 49.86 | – | – | – | – | 57.06 | 59.13 | – | – | – |
| 1996 | 48.58 | – | 59.19 | 55.06 | 56.06 | 47.08 | 48.71 | – | 52.25 | – | – | 48.54 | – | 56.31 | – | 46.24 | 43.76 | 48.79 |
| 1997 | – | 58.46 | 59.32 | 55.74 | – | – | – | – | – | – | 53.05 | – | – | 48.53 | – | – | – | – |
| 1998 | 49.84 | – | 59.23 | – | – | 48.13 | – | 53.53 | 52.17 | 55.65 | – | 48.99 | 53.85 | – | 56.52 | – | 45.18 | 49.53 |
| 1999 | – | 57.79 | 58.59 | – | – | – | – | – | – | – | 51.50 | – | – | – | 56.85 | – | – | – |
| 2000 | – | – | – | 55.36 | 57.92 | 46.60 | – | – | 51.92 | 54.97 | – | 51.87 | 50.30 | 56.56 | – | – | 44.56 | – |
| 2001 | – | – | 58.69 | – | 57.50 | 49.96 | – | – | – | – | – | – | – | – | – | – | 44.96 | – |
| 2002 | 52.52 | 60.24 | 58.23 | – | – | 49.76 | – | – | 52.32 | 55.34 | 53.97 | 49.68 | – | 56.51 | 57.98 | 54.65 | – | – |
| 2003 | – | – | 57.61 | 54.92 | 58.83 | – | 51.88 | 61.78 | 49.37 | – | 53.88 | – | – | – | – | – | – | 48.20 |
| 2004 | 51.27 | – | – | – | – | 48.03 | 51.46 | 51.83 | – | – | – | 46.05 | – | 54.88 | 55.10 | – | – | – |
| 2005 | 50.03 | 58.19 | 56.39 | – | – | 47.23 | 49.97 | 53.65 | 49.70 | – | 56.71 | 50.20 | 52.33 | 54.58 | 53.89 | 51.97 | 44.94 | 47.61 |
| 2006 | 48.77 | – | – | 52.00 | 58.49 | 48.03 | 50.76 | 53.14 | – | 53.69 | 55.31 | 48.11 | – | 54.93 | – | 49.55 | 46.24 | 43.44 |
| 2007 | – | – | 55.02 | – | – | 48.64 | 48.83 | 54.37 | – | – | 53.02 | – | – | 53.30 | 53.24 | – | – | – |

percentage has increased over time (especially in the cases of Argentina, Bolivia, Paraguay, and Venezuela), other countries have shown a steady reduction in the percentage of poor people (Brazil, Chile, Costa Rica, Ecuador, Honduras, Mexico, Nicaragua, Panama, and Peru).

4. There seems to be a clear correlation in the fluctuations in the percentage of poor people and the percentage of indigent people, across countries. The sudden rise in the number of poor people and of indigent people clearly reflects the economic and financial crises experienced by different countries in the region (for instance, Argentina in 2001–2; Mexico in 1996; Uruguay in 2003; and Venezuela in 2002).

5. Similarly, the most extreme indexes of Gini (income inequality) correlate with periods of economic crisis and stagnation: Argentina in 2002; Bolivia in 2002; Brazil in 1989; Chile in 1987; Costa Rica in 2001; Dominican Republic in 2000; Ecuador in 2003; El Salvador in 2002; Guatemala in 1989; Honduras in 1990; Mexico in 1989; Paraguay in 1995; and Venezuela in 1987.

6. In general terms, countries have performed better in reducing relative and absolute poverty than in reducing inequality, which remains a very difficult political and social problem. For instance, while there has been a steady reduction in the percentage of indigent people in Brazil, Chile, Costa Rica, Ecuador, Guatemala, Honduras, Mexico, Panama, Peru, and Venezuela, that encouraging trend has not been accompanied by a reduction in the income inequality in those countries.

We should turn now to a detailed analysis of the evolution of poverty and inequality in the region, tracing its possible causes.

*The evolution of poverty in Latin America, 1982–2008*

In the 1980s, the incidence of poverty had unquestionably increased, as opposed to the previous two decades. The preceding decline in relative poverty was halted and reversed, while the number of people living below the poverty line grew rapidly in absolute terms. Poverty in Latin America increased from 26.5 per cent in 1980 to 31 per cent in 1989; in other words, about 131 million people in the region lived on less than $2 a day. Other estimations refer to even 38 per cent of the population, or about 160 million, by 1986 (Gafar 1998, 601; and Rosenthal 1989, 66). According to the ECLAC statistics, in 1990 about 48.4 per cent of the Latin American population lived below national poverty lines (quoted in the *Economist*, 3 December 2011, 51).

In the 1990s, the picture remained bleak with a stagnation trend, which represented a negative turn in absolute terms (Filgueira 2008, 24). In terms of percentage, relative poverty in the region fell from 48 per cent in 1990 to 40 per cent in 2005, while extreme poverty dropped from 23 per cent to 15 per cent. Still, according to ECLAC statistics, the number of poor people in the region grew to 192 million in 1990, and to a record number of 225 million in 2002.

By 2005, about 40 per cent of the region's population was living below the poverty line, while over 15 per cent (about 82 million people) was living in extreme poverty (indigence). The countries with the highest percentages of the population living in poverty were Bolivia, Colombia, Ecuador, Haiti, Honduras, Nicaragua, Paraguay, and Peru. Only in Chile and Costa Rica did both national and international estimates indicate that less than 10 per cent of the population was living in poverty. Moreover, the Dominican Republic, El Salvador, Guatemala, and Panama managed to reduce poverty quite dramatically. Nowadays, the estimation of ECLAC for 2011 is that 30.4 per cent of the region's population lives below the national poverty lines, probably the lowest figure recorded ever (ECLAC statistics quoted in Harris 2008, 58–9; and Maira 2008, 502; see also Birdsall and Szekely 2003, 50; Harris and Nef 2008, 16; and Helwege and Birch 2007, 2–3).

The poverty profile for the region has several important characteristics, among them the increasing urbanization of poverty. Traditionally, much of the poverty in Latin America was concentrated in the rural periphery outside the cities, in outlying regions, or among the migrants from the countryside to the city. It is in the rural areas where we will still find the most extreme cases of poverty, such as in the northeast of Brazil, Southern Mexico (Chiapas), southern Colombia, and parts of the highlands of Peru. While the incidence of rural poverty reached about 60 per cent in 1980, it continued to be shockingly high after thirty years of liberal economic policies, affecting about 58.1 per cent of the rural population by 2004. At the same time, urban poverty has increased dramatically since the early 1980s, as a consequence of high rates of rural-to-urban migration, and the recession of the 1980s, with the concomitant inability of the cities to supply the migrant rural poor with basic welfare services and the proliferation of shanty towns (*villa miserias* and *favelas*) (see Berry 2004, 20; Burki and Perry 1997, 88; Hoffman and Centeno 2003, 370; and Kay 2008, 25).

As of 2008, the Latin American poverty rate of 36 per cent was still not much lower than that of 1980 (of about 40), while the number of poor people in the region actually increased from 136 million to almost 190 million (O'Neil 2008, 10, 14). As was previously mentioned, the decline of poverty in Latin America between 2002 and 2008 was directly related to the expansion in production and on average annual GDP growth of 3 per cent or more (Noriega 2009, 1).

### The evolution (and persistence) of inequality in Latin America, 1982–2008

As we can discern from Table 4.8, more than two decades after the return to democracy in the 1980s, income inequalities have largely persisted, if not exacerbated, in the region, following a historically stubborn pattern. Social inequality in Latin America is the highest, most extensive, and most pervasive in the entire world.

The region has become a symbol of inequality of income distribution along several dimensions and comparisons: between sub-regions in Latin America (i.e., contrast the Southern Cone of South America with Central American and the Caribbean, such as the extreme case of Haiti); within countries (i.e., contrast southern Brazil (the state of São Paulo) with the backward northeast); between rural and urban sectors, skilled and unskilled labour, and so forth (see Singer 2002, ix). It penetrates all the different dimensions of welfare and opportunities beyond just income distribution, including human capital; access to credit; access to education, health, and public services; access to land and other assets; the functioning of credit and formal labour markets; access to systems of birth control; attainment of political voice and influence; and even unequal and unfair treatment by police and justice systems (Berry 2007b, 1; De la Escosura 2007b, 291–2; Filgueira 2008, 28; and Harris 2008, 61).

What is particularly striking about the level of income inequality in the region is the fact that Latin America has reached an intermediate position among the world's nations in terms of per capita income (on average, a regional GNP per capita to be estimated at about $10,000), which, by historical standards, should presuppose a more equitable distribution of income. Furthermore, the long-term pattern of unequal distribution of income has been a constant pattern of the economies of the region and one of the most enduring features of Latin American economic and social systems, across different historical periods and divergent economic strategies adopted in their political economy, ranging from the ISI pervasive government intervention (1945–75), through the authoritarian phase of neoliberalism (1975–80s), and into the post-authoritarian (re-democratization and democratic) contemporary period since the 1980s (Glade 1996, 159; and Rosenthal 1989, 64). Thus, although a high inertia in the level of inequality is characteristic of many societies in different parts of the world, what makes Latin America atypical, compared to other regions, is its high level of inequality through periods of both ISI and openness to globalization.

High inequality in the region sustains major costs and negative ramifications. It increases poverty and reduces the impact of economic growth and development on poverty reduction. Moreover, inequality carries negative implications for aggregate economic growth, especially when associated with unequal access to capital and to education, and with social tension. Thus, a large majority of Latin Americans judge the current levels of income inequality to be inherently unfair. In political terms, inequality of opportunity is deemed unacceptable (see de Ferranti et al. 2004, 1).

It has long been acknowledged that, while globalization is supposed to lead to growth and to wealth, that wealth has not always been evenly distributed. In Latin America, a region plagued with historic and structural problems of social, political, and economic inequality, it is argued by serious empirical studies that the adoption of neoliberal economic policies since the late 1970s has in many cases served to reinforce and exacerbate the pervasive trends of socio-economic inequality. In this context, social inequality relates to processes of social exclusion and marginality, which in turn generate poverty and perpetuate inequality in a vicious circle, since the growth model adopted had inevitably exclusionary roots in its initial stages (Burki and Perry 1997, 93; Gacitúa and Davis 2001, 16; Hecht Oppenheim 2000, 9; OECD 2008, 44; and Robinson 2004, 172).

During the last three decades since its latest insertion into globalization, Latin America as a region has not experienced a substantial change in income distribution, though individual countries have. Inequality has remained very high, as a result of the increase of within-country inequality (as measured by Gini) in Argentina, Chile, and Mexico, the three countries with the highest per capita income in the region, as well as in Venezuela. This contrasts with a more encouraging process of economic convergence among other Southern Cone countries, including some significant improvement in Uruguay and Peru and a slow reduction of inequality in Brazil.

Social inequality worsened during the 1980s, partly as a result of the debt crisis. Almost all Latin American countries experienced acute and regressive redistribution of income during the 1980s, the decade of crisis and structural adjustment (Altimir 1998, 8; and Bouzas and Ffrench Davis 2004, 4). Social inequality only modestly diminished in some countries during the 1990s, as most countries underwent far-reaching market-oriented economic reforms. Only in the early 2000s have we witnessed some decline in the Gini indexes, though it has been far from been too dramatic (see Table 4.8; *Economist*, 3 December 2011, 51; Glenn 2007, 160–1; Hartlyn 2002, 103; and Mamalakis 1996, 9).

### Explaining poverty and inequality in Latin America

What explains the high levels of poverty and the exorbitant gaps in income distribution in the region? What are the major causes of poverty and inequality in Latin America? There are a myriad of explanations, ranging from the domestic realm, through the international realm, to hybrid explanations that span the domestic and international levels (including my *intermestic* explanation). There is not an overall explanation, though the focus in this section will be on the *domestic* (internal) explanations for poverty and inequality, in juxtaposition to those that derive from economic globalization and the international system.

*Domestic sources of poverty and inequality in Latin America*   Poverty and inequality in the region are directly related to the historical unequal distribution of land, the insufficient human capital and education, and the particular domestic conditions of the national economies. All those factors are directly related to the political conditions within the countries of the region, first and foremost the traditional relative weakness of the Latin American state vis-à-vis its society, coupled with wrong and counter-productive economic policies adopted by their governments (Fishlow 1998, 448; and Robinson 2003, 71).

The causes of Latin American inequality and its skewed concentration in income are partly historical in nature, going back to the Iberian colonization and conquest period, which led to an *unequal distribution of land ownership* to a relatively few beneficiaries as the reward for conquest, institutionalizing from the beginning an inequality of wealth, human capital, and political power, with an embedded discrimination between the conquerors (*conquistadores*) and the indigenous groups. Thus, land tenure patterns have remained medieval throughout the region.

In most of the Latin American countries, the landowner elite has retained high levels of political power, in the absence of significant land reforms (like in Mexico following the Revolution). This directly affects the incidence of rural poverty in the countryside. Furthermore, the sharp disparity in landholdings has been aggravated by the widespread commercialization of agriculture, the development of agro-industries, and the resulting displacement of a large number of small farmers and poor peasants from the land (see Berry 2007a, 213; De la Escosura 2007b, 291; Harris and Nef 2008a, 16–17; Hoffman and Centeno 2003, 369; Ramos 1996; and Reynolds 1996, 41).

Second, the persistence of poverty and inequality in the region is directly related to the *distorted distribution of human capital*, which is an economic and social category, where public action by the state, and other political and social institutions, can really make a difference, with a special emphasis on education. Human capital, defined as the pool of appropriate knowledge, competence, and personality traits that are embodied in the successful ability to perform labour and produce economic value, is primarily associated with education and professional experience. Unfortunately, Latin America continues to exhibit a poorly distributed and low-quality human capital, manifested in the skewed distribution of the level of education. In turn, variance in educational levels directly affects income distribution and wages. In other words, *wage inequality* becomes a major determinant of income inequality in the region, as a function of the unequal distribution in the quantity and quality of the existent levels of education (Bouzas and Ffrench Davis 2004, 6; Fishlow 1998, 455; Hoffman and Centeno 2003, 371; and Ramos 1996, 151).

Third, since income inequality in Latin America seems so resilient and resistant to change, we can infer that its sources are deeply embedded in the *structure of its national economies and societies*. In this context, we should pay particular attention to the highly *unequal distribution of labour income* in the region. For instance, the variance in the sector distribution of value added and income between agriculture, mining, industry, and services has played a crucial role in shaping poverty and inequality in the region (Mamalakis 1996, 7). Similarly, the ethnic composition of the population, its social stratification, and degree of heterogeneity might provide useful clues to understand the domestic sources of poverty and inequality.

Fourth, in Latin America one can come to the fatalistic conclusion that poverty and inequality are taken for granted in a kind of deterministic fashion. This is directly related to the *relative weakness of the state*, especially its very low fiscal capacity, which is expressed in the lack of progressive policies and the failure of social welfare. In absolute terms, on average the tax collection capacity of the Latin American state is very low – about 13 per cent only (Centeno 2002, 6; and Escudé 2006a). Moreover, with the adoption of the neoliberal policies and structural adjustment in the 1980s and the 1990s there has been a further *retreat of the state* as a leveller of last recourse, with serious detrimental implications for social welfare, an increasing decline in jobs and wages, and the gradual erosion, if not disappearance, of the middle class (Hoffman and Centeno 2003, 371).

The retreat of the state in Latin America explains why the issues of poverty and inequality are not a question of economic resources only, but rather a crucial political issue that should involve the mobilization of political will. In this sense, economic globalization is often blamed for affecting adversely poverty and inequality by limiting the power of national governments to follow certain progressive policies (Bouzas and Ffrench Davis 2004, 23).

Yet, the relatively weak Latin American state and its feeble institutions pre-existed the contemporary age of globalization, as illustrated by the inefficient fiscal policy and the inability to collect taxes, well before the insertion of Latin America into contemporary globalization. This of course does not contradict the plausible claim that globalization in itself accentuated the inherent difficulties of addressing poverty and inequality.

Finally, and related to the relative weakness of the Latin American state, one can argue that the ultimate domestic explanation for the perpetuation of poverty and especially of inequality in the region resides in some *inefficient and counter-productive policies*, such as patterns of low levels of public investment and high expenditures, adopted by certain national governments. Paradoxically, while many Latin American governments were able to promote growth, a reduction of inequality was *not* considered as an important objective of public policy.

In general terms, the reduction of inequality of wealth and income were not a priority in the social policies or the political agenda of Latin America, which focused on growth rather than equality, despite the relevance of both goals. Social policies – including the discussion of equity and justice – were intellectually and politically subordinated to the fulfilment of economic policies of modernization and development, essentially the growth of the global social product, at the expense of the marginalized sectors (see Glade 1996, 167; Maddison 1989, 95; Ramos 1996, 154; and Reynolds 1996, 44).

*International sources of poverty and inequality in Latin America* In addition to the domestic sources of poverty and inequality in the region, it is commonplace, following the radical Latin American tradition of *dependencia* approaches, to refer to *external* sources, such as the insertion of Latin America into globalization processes since the late 1970s and the incidence of international economic crises and their concomitant contagion effect, for the exacerbation of both poverty and inequality, especially in the context of foreign debt and dependence upon financial flows.

Since independence, Latin America has been exposed to occasional significant capital outflows and to substantial capital inflows at other times, whether in the form of foreign direct investment or of portfolio flows. An important observation about these capital flows is that they tend to increase in times of economic bonanza and high liquidity and to reverse subsequently as conditions change in periods of economic crisis and uncertainty. In this sense, these financial flows have had a significant, and often detrimental, impact upon poverty and inequality (Loser 2008, 35; and Mamalakis 1996, 8).

The opening up of Latin America to the international economy has been generally associated with both a widening of income inequality within and across countries, and with the persistence of poverty in many cases (De la Escosura 2007b, 292–3; Fishlow 1998, 454; and Meyer 2000, 4). This has been partly a result of the labour-saving character of technological changes and the increases in trade and capital flows, resulting from foreign direct investments (Berry 2007a, 217; see also Ramos 1996, 152). Moreover, the external imposition of social stratification, transferred from the core of the world economic system to Latin America since the colonial period, and then perpetrated under neocolonialism, left a profound mark in the form of underdevelopment, social inequality, and poverty. This created an embedded structural discrimination across social classes; exacerbating poverty and inequality in the rural, indigenous, and other less disadvantaged sectors of society (see Iglesias 1992, 101; and Maddison 1995, 52).

Intermestic *sources of poverty and inequality in Latin America: the relevance of the political model*  A third category of explanations for poverty and inequality in the region attempts to combine and converge both domestic and international factors, in a kind of *intermestic* dynamics that I previously explained in Chapter 3. In other words, by applying the political model developed above, I argue that the sources of poverty and inequality in Latin America are intrinsically related to the role of the state and other political actors that partly determine the menu of choice for their possible actions. A vicious cycle of poverty and economic inequality handicaps most Latin American countries, undermining their ability and capacity effectively to finance and deliver essential governmental services, including the provision of public security. The domestic and international results are homeland insecurity and crime, waves of migration, lack of political stability, the adoption of populist policies, and the reluctance of international investors to invest in unstable polities and societies.

In order to understand the logic behind this *intermestic* model, we should link together the historical unequal distribution of land, the insufficient human capital (especially with regard to education), the dire economic and social conditions of the national economies (including the initial Kuznets' effect of exacerbating inequality in the short term on the way to increasing growth), the adverse political institutions and conditions (especially the relative weakness of the state), and the wrong economic policies, alongside the globalization processes, the international economic crises, and the required and concomitant economic reforms and structural adjustment (see, for instance, Morley 2003, 63). In this sense, we should distinguish between the underlying sources of poverty and inequality (as features related to the society and polity) from the proximate causes (such as external shocks and international economic crises).

For instance, the Kuznets' effect precisely refers to the initial impact of growth as having a negative effect on the distribution of income, by pulling apart the wage structure. Thus, the capital-intensive technologies introduced by foreign investment lead to labour-saving changes, with a cost of rising inequalities, at least in the short term (Berry 2007a, 217; Reynolds 1996, 42). But all this economic logic does not happen out of the blue or as the result of a natural disaster; it is the deliberative decision, and (relatively free) choice, of the relevant national governments that choose particular economic policies, within the constraints of their structural position in the regional and international structures of hierarchy and power. In this context, it is the adoption of neoliberal economic policies that has served to reinforce the tendency of economic and social inequality (Hecht Oppenheim 2000, 9).

Similarly, it is the adoption of trade liberalization that might affect employment trends, producing a significant loss of jobs in the region, at least in the short term. With a similar logic to that of the Kuznets' effect, economic liberalization reforms might create new jobs in the long term, but there is a clear asynchrony between the process of job destruction and that of job creation (Bouzas and Ffrench Davis 2004, 13). Thus, partially competing interpretations of why inequality has risen in Latin America are the labour-saving character of technological change and the increase in trade and in capital flows.

As a result of the retreat of the state and the transformative shift away from statist policies to market-driven liberalization policies, new economic and social actors have emerged in the region, including export-oriented entrepreneurs and foreign capital agents, who encapsulate the logic of this *intermestic* explanation. In other words, there are new winners and losers from the expansion of globalization in the region. Among the *winners* of globalization in the region we can recognize the owners and executives of the big domestic conglomerates and transnational corporations that were able to modernize and obtain export markets.

Among the *losers* we might identify small and medium companies, where the bulk of employment has been concentrated, leading to the dwindling of the middle class. Thus, in most of Latin America it is the poor and the newly impoverished middle classes – the teachers and health workers who lost their jobs, the pensioners who lost their pensions – who articulate the opposition to economic globalization. Hence, the *erosion of the middle classes* has been both a consequence of new inequality patterns, and also a cause of a deep political and moral sense of *fracasismo* or *fracasomanía*, a sense of cultural despair and criticism that blames the Latin Americans themselves for an inherent incapacity that leads to social, economic, and political failures (Hoffman and Centeno 2003, 369). We can now assess the links between globalization, poverty, and inequality in the Latin American context.

## Links between globalization and the distribution of wealth in Latin America: are the paradigms relevant?

It is a very difficult task to assess the direct consequences of economic globalization upon the distribution of wealth in Latin America, due to the contradictory accounts put forth by scholars (see Kacowicz 2007; and Chapter 3). The discussion here continues the debate about the alternative sources of poverty and inequality, by focusing on the contradictory answers to the question: who is responsible for the economic disasters and crises in the region? Ideological and theoretical positions divide between those who blame globalization – embodied in the role played by the IFIs and the structural characteristics of international financial markets – and those who blame the Latin American governments themselves for their lack of commitment, capacity, and willingness to carry out the adequate and necessary structural reforms (Margheritis 2003, 13).

### The Liberal argument and the Latin American experience

From a Liberal perspective, there seems to be a direct and positive (reversed) relationship between globalization and the distribution of wealth. In theory, the more globalization takes place, the less poverty there will be. Thus, the best Liberal policy prescription to reduce poverty and inequality in Latin America is to remove regulatory impediments to growth in the region and allow the market to play itself freely, benefiting all the sectors of society, including the less advantaged.

In the Latin American context, the big question remains whether the region can harness the new opportunities brought about by economic globalization, while safeguarding against the possible risks. According to the Liberal interpretation, the wave of economic reforms in the 1980s and the early 1990s did produce some spectacular economic successes, such as the taming of previous astronomic inflation. Furthermore, trade and investment liberalization fostered significant, though heterogeneous, technological modernization.

According to neoliberals, in terms of capital flows, the insertion of Latin America in the global economy has been overall positive in terms of growth and poverty reduction. At the same time, even Liberals are aware that the Latin American countries have been traditionally subject to large external shocks stemming from terms of trade fluctuations, and especially from the volatility of capital flows.

Financial volatility, directly related to the contagion effects of globalization, is higher in Latin America than in the industrial world and in the more stable developing regions, such as East Asia, and it has been magnified by the region's thin domestic financial systems. Since the processes of globalization mean that national policies are forced to adapt and to dovetail to the global market expectations, there is not much room for discretion in fiscal, monetary, and other economic policies for the Latin American states (Bouzas and Ffrench Davis 2004, 14–17 and 20–4; Potter 2003, 266; and Sanchez 2003, 8).

To sum up, we might conclude that in the Latin American context of the last two decades of the twentieth century, more liberalized economies have performed better in terms of economic growth than less liberalized economies. Nevertheless, such economies suffered higher volatility, experienced higher levels of poverty, and saw greater increases in inequality, which point out the difficulties, if not failures, in linking economic neoliberalism to the construction of sustainable and strong social safety nets.

There is some empirical evidence for the relevance of the Liberal argument. For instance, in a recent study about the economic effects of globalization upon poverty in individual households, Guido Porto compared the poverty impacts of world trade liberalization in agriculture on the Argentine poor population with the welfare impacts of the Central American Free Trade Area (CAFTA) upon the indigenous population in Guatemala. In the Argentine case, liberalization would cause export prices to increase, and thus would affect consumer prices of food items and market wages. While higher agricultural export prices would make the domestic food basket more expensive (hence, increasing poverty), it would also boost labour demands and wages, thus alleviating poverty. In the final analysis, the labour (positive) income effects are higher than the (negative) poverty-line effects. Similarly, since liberalization of agricultural trade with the United States would bring the prices of agricultural products down, CAFTA would result in welfare gains for the average Guatemalan indigenous household (Porto 2007, 1454–5).

## The Radical argument and the Latin American experience

According to its Radical critics, economic globalization leaves the poor behind: it causes and deepens poverty and exacerbates inequality. In the Latin American context, the region's subordinated position of structural dependency upon the global economy has had serious negative consequences for the distribution of wealth. The financial vulnerability of Latin America, together with the globalization of capital flows, left the region dangerously dependent upon the whims and reversals of fortune of the international economic system.

Thus, the development of the Latin American economies has been severely constrained, restrained, and curtailed by the international financial and trade regimes that regulate the global economy. Furthermore, the increased openness of the Latin American economies to globalization has been at least partly to blame for the increased indexes of inequality in several Latin American countries, including Argentina, Colombia, Mexico, Ecuador, and Chile (Berry 2007b, 64; Harris and Nef 2008b, 283; and Teichman 2001–2, 16).

Radicals would argue that the initial policies of neoliberalism in the region, institutionalized in the stabilization and structural adjustment policies advocated by the IFIs and by the US government, were initially implemented after 1973 by the military dictatorship of Augusto Pinochet in Chile. Later on, the ideology of 'market fundamentalism' became the contemporary official capitalist ideology in the 1980s and the ideological foundation for the 'Washington Consensus' of the late 1980s and early 1990s. With the benefit of hindsight, Radicals conclude that, with the possible exception of the Chilean case, market reforms within the context of globalization have not brought the Latin American countries into the developed world (Harris 2008, 86–7; Klein 2008; and Teichman 2001–2, 7).

According to the Radicals, the aftermath and the after-shocks of the debt crisis of 1982 exacerbated poverty and inequality by the need to renegotiate that debt, at the price of restructuring the economy, reforming the state, and running regressive social welfare policies. The debt crisis contributed to establish a fundamentalist liberal vision of globalization. The concomitant market reforms inhibited and prohibited policies that were crucial for the alleviation of poverty and inequality in the region, leading to important contingents of winners and losers from globalization (Ferrer 1998, 199; Hoffman and Centeno 2003, 371–2 and 381–2; and Teichman 2002, 2).

As mentioned above, the financial vulnerability of Latin America and the globalization of capital flows left the region dangerously exposed to the problems of other economies, including the contagion effect of global economic crises, such as the Mexican 'Tequila crisis' of 1994, the East Asian crisis of 1997, and the most recent US-induced financial crisis of 2008–9. These external shocks not only substantially altered the international economic environment of the region, but also directly affected the domestic economic conditions within the Latin American countries (Harris 2008, 82; and Meyer 2000, 6).

If the region's comparative advantage in economic terms does not reside in its low-skilled labour force but rather in its vast natural resources, then Radicals would argue that the Prebisch–Singer thesis on the unequal terms of trade explains the lingering underdevelopment and dependency of many Latin American countries. Since trade is so important to the economies of almost all of the Latin American countries, fluctuations in their foreign trade are one of the most important determinants of their economic instability and dependency, the United States and Europe (and lately China and India) being the primary destinations for their exports (Harris 2008, 63–5; and Sanchez 2003, 3–4).

In addition to the fluctuations of capital and trade and their negative consequences, Radicals emphasize the disastrous effects of globalization in the region in social, political, and economic terms in the last thirty years. The 1990s were the years of triumphant neoliberalism, characterized by de-industrialization, deteriorating labour conditions, and stagnation. In the Radical interpretation, globalization has destroyed many national industries, especially the traditional ones, generating a large number of unemployed, exacerbating poverty and inequality. Trade liberalization and financial flows had the effect of increasing unemployment by making it easier to dismiss workers following the dismantling of workers' unions and the passing of reformed labour legislation.

Finally, the adoption of the neoliberal ideology of globalization increasingly denied the countries of the region the possibility of building and furnishing their own national economies. In other words, globalization limited the power of national governments to mould and to follow certain anti-cyclical policies, thus limiting the role of the state (already limited itself) in Latin America. Both the IMF and the World Bank developed a variety of policy-based instruments to encourage Latin American governments to reduce the role of the state in their national economies.

In the context of the 'Washington Consensus', notions of nationalism and a national project were abandoned in favour of the neoliberal insertion into globalization, leading to social discontent and political protest that engendered several crises of governability (for instance, in Argentina in 2001–2) and led to the rise of the left in many countries of the region in the early 2000s. Furthermore, a grassroots opposition to globalization from below materialized in the region in the form of the World Social Forum initiated in Porto Alegre, Brazil (see Bouzas and Ffrench Davis 2004, 24; and Teichman 2001–2, 2).

### The statist (Realist) argument and the Latin American experience

A third theoretical approach, neither Radical nor Liberal, but rather Realist (or better, statist), does not identify a necessary or clear direct link between globalization and the distribution of wealth in the region. This approach suggests that serious problems that have affected the fate of peoples and states in Latin America, such as poverty and inequality, are first and foremost directly related to the performance of its national governments and to national policies rather than to the supra-national or supra-territorial forces of the global market.

From this perspective, the forces of globalization as such are not inherently beneficial or deleterious for development prospects in Latin America; they carry both risks and opportunities (the Radicals emphasize the risks; the Liberals, the opportunities). Thus, the causal links between globalization and the distribution of wealth are far from being straightforward. Higher mobility of goods, factors of production, and technology will indeed affect relative prices and factor returns, thus influencing poverty and inequality, but the direction and effectiveness of these factors is always policy-dependent, as a function of the role of the state in mediating and translating the effects of globalization in the region (see Bouzas and Ffrench Davis 2004, 8–9; and Sanchez 2003, 2).

Unfortunately, the Latin American state's capacity to act as a powerful and active 'transmission belt' has been actually quite limited in itself, partly as a result of the effects of globalization. In this context, one can find a direct link between the institutional power and the political authority of the state and social inequality across countries in the region. In other words, we can posit that the weaker the state the higher the levels of social inequality. It seems that only a strong state in Latin America can implement adequate social and economic policies to cope with globalization, and to help the disadvantaged sectors in the society (see Hoffman and Centeno 2003, 383; Nudelsman 2006, 12; and Sanchez 2003, 4).

Hence, according to this statist approach, there is a political economy rationale to make the state more effective, since market mechanisms can function properly only if they are regulated, or monitored, by the state. Thus, paradoxically, states in the region should take on new roles in order to meet the demands of globalization, including political and economic modernization (Berry 2007b, 41; and Hecht Oppenheim 2000, 10).

There is no doubt that globalization has brought about a certain degree of de-politicization of economic policies, at the expense of the traditional role of the welfare state. In other words, economic policymaking is less of a discretionary political instrument in the hands of the state to regulate and impact its economic environment; for instance, in relation to fiscal and monetary policy management. Fiscal policy is particularly relevant in Latin America due to the character and recurrence of globalization crises. In many of these countries, the state has borrowed too much and is prone to situations of insolvency, illiquidity, and to a political, economic, and psychological lack of confidence (Nudelsman 2006, 12 and 16).

In contrast to the view predominant in the 1990s, national policies and domestic politics are considered again crucial determinants in explaining the impact of globalization upon economic performance, partly as the result of the 2008–9 global economic crisis. In a nutshell, the argument of this political approach is that *Latin American governments are no longer prisoners of markets*; national governments in the region should be able to determine the proper social and economic policies. In fact, the realities and processes of globalization demand an active participation of the state in the national scene in the different countries of the region. This encapsulates the logic of the *intermestic* model in the Latin American context (see Berry 2007b, 53; Bouzas and Ffrench Davis 2005, 348; Ferrer 1998, 201; and Robinson 2003, 74).

### The *intermestic* model: bringing politics back to the fore in Latin America

Economic globalization and the regional and international structures indeed restrict the menu of choice available to the political actors in the region, by affecting the bargaining power of the state and other domestic actors, who in turn use globalization to increase their political power both in the domestic and in the international realm (Robinson 2003, 72; see also Figure 3.1). Yet, since not all the countries in Latin America are affected by globalization in the same way and with the same intensity, and there is a clear variance in terms of poverty levels and Gini coefficients of inequality in the region, we should pay particular attention to the *political context* as represented by the state and other political actors and institutions, who shape national decisions and policies that help us to explain that variance across countries.

For instance, as derived from *Hypothesis 1*, we should expect the strongest states in Latin America (Chile, Uruguay, and Costa Rica) to cope better with economic globalization in terms of achieving better (meaning lower) indexes of poverty and inequality in the region. In the next chapter, I examine in empirical and comparative terms the performance of the 'ABC countries' (Argentina, Brazil, and Chile) in this respect.

Institutions have played a crucial role in shaping the Latin American economies; moreover, political considerations – including, in particular, distributional struggles – have been paramount in determining economic and political outcomes in the region. For instance, economic globalization might have negative or positive effects upon income distribution and levels of poverty, depending on domestic variables such as the level of public sector spending or investment in education and other relevant social welfare policies (Bouzas and Ffrench Davis 2004, 26–7; and Edwards et al. 2007, 1). This argument follows the logic posited in *Hypothesis 2*.

Among the relevant (and efficient) social policies implemented by several Latin American countries we can point out the following: (a) conditional cash-transfer programmes, such as *Bolsa Família* in Brazil, which pay households that engage in socially useful behaviour such as keeping children in school; (b) reforming the labour market, by improving the quality of workforce integration in the labour market and increasing real wages; (c) reforming education, especially at the secondary level, given the demographic conditions of the region; (d) using public expenditures to redistribute wealth and ameliorate sub-standard living conditions; (e) turning social expenditures into more progressive policies through the refurnishing of pension coverage and the provision of public services for more economically depressed or remote geographical areas; and (f) improving fiscal policy, through more transparent and progressive tax systems (see Bárcena 2011, 21; ECLAC 2009; and OECD 2008).

In this context, the improvement in income distribution and poverty reduction in the region can be explained in large part by economic growth and adequate government policies, and the interaction between them.

Many economies in the region have made significant efforts to increase the resources available to implement social policies, in order to reduce poverty and inequality. Thus, on average, social spending rose in the region from 12.2 per cent of the GDP during 1990–1 to 18 per cent of the GDP during 2007–8. Moreover, as a share of overall public spending, social programmes grew from 45 per cent to 65 per cent (Bárcena 2011, 20–1).

The rationale of the *intermestic* model for Latin America implies that we should look for political and institutional variables to make sense of the Latin American political economy, including the economic malaise as represented by the high indexes of poverty and inequality. These variables include: the relative weakness (or strength) of the Latin American state in general; the weakness (or strength) of democratic regimes since the 1980s; the implementation (or not) of populist policies, which tend to be extremely inefficient in economic terms; and the weakness (or strength) of political institutions, such as the Congress, the judiciary, and the fiscal and taxation administrations. Political parties in the region are generally weak and fragmented, which makes the formulation of a stable economic policy very difficult in the long term. Populist policies generate lack of efficiency; economic crises are caused in the fiscal sector due to uncontrolled public expenditures.

Furthermore, Latin America includes many unequal national societies since people do not pay enough taxes, and the tax administrations in general are very weak. In the cultural realm, there is even some degree of tolerance for the violation of the law and for tax evasion. All these features might explain the regional variation between countries like Chile and Costa Rica at one positive end of the continuum (strong states), in contrast to Venezuela, Ecuador, and Argentina, at the negative pole (weak states) (*Hypotheses 1 and 2*).

The panacea recommended by international institutions such as the World Bank and the IMF to cope with the inherent weaknesses of the Latin American political institutions include nowadays measures of *political conditionality*, such as the slogan of 'good governance' and the strengthening of political institutions that should fight corruption and invest in their own people. And, yet, there might be an apparent contradiction in the demands for good governance in political and institutional terms, since the previous demands in the 1980s and early 1990s for *economic conditionality* had led to the retreat and weakening of the state in economic and social welfare terms, as the logical economic consequence of the insertion of the Latin American economies into globalization (Aninat 2000, 3; Berry 2007a, 221; and Stallings 2003, 78). This contradiction is sometimes more apparent than real, since shrinking government and good governance are not by definition an oxymoron. Thus, one can advocate *both* a better and a smaller government (following the 'small is beautiful' argumentation).

The *intermestic* model in Latin America can be examined and applied at the three levels of analysis – the *domestic/national* level, that focuses upon the role of the state, state–society relations, the functionality of the state, and other domestic political institutions; the *regional* level, which refers to several frameworks of regional integration; and the *international* level, which focuses upon the interactions with the IFIs and grassroot forms of globalization ('globalization from below'). The combination and interaction among the three levels of analysis might explain the variance regarding the policy attention (and effectiveness) of different countries in the region, addressing the problems of poverty and inequality. Let us examine each of these levels in turn.

### *The domestic/national level: the role of the state as an active 'transmission belt'*

In prescriptive rather than in descriptive or real terms, the state in Latin America should play a crucial role in recreating a process of economic growth to be compatible with a gradual elimination of poverty, the reduction of inequality, and the management of economic globalization. As a matter of fact, the need to foster good governance and political and economic transparency has to be translated from the trendy political slogans of the World Bank into effective and progressive social policies to be pursued by the state. Yet, the policies necessary for the reduction of poverty and inequality cannot be expected to prosper and develop if the state's social basis remains a narrow one – as a result of implementing neoliberal economic reforms in the 1980s and the 1990s that shrunk the Latin American state in the first place (Teichman 2002, 5).

The basic argument of the *intermestic* model at the domestic/national level is that the principal culprits (and saviours) of increasing (or reducing) poverty and inequality and coping with globalization are the national governments of the region themselves, through their decision-making procedures and implementation. Yet, their 'degrees of freedom' are conditioned by the international and regional distribution of power, and by the constraints of economic globalization upon the autonomy of the states (*Hypothesis 4*).

In descriptive and real terms, an essential feature of the Latin American domestic political scene has been the *relative weakness of the Latin American state* (with a few exceptions, such as Chile, Costa Rica, and Uruguay). Although the Latin American state has been ubiquitous and omnipresent in many economic, political, and social areas, it still remains weak in institutional terms and in relation to its own society.

Moreover, historically, most of the Latin American states have been highly *despotic*, yet weak in terms of infrastructures. They have been 'despotic' to the extent that state elites were able to undertake decisions without negotiating with the civil society. Yet, paradoxically, they could not mobilize enough power and domestic legitimacy to mobilize resources and development, or to become truly democratic. The infrastructures of police and justice have been weakened by domestic violence, corruption, and the absence of the rule of law; the authority and legitimacy of the state have been fragmented; while the fiscal infrastructure and the social services have been also weakened by corruption, nepotism, clientelism, and populism. Hence, the challenge for the Latin American states in their 200 years of existence remains how to create a true community of citizens that could support stronger states and become truly democratic (Franko 2007, 147; Mann 2004; Rojas Aravena 2005, 65–7).

This relative weakness could be considered as a valid explanation for the 'long South American peace' since 1881 (see Centeno 2002; and Kacowicz 1998 and 2005). Paradoxically, a similar argument can be presented here regarding poverty, and especially with reference to the high levels of inequality in the region. Particularly weak states tend to be poorer and more unequal than stronger states; for instance, contrast the appalling cases of Haiti and Bolivia with those of Uruguay, Chile, and Costa Rica. These latter three countries exhibit moderately high taxes and significant redistributive public policies (De Ferranti et al. 2004, 11). Thus, one might argue that the stronger the state in Latin America the better chances are for *domestic* peace and stability, not just international peace. Thus, the stronger the state vis-à-vis its own society, the richer and more equal it will be. At the risk of over-generalization, one can argue that a strong state is a necessary but not sufficient condition successfully to address poverty and to reduce inequality (*Hypothesis 1*).[3]

The Latin American state has been traditionally weak in fiscal and financial terms, with a low capacity to extract money, distribute it, and mobilize populations and markets. According to Centeno (2002, 6), on average the state in Latin America managed to collect only about 13 per cent of its possible taxes. The state has served the elites, and at times nationalized enormous private debts. Hence, poverty and inequality are actually indicators of the weakness of the state. The neoliberal political economy narrative of the region in the last three decades has wrongly assumed that the economic problems of Latin America resided in the

---

[3] I would like to thank Moses Shayo and Moshe Bargil for their comments on this point.

state, the solutions being in the market. As a matter of fact, the public sector in the region is roughly half the size of the industrial countries in the Western world.

The political economy problem is a composite one – of *both* markets (at times asymmetrical, rentist, and inefficient) *and* of inefficient and weak states (Escudé 2006a and 2006b; and Filgueira 2008, 29). Hence, the solution, although not exclusive or perfect, should be to strengthen the state in order to foster *good governance and transparency in economic policymaking* (Aninat 2000, 3; Wade 2004).

As Guillermo O'Donnell argued, a strong state in the region means 'a reasonably well-motivated, non-corrupt, and skilled civil service, capacity to formulate and implement policies; openness to, but not colonization by, society; at least some transparency and accountability; and responsiveness to goals and priorities formulated through a democratic political process.' (O'Donnell 1998, 53; see also Kuczynski 2003b, 34). In other words, there is a need for a 'smart state' to address redistributive crises. Paradoxically, two broad forces indicate a possible increase in state intervention and its potential reinvention: globalization and the social challenges in the region (see Franko 2007, 147).

At the domestic level, and in tandem with the strengthening of the state, we should also emphasize the need to strengthen *civil society elements*, including civic actors, interest groups, NGOs, social networks, and voluntary associations, since state–society relations are not necessarily zero-sum. Citizens need more space for participation in decision-making, within a democratic framework and beyond the political machinery and apparatus of the state. In the last two decades, we have witnessed in the region the rise of identity politics and significant social movements ('Sin Tierra' (landless) in Brazil, the *indigenistas* in Bolivia, the Mapuches in Chile, and the Zapatistas in Chiapas, Mexico), as well as several environmental and pro-developmentalist groups. They all offer new forms of political and social mobilization, challenging the moral responsibility of the state. Some of those forces are centrifugal movements, which both resist globalization and take advantage of it to advance their sub-national and transnational agendas (Hecht Oppenheim 2000, 15). The different political trajectories of Latin American democratic regimes in the last decade prove the point that we should discount cultural and structural determinism, and that institutional change is possible through policy change. For instance, social democracy, as advocated and implemented in Chile, Brazil, and Uruguay, has managed to alleviate poverty, and, to a less extent, inequality, by finding a delicate compromise between the economic logic of the market and the political and moral logic of the welfare state (Lustig 2009, 21) (*Hypothesis 2*).

*The regional level: Latin American frameworks of regional and sub-regional integration*

In addition to the domestic or national level, it is important to mention that several *regional actors* – such as Mercosur, the Andean Group, the Union of South American Nations (UNASUR), and the Rio Group – can play a significant role in discerning and affecting the possible links between globalization, poverty, and inequality in Latin America in an *intermestic* fashion. Regionalism has emerged in recent decades as another potent force affecting the processes of economic globalization.

If globalization is regarded as the compression of the temporal and spatial aspects of social relations, then regionalism may be understood as one important component of globalization. According to this view, by helping national economies to become more competitive in the world market, regional integration schemes might lead to multilateral cooperation on a global scale, the adoption of liberal premises about cooperation, and the opening of the domestic markets, with positive implications for the eradication of poverty and the reduction of inequality as well. Thus, processes of regional integration can be interpreted as part of the global economic order. Conversely, regionalization might stem from a reaction and challenge to the amorphous, undemocratic, and inexorable economic rules of globalization (see Kacowicz 1999).

At the regional level, Latin American states, at least rhetorically, have acted collectively and in cooperation and unison, through the promotion of regional frameworks of integration and the institutionalization of international organizations, in order to cope simultaneously with globalization while addressing the problems of poverty and inequality. In the Latin American context, the Organization of American States (OAS) at the Pan-American level, the Rio Group at the Latin American level, the recently created UNASUR at the South American level, and Mercosur at the sub-regional level in the Southern Cone of South America all include in their rhetorical mandates specific references to promote growth and to reduce poverty and inequality (*Hypothesis 3*).

In a recent lecture at the ECLAC, José Miguel Insulza, the secretary general of the OAS, referred specifically to the *intermestic* links between poverty, inequality, democracy, and development in the region. In his own words, 'Poverty and inequality militate against the quality of democracy and impede its full exercise in the region' (Insulza 2010). Thus, democracy in the region is being undermined by social inequality. In order to intensify the inter-American cooperation in the fight against poverty and inequality, in September 2009, the OAS established an Inter-American Social Protection Network, with the intention to improve the well-being of people throughout the Americas. That initiative includes governments, international organizations, international agencies, the private sector, academia, and international non-governmental organizations (INGOs).

Similarly, at the level of Latin American cooperation, the Rio Group includes in its vast political and security agenda the 'war against poverty' as one of its over-arching goals, calling for the full implementation of the Monterrey Consensus of 2002 and other international agreements to help the developing countries in their fight against poverty and hunger, alongside a further democratization of the IFIs. An almost identical rhetoric and very similar plans for action can be found also in the new UNASUR, that includes the goal to 'eradicate poverty and overcome inequality' among the paramount objectives of the South American Union, including 'strengthen[ing] political dialogue, universal literacy and access to education, sustainable energy integration, development of infrastructure, financial integration, protection of bio-diversity, social security and health services, and consolidation of South American identity'. As for Mercosur, the sub-regional integration scheme of Argentina, Brazil, Bolivia, Paraguay, and Venezuela, the fight against poverty and inequality is also mentioned as a paramount goal, even though any link between the reduction of poverty and the Mercosur trade policies remains ambiguous at best (*Hypothesis 3*).

What emerges as a clear pattern for those different schemes of political cooperation (OAS, Rio Group) and integration (UNASUR, Mercosur) is the strong links between politics and economics in Latin America. Economics can be considered as 'high politics', and schemes for integration are predicated upon political motivations such as the consolidation of democracies, the attempt to establish interdependence, and the management of globalization. From the almost identical rhetoric, we can infer that there is an overwhelming concern with issues of economic development, human development, and human security, as illustrated by the lingering astronomic levels of poverty and inequality, which affect and retard the flourishing of democracies. The success in reducing poverty and inequality, like the schemes of regional integration, still remains a work in progress (hence, *Hypothesis 3* is neither proved nor discarded).

### The international level: Latin America meets the world

At the international and global levels, the focus turns to the role of the international and global institutions – the United Nations, the World Bank, the International Monetary Fund, and the World Trade Organization – that are considered harbingers of globalization and pillars of the global economy. In the Latin America context, institutions such as the IMF have a long and not very illustrious record of political interference and intervention in the domestic politics and the political economy of the Latin American states.

The IMF has not performed ideally, to say the least, in the debacle of the debt crisis of the 1980s and the exchange rate management of the 1990s and the early 2000s. Capital market liberalization led to a series of financial and currency crises in the 1990s and the first decade of the twenty-first century, when macroeconomic fluctuations that had been generated outside of the region brought severe shock effects to Latin America (Berry 2007a, 228).

At the international or extra-regional level, the essential political problem that Latin America has confronted in its relations with the rest of the world is that of *asymmetrical significance* (Smith 2008). This means that the rest of the world (for instance, North America, Europe, or Asia, or specific countries such as China, the United States, and India) is more important to Latin America than Latin America to other regions and countries in the international system, both in political and economic terms. In this sense, Latin American countries (with only a few exceptions, such as the most recent case of Brazil) are usually onlookers and passive recipients of globalization, rather than shapers of the international system.

In this context, several *international and global actors* have played a key political role in the development of the Latin American political economy, including officials of multilateral lending institutions and representatives of big business conglomerates, who work assiduously to promote the political power of the local economic and political elites in the region, as an example of the *intermestic* model, mimicking a kind of neodependency model where the local elites are transnational allies of external actors from the global economic scene (usually located among the developed countries) (Teichman 2001–2, 16).

Moreover, international institutions might provide certain economic and political incentives for countries in the region to adapt and to adopt norms and rules of economic behaviour, including specific measures to eradicate poverty and to reduce income inequality, as a condition to 'join their club'. This has been evident in the cases of Mexico and Chile joining the very exclusive club of the OECD (*Hypothesis 4* is corroborated here).

In addition to these formal institutions, this level of analysis also investigates the role of multinational corporations and of grassroots organizations, which promote 'globalization from below'. While multinational corporations pursue private wealth, they affect the economic and social fate of millions of people in the region, while playing a very important political role, sometimes as a domestic actor, within the affected states and societies. As for the grassroots organizations, they promote an alternative agenda for globalization, and the possibility of a new 'Latin American Consensus' that encourages regional integration and cooperation, brings back the welfare state, promotes government-oriented macroeconomic and productive development, and the evolution of a pragmatic developmentalist state, in juxtaposition to the 'Washington Consensus'. This is the agenda of the Porto Alegre alternative World Forum, and of transnational networks of advocacy that oppose the neoliberal version of globalization. The effects of these grassroots movements are not uniform and evident, and they change from country to country according to different political contexts.

*Summing up: the inter-relationship between international and domestic factors in the* intermestic *model*

The different variables and actors presented in these three levels of analysis are deeply and intrinsically inter-related. One can posit that the international (structural) variables set the limits of choice for the national policies enacted by the different Latin American countries. At the same time, there is room and relevance for the variance across the region (in the formulation of social policies), when the international structure is less omnipresent, in either negative or positive directions. For instance, in empirical terms, in both the 1980s (the 'lost decade') and in 2003–8 (the period of economic boom), the effects of globalization were paramount and overwhelming, bringing about both negative and positive outcomes (the 1980s and the 2000s respectively). By contrast, in the 1990s, we can trace different national responses that led to different results across the region, as a function of divergent economic and social policies formulated by different Latin American countries (see Chapter 5).

One plausible explanation for the evolution of inequality in the last two decades is that globalization has limited the power of governments to follow certain (developmentalist and populist) policies, while promoting the adoption of other (neoliberal) policies. Yet, globalization could have negative or positive effects upon income distribution, as a function of variables such as the level of public sector spending, or the national investment in education. Hence, there is also a paramount role for the domestic context, and for the formulation of specific national policies (Bouzas and Ffrench Davis 2005, 23 and 26).

Structural factors other than economic globalization have shaped the different and distinct configurations of economic and social policies in the region. Some of these factors are fixed, like the size of the country and its economy, its geographic location, and its natural resources. Other structural factors might be domestic, like the political culture and political system of any given country (see Fajnzylber 1990, 7). In my *intermestic* model, I posit that although the international and regional contexts set the parameters for the political and economic choices, the role of different economic and social policies articulated by different political regimes and governments in different states across the region is still very relevant. For example, if we examine the initiatives taken by governments of the left in Latin America in 2003–8, we might recognize some positive movements in the direction of more citizenship-based rights and lower income inequality. In more specific terms, Nora Lustig recently has found that under social-democratic regimes from the left (in Brazil, Uruguay, and Chile) public social spending tended successfully to reduce inequality in better ways than populist or centre-right regimes (Lustig 2009, 1–5).

## Conclusions

In this chapter, I have assessed the complex links between globalization, poverty, and inequality in the context of the Latin American political economy between 1982 and 2008. To understand the complexities of these possible links, beyond the economic discussion about the merits or pitfalls of globalization, I preferred to focus upon the role of the state and its strength vis-à-vis society as a vital and active 'transmission belt' (or intervening variable), between the structural forces and constraints of globalization (external variables), and the domestic, societal variables (within the state). Thus, to make sense of whether and how globalization might affect poverty and inequality in the Latin American region, I applied here an *intermestic* political model that stresses the role of the state and other political institutions (domestic, regional, and international) in coping with globalization, poverty, and inequality.

The external, international dimension is related to the Latin American position in the international structure as one of dependency, characterized, for instance, by the financial vulnerability and volatility of the Latin American economies vis-à-vis the international capital market. The domestic, socio-political dimension refers to social and economic stratification, as well as political divisions within the different states, alongside state–society relations, which determine the level of strength (or weakness) of any given state. States in the region then fulfil (or better, *should* fulfil) a major role in regulating the national economies, in competition and cooperation with other non-state, political, and economic actors, at different levels of analysis (domestic, regional, and international).

In normative terms, the paramount goal of successfully coping with poverty and inequality under the structural constraints of globalization should be not to dismantle or to reduce the state, but rather to strengthen the political instruments and institutions necessary for the promotion of both development and equity, perhaps within the context of a social-democratic alternative (Ferrer 1998, 204). In other words, the ideal model should be a strong state that pragmatically adopts the economic logic of the market, promotes equity policies, enacts land redistribution, tax-supports social security, transfers welfare, and guarantees access to health and education (De Janvry and Sadoulet 2001, 38).

Perhaps it is time for Latin America to draw a new social contract, this time based on political will and mutual tolerance, which would combine economic efficiency, rationality, and social justice, by promoting economic development with social justice, but not necessarily with populism. While not eluding economic globalization, which remains an inevitable if not indispensable process, the emphasis should be on achieving a pro-poor pattern of growth and strong poverty-readdressing policies, by creating a strong demand for unskilled labour (Berry 2007b, 4; and Reynolds 1996, 45).

Is the Latin American case an exceptional example of the profound impact of globalization upon a specific region of the world, in terms of poverty and inequality? It is obvious that globalization is no longer a simple political choice, but a given structural constraint. Technology makes it impossible for countries and regions nowadays to survive as economic islands (Price and Haar 2008, 15). It is also evident that the economic policies of the Latin American countries have been conditioned, in one way or another, by the external forces of globalization, such as financial globalization. Yet, the challenge of Latin America remains to find its own responses and its own menu of choice in order to promote development, eradicate poverty, and reduce inequality, within the structural constraints and the 'degrees of freedom' that globalization processes enable, by fostering the role of the state and other political and social institutions (see Ferrer 1998, 203, and 1999, 77–8; and Hoffman and Centeno 2003, 381–2).

# 5　The Argentine experience in a comparative perspective, 1982–2008

This chapter addresses the complex links between the phenomena of globalization, poverty, and inequality by focusing upon the peculiar case of Argentina between 1982 and 2008, with a particular emphasis on its 2001–2 economic and political crises. The chapter also presents a brief comparison of Argentina with its two most important neighbours in the Southern Cone, Brazil and Chile (the three countries together are called the 'ABC countries'). The parallel but different cases of Brazil and Chile allow us to discern common patterns and characteristics among the 'ABC countries', alongside significant differences in the formulation and implementation of their economic and social policies.

To what extent can Argentina be considered as a useful case study to explore the relevance of those links? Argentina offers an extreme illustration of the implementation of the neoliberal ideology in many economic and social dimensions, including growth instability, growing inequalities of income between capital and labour force, informal employment, growing poverty, low formation of capital, and rentist behaviour of the private sectors that have used and abused the Argentine state throughout its long political history (see Salama 2003, 119–20). At the same time, this case study also reflects the other possible links between globalization and the distribution of wealth, and it is an extraordinary example to test the validity of the *intermestic* model, including a within-case variance throughout the last three decades.

Argentina's road to default and to both economic and political crisis in 2001–2 has been considered by the critics of globalization as an example of how the dynamics of globalization might have devastating effects upon developing countries. As Leonard suggested, Argentina's tango with the IMF was a dance to the tune of globalization, where the IMF has indeed become a key player in determining the fate of many developing countries, such as Argentina, in the global environment of US-dominated economic globalization and neoliberal restructuring (Hershberg 2002, 31; and Leonard 2006, 1).

In 2001 and 2002, Argentina's poverty and unemployment rates soared as the country defaulted on its astronomic foreign debt, precipitating a social, economic, and political crisis that led the country to the verge of institutional and economic breakdown. The painful collapse of the Argentine economy was one of the most spectacular phenomena in modern history (Blustein 2005, 1; and Escudé 2006a and 2006b). Critics of globalization saw the Argentine crisis of 2001–2 as a confirmation of their deep scepticism regarding the implementation of the 'Washington Consensus'. Conversely, defenders of globalization pointed out that the causes of the Argentine crisis of 2001–2 were inherently rooted in its domestic political conditions, without any direct link to economic globalization.

Even prior to the 2001–2 disaster, Argentina's political economy story has been one of a decline unparalleled in modern times, or what Carlos Waisman referred to as the 'reversal of development' (Waisman 1987). About one hundred years ago, Argentina ranked among the ten richest countries of the world, even ahead of France and Germany at that time. Since then, it has been a downhill trajectory most of the time. Hence, the extraordinary crisis of 2001–2 should be explained and understood within the larger context of the evolution of the Argentine economy and its insertion into economic globalization. Furthermore, the economic crisis of 2001–2 is an opportunity to examine the Argentine distribution of wealth, in terms of poverty and inequality, and its causes and consequences.

In slightly more than half a century, Argentina has suffered an almost unparalleled economic involution: the percentage of its population below the poverty line has risen steadily from approximately 10 per cent in 1950 to 45 per cent in 2005. This astonishing trend has been the product of political economy processes that have taken place under both democratic and military regimes, irrespective of which political party governed while under constitutional rule, and it was accompanied by a steady deterioration of its social structures and political institutions (Escudé 2006a, 36, and 2006b, 125).

Since the early 1970s, even a few years before the 1976 military coup, Argentine economic policies have been predominantly – though not exclusively – oriented by what may be called the adoption of a neoliberal economic model. Since the early 1990s, Argentina incarnated one of the most radical applications of neoliberalism in Latin America, and provided one of the best examples of a harmonious partnership between the IMF, the World Bank, and its national government (López-Alves 2007, 49; and Nochteff and Abeles 2000, 7). Less than ten years later, by the end of 2001, the 'payoff' for being the poster child for the neoliberal agenda of the 'Washington Consensus' was an unprecedented collapse of Argentina's economy, and the impoverishment of about half of its population.

What caused the economic disaster in Argentina and what were their social, economic, and political ramifications? The analysis of the Argentine crisis is particularly complex because of two reasons. First, the crisis occurred in a country that, during most of the 1990s, was considered as a successful model of economic insertion in the global economy. Second, my analysis refers to the socio-economic and political effects and repercussions of the collapse, rather than merely to its economic consequences (Chudnovsky et al. 2003, 61). Thus, the causes of the 2001–2 crisis encompass an array of economic and political reasons, both external and domestic: a vicious circle of external shocks, domestic vulnerabilities, currency appreciation, economic policy mistakes, a restrictive monetary policy that was badly implemented, fiscal (over)spending, problems of good governance (i.e., political corruption), and even bad luck. Domestic political causes include institutional elements, patronage and corporatism, cultural explanations such as corruption, and the dynamics of sub-national federal politics (central government–provinces' relationship). The external international economic causes include the overarching context of external shocks and contagion effects of global financial crises. Finally, *intermestic* explanations include monetary and fiscal policies, fiscal mismanagement, and false (psychological) expectations.

As for the political dimension, we should emphasize the relative weakness of the Argentine state and the fact that powerful private interests captivated it through legal mechanisms sometimes in connivance with the armed forces (see Escudé 2006a, 24). In addition, between 1930 and 1983 the direct political involvement of the military in recurrent coups d'état demonstrated a failure in conflict management and resolution of domestic political crises that reflected political and social polarization confronting Peronism and anti-Peronism (see Collier and Collier 1991, 736–41). Thus, through a series of military coups that produced significant political discontinuities, the Argentine military removed from power the middle classes and their representatives (in 1930), the export agriculture oligarchy (in 1943), the labour union and populist parties identified with Peronism (in 1955), the industrial sectors (in 1962), the traditional political parties (in 1963 and 1966), and again Peronism and the unions in 1976 (see Rouquié 1987, 287). As O'Donnell suggests, in the peculiar Argentine case, there has been a continued crisis of the state as a system of political domination, so the state was repeatedly razed to the ground by civil society's changing coalitions (see O'Donnell 1988, 201). Likewise, Argentina is considered one of the countries with the lowest level of trust on the ethical standards of its politicians, who sustain a high level of political corruption. In 2009, Argentina got the eighty-fifth ranking in

terms of economic competitiveness by the World Economic Forum, due
to the lack of trust of its private sector regarding the Argentine government's respect for the rule of law (Galak 2009). Hence, we can argue that
the major problem of Argentina is rather *political*, not economic, while
the solution lies in the hands of its own politicians and citizens (Bertucci
2001, 29; and García-Heras 2009, 280).

Yet, it is possible to trace a certain variation in the degree of state
strength throughout different time periods, with a notable recovery and
strengthening of the Argentine state after 2003, leading to a significant
improvement in the distribution of wealth, in terms of a reduction of
both poverty and inequality. This improvement is related to the parallel
strengthening of both the state apparatus and of civil society, as well as to
the substantial recuperation of domestic legitimacy by the state vis-à-vis
its society, leading to greater and more effective governance.

A recurrent pattern in the conflictive nature of Argentine political
history has been the presence of political veto players, including the military, trade unions, provincial governors, and rival politicians within the
same ruling party, who had contributed together to the political paralysis of the country. This political paralysis helps us to understand why
and how countries like Chile and Brazil have performed much better
than Argentina in the articulation of their economic and social policies,
despite confronting similar political, social, and economic problems in
the 1970s and 1980s, and despite also having despicable military dictatorships in the not so distant past (Veigel 2009, 4, 8–9, 205–6). Thus,
in comparative terms, Chile and Brazil can be considered stronger states
than Argentina, with a more coherent political and economic model,
better capacity of regulation and governance, and more social inclusion.

In the following pages, I locate the Argentine crisis of 2001–2 within
the larger temporal context that preceded and followed it. The second
section of the chapter addresses the alternative explanations for that crisis.
The third part of the chapter reintroduces the links between globalization
and the distribution of wealth in the Argentine case. Finally, the last part
of the chapter briefly discusses the cases of Brazil and Chile in 1982–
2008, with a focus on state strength and the articulation of economic as
well as social policies to address poverty and inequality.

### Explaining the political processes and economic policies adopted by the Argentine state

It is not a coincidence that Argentina's greatest economic success
occurred during the first period of globalization under the gold standard,
by the end of the nineteenth century, while its economic decline reached

the bottom with the onset of the second globalization period, in the late 1970s and early 1980s, culminating with the crisis of 2001. For most of the twentieth century, Argentina stood out in Latin America for its high levels of social integration and relatively low levels of income inequality, including the presence of a significant middle class. Yet, between 1950 and 2000, Argentina's per capita income declined in relation to the industrialized countries, while it approximated that of its neighbours. As a result, Argentina, once considered a promising economy that would join the club of the most advanced countries in the world, became more of a developing country. This 'reversal of development' (in Carlos Waisman's terms) is one of the puzzles in the political economy of this intriguing country (see Del Cueto and Luzzi 2008, 17; and Fernández Valdovinos 2005, 2).

From 1880 to 1930 Argentina adopted the economic model of export of primary agricultural products. This model was based upon a myriad of factors of production, huge agricultural resources, the flow of external capital, and inflow of masses of migrant population from Europe. The rapid economic growth in Argentina in the half-century after 1880 can thus be attributed to its full integration with the international markets of the global economy by exporting commodities. Despite its limited democracy and oligarchic political system that lasted until 1916, the country enjoyed both economic growth and political stability. Indeed, Argentina was the tenth largest trading country in the world and was ranked the sixth in terms of per capita income. During the so-called 'golden years' of 1900–13 the country had the fastest-growing economy in the world at an average growth rate of 7 per cent annually. Furthermore, the successful 'agro-exporting' model was accompanied by a significant development of the Argentine infrastructure, providing the country with a position of primacy and relevance in the world economy.

Argentina was the fastest-growing economy in 1880–1930 not because of its institutions or political stability, but rather due to new technological developments. The advent of railways made the transport costs of cereal production very profitable, turning Argentina into the 'granary of the world' (*granero del mundo*). Unfortunately, the oligarchic elites that ruled Argentina at that time did not manage to translate that amazing wealth to build a balanced and technologically advanced economy (see Gerchunoff and Llach 2009, 112; Larson 2003, 7–8; Lewis 1978; and Rapoport 2006, 157).[1]

In the mid-1970s, Argentina returned to embrace globalization, after four decades of the adoption of an Import Substitution Industrialization

---

[1] I would like to thank Tullo Vigevani for his comments on this point.

(ISI) model of development since the 1930s. The ISI model worked particularly well in its first two decades, but it eventually exhausted itself and precipitated a series of economic crises by the end of the 1960s and early 1970s. In spite of a respectable growth rate since 1963, by the early 1970s, Argentina's ISI was showing clear signs of stress. The inflation rate, which was around 60 per cent in 1972–3, was its most notorious symptom. The countries that had suffered the most with the failures of ISI, like Argentina, were the ones more prone to adopt and apply the most aggressive and abrupt liberalizing market reforms in its aftermath (see Gerchunoff and Llach 2009, 15; and Larson 2003, 10).

The renewed economic opening and liberalization of the Argentine economy took place one year before the brutal military coup of 1976, under the *Rodrigazo* of 1975, named after the Argentine economic minister who re-established the economic model under the neoliberal premises of Milton Friedman's 'Chicago School'. This model systematically dismantled the industrial and developmentalist policies of the previous decades. Simultaneously, there was the emergence of the *patria financiera* ('fatherland of financiers'), an economic system that benefited particularly a small segment of society, leading to the proliferation of speculative financial schemes to the benefit of the ruling elites. Yet, during the first years of the military rule, the economic model led also to a populist (and popular) period of *plata dulce* ('easy and sweet money') that apparently benefited also broad sectors of the population, at least in the short term.

Since 1975, Argentina has lived in a system of 'indebted economy', which destroyed a great part of its productive system, and could endure only with the continuation of the external flux of capital and credit. Thus, an economy of financial rent was built at the expense of real production, at least until the aftermath of the crisis of 2001–2. The military coup of March 1976 embedded the institutional end of the corporatist, inward-oriented, ISI model, and the adoption of a new paradigm of economic opening and liberalization alongside a brutal political repression and dictatorship. The military regime that took power in 1976 initially appeared to be strongly committed to the market, but unlike Chile and Brazil, the liberalization process became stalled and ultimately collapsed during the debt crisis of the early 1980s. Moreover, the economic and social policies of the military regime led to a drastic negative redistribution of wealth at the expense of organized labour, with a significant fall in real wages (see Del Cueto and Luzzi 2008, 18; and Gerchunoff and Llach 2009, 16).

The return to democracy in 1983 did not change basically the contours of the neoliberal economic model; though only after the failure of a more heterodox programme of President Alfonsín in 1983–8 did Peronist President Carlos Menem implement further significant liberal reforms in the early 1990s. Ten years later, the resignation of President de la Rúa in December 2001 would epitomize the ultimate failure of the neoliberal economic model (see Escudé 2006b, 128–30; Ferrer 2008, 390–1; Godio 2002, 14; Rapoport 2006, 166–78; Teichman 2001, 97; and Veigel 2009, 4–8). In the following pages I analyse the evolution of the Argentine political economy from the early 1980s until 2008.

## The debt crisis of 1982 and the 'lost decade' of the 1980s

When in the late 1970s and early 1980s the United States raised interest rates to nearly 20 per cent, Argentina found itself unable to meet its debt repayments, leading to the so-called debt crisis of 1982. In the aftermath of the August 1982 crisis, which affected Brazil and Mexico as well, debts were restructured, though there was inadequate debt forgiveness, so for much of the 1980s money flowed the other way around, this time from Argentina to the United States and other advanced industrial countries, bringing about economic stagnation.

During the military dictatorship of 1976–83, major private contractors in the country consistently failed to pay their creditors, so the national treasury picked up the bill and nationalized the private debts. Consequently, and also paradoxically, the taxpayer had to pay for the foreign debts of many of the major and even more solvent Argentine economic companies, similar to the recent economic situation in the United States and in Western Europe. Moreover, high inflation and massive foreign debt led, in turn, to severe disinvestments, which resulted in Argentina suffering negative growth rates for at least five years during the 1980s. All these problems, combined with the exhaustion of the previous ISI model of economic development, fostered a process of de-industrialization (Escudé 2006b, 131; Powers 1995, 91; and Stiglitz 2007, 220–1).

After the Argentine military debacle in the Falklands/Malvinas War in June 1982, there was a swift transition back to democracy about a year later. The new democratic regime of President Alfonsín in 1983 was faced with the double challenge of fixing the economy and meeting urgent social demands, though it miserably failed on both grounds. That failure could be attributed, in large part, to the burden of external debt obligations. As a result of the nationalization of the private external debt of 1982, the Argentine state became responsible for making the bulk of interest payments, which amounted to approximately 12 billion dollars between 1980 and 1990. By 1989, hyperinflation in the country had reached an annual level of 4,924 per cent, creating sufficient economic and social hardship and disappointment to pave the way for the victory of the Peronist leader, Carlos Menem (Lloyd-Sherlock 1997, 23; and Powers 1995, 91).

The economic failure of the Alfonsín administration (1983–9) reflected the long-term structural weaknesses of the Argentine economy, which had engendered cyclical balances of payment problems and an inconsistent pattern of stop-and-go economic growth, oscillating between adopting Keynesian welfare strategies and sponsoring neoliberal stabilization policies. As mentioned before, the 1980s also witnessed the final and definitive sea change in the economic paradigm regarding the appropriate policies that should lead to economic development.

The previous paradigm of 'growth and development', which corresponded to the ISI model and aimed at full employment, redistribution of income, satisfaction of basic needs, and reduction of poverty, was finally buried and replaced by the prevalent neoliberal paradigm, which allowed for the possibility of 'growth without development'. This new paradigm particularly referred to adjustment concerns, liberalization of the economy towards the global market, and economic stabilization to facilitate the payment of the external debt (Lischinsky 2002, 132; and Lloyd-Sherlock 1997, 24). Yet, by 1989, Argentina was again on the edge of the abyss, with null growth, hyperinflation, fiscal debacle, and a huge flight of capital. The external debt did not diminish; to the contrary, it kept growing, along with unemployment rates, poverty, and inequality (Castro 2000, 34–5).

*The 1990s: Menem, neoliberalism* à outrance, *and the 'Washington Consensus'*

In contrast to the 1980s, many analysts considered the first years of the 1990s as a remarkable economic success for Argentina, with growth rates of about 4.2 per cent to 7.9 per cent per year, with a concomitant overall GDP growth of about 40 per cent between 1990 and 1994. During those years, Argentina outperformed Brazil and Chile, reaching records of economic growth. Furthermore, Argentina became well known as the economy hosting the highest foreign investment and the largest number of foreign-owned firms in the whole of Latin America (see Gerchunoff and Llach 2009, 17; and López-Alves 2007, 55).

In 1991, Carlos Menem, the pragmatic Peronist President, and Domingo Cavallo, his powerful economy minister, set out to reverse the economic decline of Argentina through extensive free-market reforms, including open trade, unrestricted financial opening to international markets and free inflows of foreign capital, reduction of tariff rates, removal of quantitative controls on imports, and drastic cutbacks in state expenditures, along with the privatization of public enterprises and state companies (such as telecommunications, the national airline, railways, petroleum, and steel), following the guidelines and recommendations of the 'Washington Consensus'.

Thus, Argentina began the 1990s by implementing economic policies aimed to dominate the previous macroeconomic instability and consolidating structural reforms that drastically changed its economic regime. These goals were largely achieved. As for stabilization, inflation was controlled, there was an expansion of the economic activities, and the fiscal account was notably improved. Moreover, the structural reforms shaped a new and distinct economic reality, where there was a change in the relative importance of the productive sectors and the composition of capital, and the Argentine state substantially reduced its involvement in the national economy (see Beccaria 1998, 23).

The most significant economic policy articulated by the first Menem administration, which was not stipulated in the 'Washington Consensus' itself, was the establishment of a currency board (the 'convertibility law'), by which the Argentine peso was fixed by law at a parity of one to one to the dollar, so the money supply was restricted to the level of hard-currency reserves (in dollars). The exercise of a strict economic discipline regarding monetary policies actually killed hyperinflation, and stabilized the economy until 1998, spurring a significant increase in foreign investment.

At the beginning, the monetary scheme seemed to work very well, at least until the second half of the 1990s. Inflation was drastically reduced, from about 5,000 per cent in 1989 to 0.16 per cent in 1996. With all risks of devaluation apparently removed, capital poured in from abroad. New confidence in the Argentine economy meant that foreign banks and other lenders were willing to lend, even to finance local consumption. The success of the stabilization process after 1991 led to a great influx of foreign capital. This allowed it to re-establish and expand the level of economic activity and to increase productivity. Yet, the main orientation of the economic policy during the 1990s essentially reflected the demand for international capital as a crucial ingredient to keep the Argentine economy in motion. This was expressed by the privatization and the deregulation of the economy and the free inflow of foreign capitals, with a flux of a net balance of 100 billion dollars. Unfortunately, that astronomic amount was in fact counter-balanced by the formation of external capital accounts of Argentines overseas in the form of capital flights up to the sum of about 190 billion dollars (see Beker 2000, 1; Castro 2000; *Economist*, 28 February 2002; Gambina and Crivelli 2005, 392; Stiglitz 2007, 221; Teichman 2001, 111; and Weintraub 2003, 117).

A major assumption behind the Argentine neoliberal economic policies of the 1990s was that 'globalization was unstoppable'. But the strategy adopted by the Argentine government ended up being too risky: a volatile international economic environment requires frequent adjustments of exchange rates to potential damaging external shocks, which the Argentine economic regime did not allow, due to the rigidity (and stability) of its convertibility law. Having voluntarily renounced to shape its own independent monetary policy of exchange rates, the Argentine government was left with few available tools, if any, to respond to outside events, such as external shocks and contagion effects from the global economy.

These external shocks did indeed hit hard in the second half of the 1990s. The prices for Argentina's commodities stopped rising; the cost of mobilizing capital for emerging economies began to go up; the dollar appreciated against other currencies (and, concomitantly, the Argentine peso pegged to it, so it became over-valued); and finally Brazil, Argentina's major trading partner, devalued its national currency following the East Asian crisis of 1997. As a consequence, global interests to emerging markets soared, and Argentina's debt service increased from 13 billion dollars in 1996 to 27 billion dollars in 2000, while the total external debt grew from 90 to 180 billion dollars between 1995 and 2001.

The rigidity of the Argentine currency board led to a deep recession, with a negative growth of 3.4 per cent by 1999. The end of the easy influx of foreign capital and the withdrawal of speculative financial funds, which had started to be noticeable in 1997, marked the limits of Menem's success. The predictable collapse of the Argentine economy would fall upon Menem's successor's shoulders, Fernando de la Rúa (1999–2001), whose last-minute economic measures precipitated the crisis of 2001–2 (see Llach 2004, 44; Romero 2004, 30–1; and Stiglitz 2007, 16–17, 221).

While the early 1990s witnessed great improvements in terms of economic growth and low inflation, the late 1990s experienced catastrophic consequences in terms of social welfare and the distribution of wealth, including the exacerbation of poverty and inequality. The fast growth of the economy until 1998 did not coincide with the behaviour of the labour market, due to the asymmetry in the growth of its demand and supply. In other words, the slower growth in the labour demand was directly related to the privatization and lay off of a large number of workers. Thus, the 1990s witnessed a decade of economic growth without employment, in contrast to the previous decade of employment without growth (Beker 2000, 3–4; and Bouzas 2002, 23–5).

Following the adoption of the 'Washington Consensus', there was an overall retraction of the welfare state in Argentina. Thus, market-oriented neoliberal reforms under the Menem government eliminated state institutions that traditionally had long insulated Argentine workers and local firms from the external shocks of the global economy. As a result, these neoliberal policies produced massive unemployment in formerly state-owned enterprises and the impoverishment of large sectors of labour and the middle class, all in the name of efficiency and liberalization. Unemployment rates rose from 6 per cent in October 1991 to 12.2 per cent in October 1994 and to 17.3 per cent in October 1996.

This was also the most regressive period in terms of the distribution of income in Argentina, leading to a rise of inequality by 57 per cent and the polarization in the distribution of wealth, with a larger concentration of the income among the richest sectors of the population. The sharp rise in inequality in this period contrasts with the impressive economic growth in the early 1990s, as can be examined in the continuous (regressive) increase of the Gini coefficient for most of the 1990s. For instance, the Gini coefficient for urban Argentina rose from 0.452 in 1992 to 0.507 in 2000 (Cruces and Gasparini 2009a, 409). Perhaps this contrast between economic growth and rising inequality can be explained by reference to the escalating rates of unemployment throughout the 1990s, as a consequence of the neoliberal policies adopted (Beker 2000, 1; Bertucci 2001, 27; Carranza 2005, 67; Larson 2003, 14; and Lo Vuolo 1997, 43).

*The economic crisis of 2001–2*

By the end of the 1990s, Argentina was constrained by a total external debt of about 50 per cent of its GDP, a high fiscal deficit, and a 14 per cent rate of unemployment. After that, the debt burden increased and unemployment reached more than 30 per cent of the labour force. Hundreds of local and foreign firms went bankrupt, while output and tax revenue contracted. From 1998 to 2002 the Argentine economy shrank by 20 per cent, taking real GDP to levels last recorded back in 1992–3. A significant recession began in 1999 and worsened as Brazil's currency further depreciated in 2001, making the mismatch between the Argentine fixed exchange rate and the Brazilian currency more evident than ever.

In December 2000, the Radical administration of President de la Rúa negotiated a substantial package of external help so as to be able to postpone fiscal adjustments for the future. Yet, the financial markets panicked. In March 2001, the Argentine financial system suffered the most intense outflow of deposits in the whole decade of convertibility. The domestic run was followed by a precipitous foreign capital flight. By July 2001, the drop in investment had reached every sector in the economy, while extremely high interests suffocated every attempt at economic recovery. In November 2001, the government conducted a swap of old debt for new issues with lower rates of interests. In early December 2001, facing a massive flight of deposits, the government imposed limits on the withdrawal of funds held in banks and on capital transfers out of the country (the *corralito*) (see Carranza 2005, 66; and Llach 2004, 45).

Finally, the crisis exploded with the resignation of President Fernando de la Rúa and a huge devaluation of the peso that took place. Parallel to this, the social protests and the massive demonstrations against the political establishment led to a vertiginous succession of five presidents between 21 December 2001 and 1 January 2002, setting probably a world record of democratic presidential succession under the popular slogan of *Qué se vayan todos!* (Everyone must go!).

It was probably the worst and deepest political crisis since the return to democracy in 1983. And yet, despite the virulent hostility of the general population towards the political elite and the existing political institutions, the fragile Argentine democracy managed to survive this economic cataclysm and political paralysis, probably assisted by the lingering vitality of its civil society (Klein 2004, 2–5; and Romero 2004, 15 and 35). By the end of 2001, Argentina defaulted on its public external debt, causing the biggest default in history and letting its exchange rate finally float. The value of the peso quickly fell by two-thirds. In the economic chaos that followed suit, the official unemployment rate grew to over 20 per cent, while the GDP fell by 12 per cent (Stiglitz 2007, 222).

The crisis manifested itself in several ways: the lack of a legitimate national currency and the proliferation of provincial bonds of dubious value, the questioning of business agreements, the rise of insecurity and crime, and a questionable judicial order. By 2002, the illusion of convertibility was finally gone. The crisis involved the deepest peace-time fall in GDP experienced by any capitalist country of some significance, at least since World War II (see Llach 2004, 40; and Romero 2004, 35).

Yet, Argentina, as a nation and a society that reached the edge of the abyss in 2001–2, managed to temper the crisis, and even to recover since. In the last third of 2002, there was already a sense that the final collapse of the Argentine economy was not imminent, along with the perception that the state retained some sort of capacity for negotiations. Apocalypse after all never arrived on Argentine soil. Furthermore, following the presidential elections of April 2003, it began a period of political normalization under the Kirchner administration (2003–7). Thus, the crisis of 2001–2 displayed an intriguing political paradox: despite the decline of the state and the impoverishment of its society, the democratic regime reinstalled in 1983 did not disintegrate and managed to survive until today (Romero 2004, 15–16).

*Back from the brink, 2003–8*

The presidential elections of April 2003 epitomized the beginning of what seemed to be an economic and political recovery. The country became (literally) cheap for foreign tourists and full of potential economic opportunities. The economy stopped falling after the default and the pesification of the debt. After falling 10.5 per cent in 2002, much of which was explained by the acceleration of the recession in 2001, by late 2003, the Argentine economy was surging ahead at around 7 per cent per year. Sparked initially by increased exports and a gradual expansion of consumption spending, a demand-led recovery emerged. This recovery has had a positive impact on the living standards of the Argentine population, by reducing poverty and even inequality. Since then, Argentina has become, once again, one of the fastest-growing economies in the region. So far, the indicators have been very positive: the GNP improved about 84 per cent between 2003 and 2011; unemployment dropped from 25 per cent in 2002 to only 7 per cent in 2011; and the Gini coefficient improved (i.e., diminished) from 0.55 in 2002 to 0.44 in 2011, though it is still very high in historical terms (see Fernández Valdovinos 2005, 1; Levy Yeyati and Valenzuela 2007, 115; Llach 2004, 47; Oliveto 2011, 15; and Romero 2004, 15).

What led to this surprising economic recovery? There were a series of favourable factors, at least in the short term: the transfer of capital income through the pesification of the debts, low real salaries, the freezing of tariffs, and especially very favourable external conditions, such as low interest rates and high prices for commodity exports. Prices for Argentine agricultural exports were extremely high due to the growing demands from China and India that led to an agricultural boom, which substantially contributed to the speedy elimination of Argentina's fiscal deficit (Levy Yeyati and Valenzuela 2007, 332; and Veigel 2009, 13).

Moreover, the significant economic (and concomitantly social) recovery since 2003 is directly related to the economic policies implemented after 2003, based on three fundamental pillars: first, the change of the monetary exchange regime, in an attempt to establish a more competitive and real exchange rate (after the devaluation of the peso); second, a heavy taxation on agricultural exports that led to fiscal surplus; and third, an implementation of tight controls over the influx of foreign capital (see Raus 2008, 86).

Néstor Kirchner, the Peronist President elected by a minority of the Argentine electorate in April 2003, adopted a revisionist position vis-à-vis the IMF, blaming it for the economic crisis of 2001–2 and implementing a hard-bargaining negotiating style towards the renegotiation of the defaulted debt, which amounted to about 150 billion dollars. This was a very dangerous gambit, in terms of sacrificing Argentine international credibility in the long term for a quick fix in the present. Yet, from the standpoint of Kirchner, the negotiations were very successful in political terms. Argentina eventually defaulted on billions of dollars of its international debt in 2001, and then, despite harsh entreaties from the IMF, agreed to pay only about 30 cents on each dollar to its creditors in 2003. In this sense, Kirchner's economic policy challenged the wisdom of the traditional IMF method of structural adjustment, no matter what the immediate social and economic costs would be (Gaudin 2006, 79; Leonard 2006, 1; López-Alves and Johnson 2007, 5; and MacLachlan 2006, 180).

The surprising economic recovery posed the question about how long the growth could continue (before the explosion of the financial global crisis of 2008–9). The relevancy of this question is up to date, as it carries a clear ideological edge. Traditional free-market Liberal economists remain highly sceptical about the long-term sustainability of the recent economic recovery, since they attribute it to external factors rather than to the proper economic policies of the Peronist government.

By contrast, critical observers of globalization suggest that Argentina can continue to grow apace *contra* the neoliberal remedies of the IMF and following heterodox policies, in part by ignoring and even defying the economic and political orthodoxy of the 'Washington Consensus'. Rather than moving instinctively immediately to satisfy the requirements of the IMF, the private banks, and the foreign bondholders, the Kirchner administration chose first to concentrate on reviving domestic employment and stimulating internal consumption, and only then told the creditors to get in line with everyone else (see Rohter 2004). In this sense, the Argentine case, by presenting a clear discontinuity and showing heterodox economic policies since 2003, is very different from the Brazilian and Chilean ones, which show much more continuity across different regimes and political parties, and even in the transition from military regimes back to democracy, in the implementation of neoliberal economic policies.

Ironically, it was the dynamics of economic globalization that responded to the weakened peso and contributed to the new Argentine bonanza by creating jobs and by encouraging exports. Moreover, this economic bonanza, related to the high commodity prices that benefited Argentina, demonstrated that the 'terms of trade' theory of Prebisch and Singer could be actually proven wrong. These exports, made cheap by currency devaluation, resulted in a trade surplus and even led to a budget surplus. The GDP expanded annually by about 7 per cent, while inflation was held at only 3 per cent (according to the not-always-reliable official figures). The Argentine economy, with its debts unpaid, continued to recover until the global crisis of 2008–9 (MacLachlan 2006, 177–8).

There was also encouraging news regarding the distribution of wealth. By 2004, unemployment rates declined from more than 20 per cent to about 13 per cent, and the number of Argentines living below the national poverty line fell by nearly ten points from the record high of 53.4 per cent early in 2002. At the same time, the country's successful passage through default obscured the reality that Argentina managed to stabilize its economy at a lower socio-economic level than that of 1998. Real wages fell by 30 per cent, and about 40 per cent of the population still remained poor. The formal economy, with its social safety-net benefits, fell to its 1980 level. Meanwhile, the informal economy, including the estimated 8,000 rag pickers (*cartoneros*) that recycle items from the garbage, actually doubled. Moreover, the Argentine economy remained very vulnerable to external shocks, as it continued to rely excessively upon the prices of its agricultural commodities for export. Thus, the country's economic wealth, like 100 years ago, still depends upon the prices of its commodities, while there is an energetic deficit, as illustrated by the current need to import gas and electricity to keep the Argentine industry rolling (see MacLachlan 2006, 180; and Rohter 2004).

*Summing up: the evolution of the Argentine economy between 1982 and 2008*

As a way of summary, I depict in Figure 5.1 and in Table 5.1 the evolution of the Argentine economy between 1982 and 2008 in graphic terms. Figure 5.1 and Table 5.1 include a series of globalization and economic indicators for the country, such as the GDP per capita based on purchasing-power parity, the real GDP growth rate (in percentages), trade as a percentage of GDP, FDI net inflows in the country (as a percentage of the GDP), and the overall economic globalization index.

From the reading of Figure 5.1 and Table 5.1 the following conclusions can be drawn:

1. In terms of GDP per capita, there has been a steady economic growth between 1982 and 2008, with the exception of a notable reversal during the recession of 1998–2001, which culminated in the economic crisis of 2001–2.

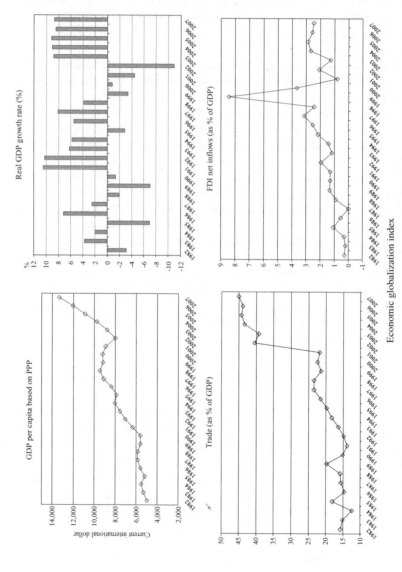

Figure 5.1 Globalization indicators for Argentina, 1982–2007

Table 5.1 *Globalization indicators for Argentina, 1982–2007*

|  | GDP per capita, PPP (in current international dollar) | Real GDP growth rate as a percentage | Trade as a percentage of GDP | FDI net inflows | Economic globalization index |
|---|---|---|---|---|---|
| 1982 | 4,976 | −3.1 | 15.6 | 0.28 | 43.0 |
| 1983 | 5,291 | 3.7 | 15.0 | 0.21 | 42.0 |
| 1984 | 5,505 | 2.0 | 12.3 | 0.29 | 43.9 |
| 1985 | 5,189 | −7.0 | 18.0 | 1.04 | 41.1 |
| 1986 | 5,611 | 7.1 | 14.5 | 0.54 | 39.1 |
| 1987 | 5,853 | 2.5 | 15.4 | −0.02 | 40.0 |
| 1988 | 5,864 | −2.0 | 15.7 | 0.90 | 40.3 |
| 1989 | 5,589 | −7.0 | 19.6 | 1.34 | 45.8 |
| 1990 | 5,610 | −1.3 | 15.0 | 1.30 | 41.6 |
| 1991 | 6,333 | 10.5 | 13.8 | 1.29 | 44.6 |
| 1992 | 7,054 | 10.3 | 14.7 | 1.94 | 48.1 |
| 1993 | 7,548 | 6.3 | 16.2 | 1.18 | 51.6 |
| 1994 | 8,054 | 5.8 | 18.1 | 1.41 | 55.0 |
| 1995 | 7,890 | −2.8 | 19.7 | 2.17 | 59.8 |
| 1996 | 8,384 | 5.5 | 21.5 | 2.55 | 60.7 |
| 1997 | 9,118 | 8.1 | 23.3 | 3.13 | 61.9 |
| 1998 | 9,469 | 3.9 | 23.3 | 2.44 | 60.7 |
| 1999 | 9,183 | −3.4 | 21.3 | 8.46 | 63.2 |
| 2000 | 9,210 | −0.8 | 22.4 | 3.66 | 61.1 |
| 2001 | 8,913 | −4.4 | 21.7 | 0.81 | 53.7 |
| 2002 | 7,993 | −10.9 | 40.5 | 2.11 | 58.5 |
| 2003 | 8,804 | 8.8 | 39.2 | 1.27 | 56.8 |
| 2004 | 9,759 | 9.0 | 43.4 | 2.69 | 58.5 |
| 2005 | 10,872 | 9.2 | 44.3 | 2.87 | 54.5 |
| 2006 | 12,058 | 8.5 | 43.9 | 2.58 | 54.3 |
| 2007 | 13,345 | 8.7 | 45.0 | 2.47 | 64.12 |

2. A better indicator of the fluctuations of the Argentine economy can be grasped by looking at the percentage of the annual real GDP growth rate. Thus, the negative growth rates of 1982, 1985, 1988, 1989, 1990, 1995, 1999, 2000, 2001, and 2002 correspond to the economic crises described above. The overall picture is that of a roller coaster trajectory, oscillating between positive and negative growth rates. The record positive growth rates correspond to the first three years of the Menem administration (1991–3), following the implementation of the convertibility plan; and to the astounding economic recovery of the country after the debacle of 2001–2 during the Kirchner administration (2003–7).

3. The trade curve (as a percentage of the GDP) shows a slow and steady projection upwards, with some fluctuations downwards that

correspond to periods of recession, stagnation, and crises (1982–4, 1987–8, 1999–2002). Again, there is a quantum leap in the volumes of trade after the crisis of 2000–3, which in an abrupt way prioritizes the importance of trading commodities as a percentage of the GDP.

4. The FDI net inflows curve (as a percentage of the GDP) is even more illustrative of the fluctuations and volatility of the Argentine economy, exposed and vulnerable to external shocks. There is a steady increase in net inflows of FDIs in the 1990s that culminated in 1999, with a vertiginous drop between 2000 and 2003.

5. As for the overall economic globalization index, the 'lost decade' of the 1980s shows the lowest point in the scale (1987–9 under the Alfonsín administration, which shied away from fully embracing globalization). During the two Menem administrations (1989–99), Argentina steadily climbed to the peak of its globalization index (1998–9), followed by a drop during the economic crisis (1999–2002), and a partial withdrawal from globalization policies, as displayed by the Kirchner administration (2003–7).

### The Argentine malaise

Before we turn to a detailed examination of the possible causes for the Argentine economic crisis of 2001–2, we should examine the broader picture of the so-called 'Argentine malaise' (or even anomie) that has characterized the country in the last half-century. We should look at the political and socio-economic features of that malaise, searching for some clues in order to make sense of the Argentine puzzle embedded in its relative economic failure and sluggish economic growth, punctuated by high indexes of poverty and inequality.

#### A political economy analysis of the Argentine malaise

As Carlos Escudé wittily remarks, 'Cynics wonder why Argentina is a land of a chronically unfulfilled future of welfare and prosperity. Her successful insertion in the world economy towards the end of the nineteenth century, her natural resources per capita, the relatively high (albeit decreasing) education of her citizens, have sparked sarcastic remarks from wits ever since her decline began' (Escudé 2002, 453). Indeed, the list of possible explanations for the Argentine failure is rather long and complicated. We can group these explanations according to two different approaches, structural-oriented and (political) process-oriented.

The first approach to address the causes of the Argentine relative economic failure assumes that economic growth has been obstructed by *structural factors*, both material and ideational, such as colonial legacies, the external dependency and asymmetry of international relations, structural problems in capital formation, and the institutional structure of Argentine society and polity, its political culture, and the weight of its distorted political and social norms and rules. All these structural factors provide both the context and the setting that constrain the policies of the Argentine state. In this regard, we can argue that the last three decades have been characterized by institutional and political unpredictability, as a form of structural constraint. Moreover, on ideational terms, Argentina has been a singular case of a *culture of decline*, including a certain obsession with failure (or *fracasomanía*) (López-Alves 2007, 58 and 61; Miguez 2005, 485–94; and Paradiso 2002, 15).[2]

The second approach lumps together explanations that refer to *political processes and to economic policies adopted by the state*. In other words, the reference here is to the lack of state intervention, or, conversely, to the fact that many times state intervention distorted economic conditions, impairing growth. In both cases, the role of the state remains crucial, though in an indirect manner, through the implementation (or lack of) of economic reforms. For instance, social expenses and tax collection have a significant effect upon the distribution of wealth (Cruces and Gasparini 2009b, 3).

In the Argentine case, most of the emphasis has been placed upon the lack of governance and institutional weaknesses that have characterized the Argentine polity most of the time, including an extreme lack of equilibrium of the political power in society, the weakness of the state in fulfilling its basic functions, the non-existence of a reliable judiciary, and a high level of political corruption. Thus, the basic political economy problem that has affected Argentina from 1930 until 2002 has been the relative absence of the state as an effective political actor capable of intervening in a systematic and coherent way, beyond the parochial and particular interests of interest groups, including powerful economic enterprises and corporations.

For many decades, the state apparatus was used and abused by big enterprises aiming to obtain credits and to nationalize the private debts (see Polino 1998, 33). As Escudé suggests, one can refer here to a series of political (mal)practices that seem to be endemic to Argentine politics, including patronage, clientelism, pork-barrelling, log-rolling, and eventually corruption and political bribe, all characterized by the erosion

----

[2] In the realm of ideas and the shaping of economic policies, see Sikkink (1991), who draws a fascinating comparison between the developmentalist ideas and policies of Brazil and Argentina in the 1960s.

of the rule of law (Escudé 2002, 455–7; Lischinsky 2002, 130; Miguez 2005, 494–501; and Sersale 2002, 24).

Nowadays, the Argentine polity can be defined as a democracy in which the public believes that democracy is better than its authoritarian or totalitarian alternatives, but it also thinks that the political system does not work properly, so it cannot be trusted, similar to other Latin American countries. Hence, the Argentine state is still perceived as a weak actor, yielding to external (international) factors that wield most of the power, most of the time. Thus, the Argentine state has been characterized at times as 'unsustainable', 'deserting', 'impotent', and 'anorexic' (Escudé 2002, 466; Jozami 2002, 12; and López-Alves 2007, 72).

Yet, the characterization of Argentina as always being a weak state is more complicated than it seems at first sight. Thus, we should qualify this broad over-generalization about the permanent weakness of the Argentine state, as we can discern certain variations in state policies and state strength across time throughout its political history, even during the three decades examined in this book (1982–2008).

For instance, after 1930 and into the Peronist era (1946–55), the Argentine state became stronger vis-à-vis its society. Peron's regime's nationalism, its concern for industrialization, and its commitment to redistributive issues led to a dramatic increase in the role of the state. Between 1943 and 1955 the functions of the Argentine state increased dramatically as a consequence of nationalization and interventionism in issue-areas such as trade, banking, and industrial promotion (Teichman 2001, 32–3).

This state strength did not last long, as the state structures weakened gradually after 1955 and into the 1970s and 1980s, showing clear signs of malfunctioning. The economic and social policies sponsored by the military regime in 1976 were more or less maintained for the next twenty-five years, defining the major contours of the Argentine state as relatively weak, and at some points even decadent and corrupt. Yet, despite the economic and social decay, Argentina has managed to maintain its democratic regime since 1983.

Under the Menem administration (1989–99), although there was a significant retrenchment of the welfare state, with a concomitant wave of privatizations, the formulation of radical liberal policies point to a certain degree of state isolation from society, thus demonstrating a certain degree of state strength. Thus, the politics of retrenchment responded to a peculiar capacity of the Argentine state to concentrate its institutional and political power, due to the meagre veto power of significant minorities. In more specific terms, by the early 1990s, state managers had developed a technocratic cadre of economic policymakers who were able to develop a greater degree of autonomy from societal pressures than in the past, pushing for radical liberal economic reforms. Moreover, the initial success of the stabilization plans implied the strengthening of the political power of the state, its gradual recovery, and the possibility of governability of macroeconomic issues. Thus, in the early 1990s, we witness a simultaneous process of shrinking of the state, while improving its effectiveness and capabilities (see Lo Vuolo 1998, 41; Palermo 2001, 39; Teichman 2001, 98; and Waisman 1997, 229–30).

The state weakened again by the end of the 1990s, as it was losing control over the economic and political events that would lead to the extreme economic and political crisis of 2001. Finally, after 2003, under the Kirchner administration, the state became stronger again, with a record in tax collection and pro-active social and economic policies, as specified below (see Raus 2008, 85–6).

### Poverty and inequality in Argentina

As a matter of fact, Argentina remained one of the most prosperous economies of Latin America until the 1960s. Although it is true that poverty and rudimentary living conditions certainly existed in the hinterland (*interior*) in some of the least-developed provinces of the country, on any comparison of per capita gross national product, levels of poverty, or distribution of income, Argentina ranked in the past among the wealthiest and most egalitarian societies in the entire region. Unfortunately, this changed drastically after the second half of the 1970s (Powers 1995, 90).

From the 1970s on, the Argentine society has experienced a gradual deterioration regarding poverty and inequality, as measured in terms of income distribution and rise of the Gini coefficient from 0.36 to 0.49. We can identify four phases in this process: from 1976 to 1982; from 1982 to 1989; from 1989 to 1994; and from 1994 to 2002. During each of these phases, there was a worsening of income distribution. The most striking fact about Argentina is that poverty increased even in periods of economic growth and expansion, due to the unequal distribution of income. Thus, the rise in inequality and poverty was observed in periods of both growth and recession. Until 2001, poverty was related to unemployment, while afterwards, it was associated with the sharp devaluation of the peso (see Fernández Valdovinos 2005, 2).[3]

Guillermo Cruces and Leonardo Gasparini identify a series of factors that explain the strong rise in income inequality in Argentina between the 1970s and the mid-2000s as follows: severe macroeconomic crises; hyperinflation; adjustment processes and high levels of unemployment;

---

[3] Interview with Domingo Cavallo, 12 June 2008.

authoritarian dictatorships (until 1983); processes of strong trade liber-alization; episodes of fast accumulation of capital, modernization, and technological change; weak trade union institutions; and demographic changes with inequality effects. These factors are located within a structural context of the Argentine macroeconomic performance, characterized by low growth and high financial volatility (see Cruces and Gasparini 2009a, 395–404).

In the second half of the 1970s, attempts at liberal reforms and anti-inflationary policies, implemented by the military government, led to wage cuts and failure in controlling inflation. The deterioration in income distribution was thus related to the gap in the wage distribution according to different levels of skills. Unemployment later on worsened the income distribution (Altimir and Beccaria 2001, 615).

During the 'lost decade' of the 1980s, deep macroeconomic disequi-libria, recession, and hyperinflation led to high levels of poverty and inequality. Inflationary acceleration during the last part of the 1980s led to a widespread deterioration of real wages. Unemployment growth, par-ticularly affecting low-income families, was the main factor that explained the rise of household inequality (Altimir and Beccaria 2001, 618).

During the 1990s, although the Argentine economy experienced high rates of economic growth in the first half of the decade, it did not tran-spire in the reduction of poverty and inequality, but quite the opposite. The increased integration into the global economy, through trade liber-alization, encouraged production and employment in the sectors using natural resources, helped reduce the relative costs of capital, and intro-duced new skilled labour-intensive technologies in detriment of unskilled workers. Moreover, if we take a look at the state reforms that led to massive privatizations in the 1990s, then we find clear linkages between specific open market reforms and increases in income inequality and poverty. Thus, what characterized the transformation of the social struc-ture in Argentina in the 1990s was the emergence of poverty as related to the lack of income. In other words, the labour market's crisis resulted in unemployment and greater inequality (see Cruces and Gasparino 2009a, 406; and Fernández Valdovinos 2005, 3).

According to a document by the World Bank from 1999, about 36.1 per cent of the Argentine population, or 13.4 million, was considered to be living under the poverty line. In terms of inequality, the richest 10 per cent of the population earned about 36 per cent of the country's income, while the poorest 10 per cent earned only 1.5 per cent of the income (Larson 2003, 17; and Repetto 2000, 603).

Furthermore, high volatility in macroeconomic performance is an important factor in exacerbating the levels of inequality and poverty.

This is well illustrated in the Argentine case, where after three years of continuing recession, the economic and financial situation of the country reached a crisis stage during 2001, increasing the rates of poverty and extreme poverty (see Cruces and Gasparini 2009a, 395–404).

As a result of the economic crisis of 2001–2, from October 2001 to May 2003, more than 7 million middle-class Argentines, about 20 per cent of the entire population, fell under the national poverty line, becoming the 'new poor'. Taking the entire country as a whole, about 55 per cent of its urban population became poor, while the situation in the rural areas was even worse. In a country of about 36.2 million inhabitants this meant that approximately 19 million now became poor. Furthermore, there was an increase of 25 per cent from the 2.5 per cent living under the indigence line (of absolute poverty) in October 1992 to the 27.5 per cent of October 2002. The official poverty rate showed that some 53 per cent of the population was poor in May 2002, up from nearly 36 per cent just a year earlier (see Fernández Valdovinos 2005, 3; Larson 2003, 15; and López-Alves 2007, 56; see also Kliksberg 2001 and 2005).

Figure 5.2 and Tables 5.2 and 5.3 summarize a series of poverty and development indicators for Argentina between 1982 and 2008.

From the reading of Figure 5.2 and Tables 5.2 and 5.3 we can infer several conclusions, as follows.

1. The unemployment rate, as a percentage of the total labour force, is a useful proxy to discern trends in the distribution of wealth, in terms of increasing poverty and inequality. Thus, the steady rise in unemployment in the second half of the 1990s and in the early 2000s coincided with the exacerbation of poverty and the rise of inequality.
2. The percentage of poor people in the country had steadily increased between 1980 and 2002, with two peaks in 1999 and 2002 (coinciding with economic crises). Since 2002, there has been a decline in the number of poor people. Similarly, the percentage of indigent persons marked a record by 2002.
3. In contrast to the more extreme fluctuations in poverty (both relative and extreme), the Gini coefficient of inequality has remained quite steady at very high levels (between 0.45 and 0.55) during the entire period, with a slight increase in 2002 and a gradual trend downwards after that.
4. As for the indexes related to Human Development, Argentina by 2006 had a similar ranking to that of 1990, recording a slight improvement in several indicators, such as a smaller percentage of the population without access to an improved water source, or a rise in life expectancy at birth, from 70.2 years in 1982 to 75.2 years in 2007.

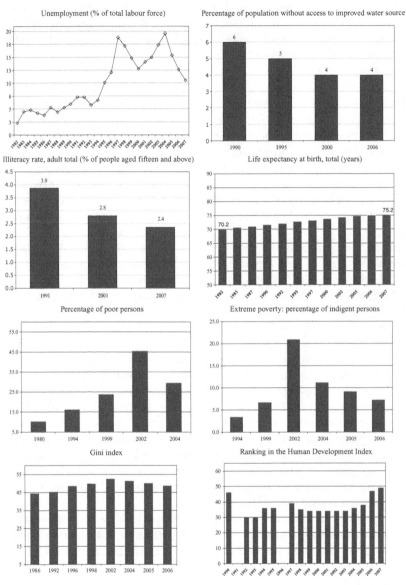

Figure 5.2 Poverty and development indicators for Argentina, 1982–2007

Table 5.2 *Poverty indicators for Argentina, 1982–2007*

|      | Total unemployment (% of total labour force) | Gini index | Poor population (% of total urban area) | Extreme poverty (% of total population, urban area) |
|------|------|------|------|------|
| 1982 | 4.8  | –    | –    | –    |
| 1983 | 4.2  | –    | –    | –    |
| 1984 | 3.8  | –    | –    | –    |
| 1985 | 5.3  | –    | –    | –    |
| 1986 | 4.4  | 44.5 | –    | –    |
| 1987 | 5.3  | –    | –    | –    |
| 1988 | 6.0  | –    | –    | –    |
| 1989 | 7.3  | –    | –    | –    |
| 1990 | 7.3  | –    | –    | –    |
| 1991 | 5.8  | –    | –    | –    |
| 1992 | 6.7  | 45.4 | –    | –    |
| 1993 | 10.1 | –    | –    | –    |
| 1994 | 12.1 | –    | 16.1 | 3.4  |
| 1995 | 18.8 | –    | –    | –    |
| 1996 | 17.2 | 48.6 | –    | –    |
| 1997 | 14.9 | –    | –    | –    |
| 1998 | 12.8 | 49.8 | –    | –    |
| 1999 | 14.1 | –    | 23.7 | 6.7  |
| 2000 | 15.0 | –    | –    | –    |
| 2001 | 17.4 | –    | –    | –    |
| 2002 | 19.6 | 52.5 | 45.4 | 20.9 |
| 2003 | 15.4 | –    | –    | –    |
| 2004 | 12.6 | 51.3 | 29.4 | 11.1 |
| 2005 | 10.6 | 50.0 | –    | 9.1  |
| 2006 | 9.5  | 48.8 | –    | 7.2  |
| 2007 | 8.8  | 47.4 | –    | –    |

## Explaining the economic crisis of 2001–2

After reviewing the evolution of the Argentine political economy since 1982 and assessing the 'Argentine malaise', we can locate the Argentine crisis of 2001–2 as part of this larger historical and political context. This crisis was a result of multiple economic and political causes, which cannot be fully understood unless we also refer to the main features of the Argentine political system and the poor quality of its institutional context, within which economic decisions were made (Chudnovsky and López 2007, 139).

Some of these causes were external (international), others internal (domestic), and still others *intermestic*. Assessing the alternative

Table 5.3 *Development indicators for Argentina, 1982–2007*

| | Population without access to improved water source (% of total population) | Total adult illiteracy (% of people aged fifteen and above) | Life expectancy at birth, total (years) | Ranking in the Human Development Index |
|---|---|---|---|---|
| 1982 | – | – | 70.19561 | – |
| 1983 | – | – | – | – |
| 1984 | – | – | – | – |
| 1985 | – | – | 70.686732 | – |
| 1986 | – | – | – | – |
| 1987 | – | – | 71.014146 | – |
| 1988 | – | – | – | – |
| 1989 | – | – | – | – |
| 1990 | 6.0 | – | 71.672976 | 46 |
| 1991 | – | 3.9 | – | – |
| 1992 | – | – | 72.112195 | 30 |
| 1993 | – | – | – | 30 |
| 1994 | – | – | – | 36 |
| 1995 | 5.0 | – | 72.771463 | 36 |
| 1996 | – | – | – | – |
| 1997 | – | – | 73.210976 | 39 |
| 1998 | – | – | – | 35 |
| 1999 | – | – | – | 34 |
| 2000 | 4.0 | – | 73.839512 | 34 |
| 2001 | – | 2.8 | – | 34 |
| 2002 | – | – | 74.258537 | 34 |
| 2003 | – | – | – | 34 |
| 2004 | – | – | – | 36 |
| 2005 | – | – | 74.834537 | 38 |
| 2006 | 4.0 | – | 75.026537 | 47 |
| 2007 | – | 2.3554 | 75.218537 | 49 |

explanations for the crisis might help us to understand the possible links between globalization and the distribution of wealth. These explanations include: (1) internal political considerations (domestic politics explanations); (2) external economic considerations (international explanations); and (3) political economy considerations (*intermestic* explanations). In terms of the previous discussion of the Argentine malaise, the domestic and *intermestic* explanations partly correspond to and overlap the approach that emphasizes political processes and economic policies adopted by the state. Conversely, the international explanations refer to the structural approach.

*Political considerations (domestic politics explanations)*

The non-economic factors behind the Argentine crisis point out to institutional, political, and even cultural elements as the critical explanations for the crisis. In this vein, the crisis is interpreted as one more step in the long history of political and economic failures, within the context of the Argentine malaise. Cultural explanations range from widespread corruption during the Menem administration, especially in relation to the wave of privatization, as well as to the lack of the rule of law and the absence of an effective political leadership and political mismanagement on the part of President de la Rúa, leading to the crisis of 2001 (Carranza 2005, 73; and Fiorucci 2004, 156). Additionally, the institutional fragility that characterized the 1990s, the profound cleavages between the state and the civil society, the scant capacity of Argentine politicians to manage public affairs or even to reach basic agreements, and even an alleged inability of the Argentine society itself to behave in a responsible, economic way, all have been advanced as possible causes for Argentina's misfortunes (Carranza 2005, 75; and Llach 2004, 47–8).

The Argentine debacle of 2001–2 was also directly related to endogenous factors such as the erosion of the state's authority and a political system of patronage and clientelism, leading to political malpractices that poisoned the relations between the central (federal) government and the provinces (regional governments) that rebelled against the central state through fiscal over-spending, as an endemic and recurrent feature of Argentine politics. The provincial governors traditionally played a preponderant role in Argentine politics. They were key political players who did not have any incentive to alter the status quo, which guaranteed fixed budget transfers from the central government to them, regardless of the country's economic performance. As the economic situation further deteriorated in 2001, and public revenues continued to fall, it became increasingly difficult for the federal government to keep the monthly transfers rolling to the provinces, thus leading to a political crisis in December 2001 that precipitated the resignation of President de la Rúa (Escudé 2002, 453; and Saiegh 2004, 108–9, 120).

To a certain extent, mimicking the previous ineptitude of the military government of 1976–83, both major political parties (Peronists and Radicals) had mismanaged the national economy since the return to democracy in 1983, continuing the nefarious tradition of squandering resources at an alarming rate. In this sense, 'bad politicians' performing 'bad politics', rather than the alleged Darwinist forces of globalization, were considered to be the major culprits of the economic and political crisis of 2001–2 (Carranza 2005, 73; and Hershberg 2002, 33).

Although these domestic political explanations seem to be crucial to understand the logic of the Argentine malaise in general, and of the 2001–2 crisis in particular, they are insufficient to the extent that they completely ignore the international dimension. After all, the economic crisis was somehow determined, if not constrained, by the external shocks of the late 1990s and the ideological hegemony of the 'Washington Consensus', which led to the implementation of pro-globalization and liberalization policies (Carranza 2005, 77–8). I turn now to assess this second set of explanations.

### International economic considerations ('external shocks')

In addition to the political domestic arguments, it is evident that the international context of the second half of the 1990s, namely the modern system of globalized financial capital, is crucial to understand the steady deterioration of the Argentine economy, following the Mexican, East Asian, Russian, and Brazilian crises (all crises of globalization) in 1994–9. Those financial crises led to 'external shocks' that swept the globe, having a profound impact upon the Argentine economy, due to its already vulnerable financial position in the world economy.

The full integration of Argentina into the international financial markets played a fundamental role in the continuing functioning of its convertibility regime, but it also laid the ground for the crisis of December 2001. As Blustein argued, foreign funds numbed Argentine policymakers into discounting the risks of their own policies. Like steroids, these influxes of foreign capital gave the economy a short-term boost while seriously damaging it in the long term (Blustein 2005, 6; and Gambina and Crivelli 2005, 393–4).

Russia's default in August 1998 deprived Argentina of ready access to foreign capital, due to the contagion effect. Furthermore, Brazil's devaluation in early 1999 destroyed Argentina's competitiveness in the foreign markets. As a result, Argentina was stuck with twin deficits, a trade gap and a budget gap, which foreigners were less and less willing and ready to finance. To right itself, the Argentine economy needed to regain competitiveness. Since the exchange rate could not fluctuate or fall (it was still fixed and pegged to the dollar), prices and wages had to fall, leading to a deep recession. As a result, peso prices edged downwards, tax revenues faltered, and Argentina's dollar debts grew harder and harder to repay (*Economist*, 3 May 2005; Weintraub 2003, 109; and Williamson 2003, 5).

The Argentine case had similarities with the Brazilian crisis of 1999 in that the fallout from external events (the Asian and Russian collapses vis-à-vis Brazil, and the Brazilian devaluation vis-à-vis Argentina) was a major precipitating cause of what followed suit. Like a house of cards or a domino effect, this is known in the globalization literature as 'the contagion effect of financial crises'. Yet, the Argentine case remained singular due to its overwhelming systemic (structural) dependence upon foreign capital inflows.

It seems that one can find a high correlation between the direction of capital flows into emerging markets during the 1990s and the evolution of the Argentine economy (Llach 2004, 49). Thus, when these capital inflows slowed down, disappeared, or became prohibitively expensive due to both internal political and international economic events, serious economic and political problems were then created for the Argentine economy and politics, with devastating social implications in terms of poverty and inequality (Calvo 2003, 113; Weintraub 2003, 119–20; and Williamson 2003, 5).

In addition to the pernicious financial effects of the external shocks, we should mention as well the external trade effects upon Argentina's balance of payments. More specifically, the combination of the devaluation of the Brazilian *real*, the appreciation of the dollar, and a deterioration in Argentina's terms of trade regarding its agricultural commodities (all of this happened simultaneously in 1999) further endangered the internal sustainability and external credibility of the country, exacerbating the recession and unemployment that reached at that time about 25 per cent of the labour force (Llach 2004, 49–50).

Although these external shocks and international explanations are equally plausible and crucial in order to make sense of the Argentine crisis of 2001–2, they also face the reversed criticism of the political explanations. That is, they cannot reveal the variance across different countries that were affected differently but simultaneously by the same external shocks. In other words, to make sense of the differences between Argentina and other Latin American countries that coped better with their external shocks, such as Brazil and Chile, we should turn now to a third set of explanations that focus upon the *intermestic* argument, by combining both external and domestic elements.

*Political economy considerations (*intermestic *explanations)*

Combining the two previous levels of analysis (international and domestic), a third set of factors focuses upon political economy considerations, which relate to domestic political decisions taken in the context and vis-à-vis the international economic system. Thus, the roots of the 2001–2 crisis resided in the excessive vulnerability of the Argentine economy to external shocks, itself a reflection of the rigid exchange regime and the fragile fiscal position adopted by the Argentine government (see Perry and Serven 2002, 375).

In more concrete terms, Argentina's monetary system and its decision in 1991 to fix the exchange rate, pegging the Argentine peso to the dollar, could be considered as another possible suspect (if not culprit) for the debacle of 2001–2, alongside the lack of a coherent fiscal policy. What made the Argentine economy particularly vulnerable to external shocks was not only its opening up to foreign trade and capital flows, like other Latin American countries. Rather, in addition to its peripheral position in the global economy, it was the monetary plan of economic stabilization that eventually worsened its external vulnerability.

The 'convertibility system' was an extremely powerful hyperinflation killer in the short term, but it brought with it unintended consequences in the long term, creating problems for both the material and the financial side of the Argentine economy; for instance, running the local import-competing industries. The convertibility plan indeed removed all scope for monetary mischief, making the peso and the dollar freely interchangeable and stabilizing the previously chaotic financial sector. Yet, the problem was that Argentina's 'monetary self-denial', as Blustein called it, coexisted uneasily with a climate of financial self-indulgence.

During the 1990s, the Argentine government sold unprecedented amounts of bonds to foreign investors, accounting at its peak for more than a quarter of all emerging market-issuance. Hence, its public debt increased from 35 per cent of the GDP at the end of 1994 to 64 per cent at the end of 2001, nearly all of it denominated in dollars (*Economist*, 3 May 2005; and Llach 2004, 50).

In political terms, the convertibility plan became much more than just an effective economic strategy to cope with inflation and to tame price fluctuations. The economic model became emblematic of the first period of true and stable economic policy in more than half a century and a symbol of political and social stability, so it gradually became both a political goal in itself and a self-perpetuating reality. Even though ominous economic signals were out there as early as 1995 that the model could not last forever, there was an obvious political reticence to change the exchange-rate regime, despite its negative consequences. Those negative effects included persistent high unemployment, increasingly uncompetitive exports (due to an over-valued peso), and diminishing access to capital for small- and medium-sized companies. Combined, these negative effects ultimately devastated the national economy and transformed Argentina from a model of development in 1991–4 to a developmental basket case by 2002 (Carranza 2005, 71; Hershberg 2002, 32; and Shambaugh 2004, 281).

Another related political economy trigger of the Argentine crisis refers to its excessive and unnecessary public borrowing and the lack of a coherent fiscal policy. According to this argument, public deficits higher than those sustainable in the long run were the main cause of the economic debacle. Although there was a substantial improvement in the fiscal position in the early years of the 1990s (following the guidelines of the 'Washington Consensus'), a coherent fiscal policy started to erode after 1993. The ratio of public debt to GDP grew from 29 per cent in 1993 to 41 per cent in 1998, all the way to 55 per cent by 2001 (Carranza 2005, 72; Llach 2004, 52; and Williamson 2003, 4).

In his second term, after dispensing the economic minister, Domingo Cavallo, Carlos Menem's government failed to tackle adequately Argentina's fiscal weaknesses, involving much spending, corruption, and an inefficient tax system. And yet, during the whole period of 1991–2000, the budget deficit of the central government averaged only 1 per cent of the GDP, whereas the principal cause of Argentina's fiscal deficits in 1999–2001 was directly related to the interest payments on its astronomic external debt.

Last but not least, a third *intermestic* factor that led to the Argentine crisis refers to the false domestic and international expectations created by the neoliberal reforms of the early 1990s, especially the convertibility plan. At the beginning, these expectations increased the perceived wealth of both public and private agents, thus inducing an expansion of public and private consumption. The assumption that the economy would keep growing and growing within the context of dollarization proved to be unsustainable in the long term, since it was based on premises that proved to be wrong: continuing growth in productivity; good international conditions for exports ('terms of trade'); consistent fiscal policies; and good will of foreign investors and creditors to keep pumping for ever influxes of foreign money.

A perverse logic of political economy guaranteed that Argentina would not voluntarily give up its strict monetary regime. By the end of the 1990s, towards the end of the convertibility plan, doubts arouse regarding the solvency of several actors involved: the Argentine government, the local banks, the individuals, and the local firms. Yet, nobody dared to change the economic and political status quo, since the convertibility plan was untouchable in political terms, so the crisis became, as any psychological event, a moral tale with a self-fulfilling prophecy (or better, self-destruction) dimension (see Galiani et al. 2003, 4–5; and Llach 2004, 54–7).

Overall, the Argentine economic crisis of 2001–2 is a case of method-ological over-determination, in terms of complementary, rather than competing or alternative, explanations. On the one hand, there was a clear impact of external factors, including the role of the financial mar-kets, domino effects (contagion) of globalization crises in the late 1990s, and the implementation of the 'Washington Consensus'. But, on the other hand, the crisis was also precipitated by a series of political and institutional domestic factors, including corruption, political inertia, and the difficult (if not impossible) relations between the central government and the provinces. In terms of *intermestic* arguments, the adoption of a fixed exchange rate (the convertibility plan) as a deliberated economic policy, joined by an incoherent fiscal policy, further exposed the vulner-ability of the Argentine economy to external shocks.

*Summing up: the relevance of the hypotheses of the* intermestic *model*

We might conclude that domestic factors exacerbated the impact of the external shocks; or, conversely, that external shocks also worsened the effects of domestic problems. This in turn created a vicious circle with devastating effects for the Argentine economy and society. In terms of the hypotheses formulated in Chapter 3, the Argentine case demon-strates the relevance of *Hypotheses 1* and *2*, the relative irrelevance of *Hypothesis 3*, and the importance of *Hypothesis 4*.

In other words, the Argentine state (and government) became 'sand-wiched' between the external effects of globalization shocks and the domestic repercussions of its social and economic policies. As a rela-tively weak state, it did not react effectively in coping with these external shocks (*Hypothesis 1*). Moreover, by enacting a monetary policy that failed in the long term, its policies helped to precipitate the economic and polit-ical crisis (*Hypothesis 2*). Finally, due to its inherent weakness, Argentina remained particularly vulnerable to the vicissitudes of the global econ-omy and the guidelines of the international financial institutions (*Hypothesis 4*). The regional context of Latin America was probably less relevant, except for the contagion effect stemming from the Brazilian crisis of 1999 (in itself, concatenated with other global economic crises in East Asia and Russia) (*Hypothesis 3*).

**Links between globalization and the distribution of wealth: the Argentine experience**

As elaborated in Chapter 3, it is very difficult to assess the direct impact of economic globalization upon the distribution of wealth. What remains ambiguous are the character and direction of the possible links between globalization, poverty, and inequality, ultimately interpreted according to the divergent paradigms of international political economy and the disparate normative views of international relations.

### *The Liberal argument: globalization reduces poverty and inequality*

The Liberal model assumes a trickle-down logic, that of the 'invisible hand' of Adam Smith, leading to the self-regulation or even to the deregulation of the economy, the cult of the efficiency and technological imperative, and the paramount rule of economic rationality (Bertucci 2001, 17–18). Many of these premises were ideologically implemented in Argentina by brutally adopting the neoliberal model launched in 1974 under the government of Isabel Perón, by the military junta in 1976–83, and especially during the Menem administration in the early 1990s.

Yet, the experiment of economic liberalization, such as the one developed in Argentina, has been rarely justified in terms of a more equitable distribution of wealth, but rather in Liberal terms of 'trickle-down' theories and traditional approaches of international trade, which predicted that commercial liberalization would improve income distribution and reduce poverty (Larson 2003, 19). That did not happen in Argentina, so there is no clear evidence that the liberalization of trade directly affected (in other words, reduced) the number of poor people in the country.

In the 1990s, the golden age of neoliberalism in Argentina, the mainstream economic assumption backing neoliberalism was that there was a counter-cyclical relationship between economic growth, on the one hand, and poverty reduction, on the other. In other words, following the Liberal logic, economic growth would lead to a reduction of both poverty and inequality. And, yet, the empirical evidence in the Argentine case for the 1990s demonstrates quite the opposite: the rapid economic growth of the early 1990s was accompanied by an increase in unemployment rates and in poverty, and by a concomitant exacerbation of the social gaps between the better-educated higher classes and the lower classes. Thus, the most striking fact in Argentina was that poverty increased even in a period of economic expansion, due to an unequal distribution of income (see Larson 2003, 17).

As for financial flows, the Argentine financial roller coaster of 1982–2008 hardly contributed to the reduction of poverty, while exacerbating inequality. The statistical evidence proves that financial liberalization and Argentina's vulnerability to the external shocks of the financial international system increased poverty, and widened its already existing inequality gap.

*The Radical argument: globalization exacerbates poverty and inequality*

The Argentine case of 1982–2008 seems more easily explained and interpreted from a Radical perspective, according to which the forces of globalization led to an exacerbation of poverty and inequality. For instance, Carranza argues that

> The triumph of neo-liberal economic ideas is the main culprit; without the blind faith in globalization fundamentalism on the part of Argentina's cultural and political elites, the Argentine tragedy would have not occurred. The crisis was created not only by corrupt governments and bad politicians but also by the myth of the sovereignty of the market, which, widely accepted by the post-1991 domestic anti-devaluation coalition, legitimized the savage implementation of neo-liberal reforms in the 1990s. (Carranza 2005, 77–8)

Thus, the exorbitant levels of poverty and inequality that affected Argentina were not only the result of the deep recession after 1999. They were also the product of a cycle of economic deterioration that started much earlier, in the mid-1970s.

This argument is rather simple, if not simplistic, and echoes early *dependencia* claims with a mixture of anti-liberalism, nationalism, and anti-globalization discourse. In a nutshell, the crisis of 2001–2 and the overall evolution of the Argentine economy in the last thirty years were, to a large extent, the result of the actions taken by global economic powers and actors, including the US government, international banks, multinational corporations, and international organizations such as the World Bank and the International Monetary Fund. These international and global actors, assisted by the subordination of the Argentine national economic and political elites, had drained the country's resources. The so-called free trade and the speculative financial or rentier capital represented altogether the dark side of globalization.

According to this logic, Argentina had been captured between 1974 and 2003 by global financial capital, which included the upper-social elites in the country, who had appropriated the state and deregulated its economy, in order to build a market economy, but instead brought about poverty and inequality. The major instrument used by the forces of globalization to perpetuate Argentine dependency had been its foreign debt, which also was the major factor triggering the 2001–2 crisis (Fiorucci 2004, 160–1; and Godio 2002, 12).

In this vein, the forces of globalization had harnessed Argentina into a deep crisis in its polity, broke the poor and middle-class sectors of its society, weakened (if not dismantled) the welfare state, promoted a perverse model of social exclusion that led to tremendous asymmetries in the distribution of wealth, deteriorated its social institutions (including trade unions and political parties), and encouraged authoritarian solutions (Bertucci 2001, 15; and Mallo 2003, 2).

As mentioned above, the Radical approach is too simple and deterministic, so it has limitations that mirror the explanatory power of the contending Liberal approach. In other words, the Radical approach cannot explain the variance in the different political efforts to deal with poverty and inequality, as a result of different social and economic policies enacted by different Argentine governments between 1982 and 2008. The key to understand that variance seems to be in the hands of the statist (Realist) approach, and in the *intermestic* model.

*The statist/Realist argument: there is not necessarily a causal link between globalization and poverty*

The Argentine case of 1982–2008 proves the point that policymaking capabilities, and the quality of economic and social policies formulated by different governments, can and do make a difference. In other words, there is an interesting variation within countries (for instance, contrast the policies of the Kirchner administration with that of the Menem administration), and, of course, across countries (as we examine below, by bringing the parallel cases of Brazil and Chile).

According to this Realist or statist argument, there has not been an obvious causal link between globalization and the distribution of wealth. The basic reason for that is that in the first place the Argentine state did not properly perform its inherent role in the political, economic, and social spheres as the crucial and indispensable intermediary and shock-absorbent player between the external forces of globalization and its possible domestic repercussions.

For instance, the policies designed to cope with poverty in Argentina from the end of the 1980s had expressed very low levels of capacity of the public domain, both at the level of the federal (central) government and of the provinces. This is explained by the deteriorated institutional quality that articulates the relationship between the domestic, national, and international actors as related to issues of poverty and inequality, as well as to the absence (or rather weakness) of political and social actors with the necessary resources in order to promote and to channel the demands of the impoverished sectors to the relevant echelons of political authority (Repetto 2000, 598).

In more specific terms, relevant social and political actors such as trade unions, political opposition, and political parties became quite irrelevant in the Argentine political scene, eclipsed by the charisma and preponderance of the political leader who creates his or her own political movement, such as Menem (*Menemismo*), Kirchner (*Kirchnerismo*), and Macri (*Macrismo*).[4] In addition, in terms of political factors that contributed to the ineffectiveness in battling poverty and inequality, we should mention a political culture that has hindered the formulation of compromised reforms at the national level (Larson 2003, 22).

## The *intermestic* model: bringing politics back to the fore in Argentina

From the discussion so far, we have learned that Argentina usually lacks a capable political class and able political institutions, in comparison to Brazil and Chile. At the same time, Argentina encompasses a very dynamic society, and its polity is more de-centralized and federalized than other countries in the region.[5] Yet, the country has a national policymaking environment dominated by presidents who tend to have too much leeway and leverage in the pursuit of their arbitrary policies, provided they obtain the support of quasi-feudal provincial governors through fiscal largesse and over-spending (see Spiller and Tommasi 2007).

Despite the fact that most of the Latin American countries were exposed to the same virulent external shocks of globalization, the particular negative repercussions in Argentina were directly related to the workings (or, better, malfunction) of its political institutions and elites, leading to the adoption of bad economic policies, or to policies that were poorly implemented. In turn, the deficiencies of Argentine public policies were the outcome of a policymaking process in which key actors had little incentive to cooperate with one another, leading to wrong political choices. In the Argentine case, the workings of political institutions led to shortsighted policymaking, and this, in turn, to low-quality policies (Lloyd-Sherlock 1997, 49; and Spiller and Tommasi 2007, 1–3). In addition, we have also learned that *fracasomanía* was widespread in the country, whether with the return of democracy under Alfonsín that led to hyperinflation, or with the implementation of the convertibility plan under Menem that led to the recession of 1999–2001.[6]

### *The Argentine state in theory: an ineffective 'transmission belt'?*

In general terms, one can argue that throughout most of its political history the Argentine state *has not* played the crucial intermediary role in

---

[4] I would like to thank Carlos Rozenkoff for his comments on this point.
[5] Interview with Marcelo Cavarozzi, 24 September 2004.
[6] Interview with José Paradiso, 28 September 2004.

the causal chain between globalization and the distribution of wealth by mediating and ameliorating the effects of globalization, or by affecting back the external domain through the feedback mechanisms. Quite the opposite, the domestic and foreign policies of Menem and de la Rúa were flawed because, based on naïve neoliberal and utilitarian premises, they aimed at reducing and even dismantling the state.

Yet, the state cannot assert itself in domestic and world politics if it is being dismantled. The relative weakness of the Argentine state stands in stark juxtaposition to its relative vital society, as displayed in instances of voluntarism and social initiatives to cope with the social and economic catastrophe of 2001–2. Furthermore, most observers who catalogue the Argentine state as weak attribute economic policy change, even during the periods of military rule (1966–71 and 1976–83), to shifts in the societal (i.e., civilian) coalitions backing it (see Teichman 2001, 98).

The Argentine state has been a relatively weak state in relation to its society, by disregarding the protection of the private property rights, malfunctioning of its judiciary, lack of transparency in the implementation of public policies, waste of public money, and legal inefficiency. Thus, the state capacity to execute its basic functions assigned within the liberal model, such as tax collection of the upper and middle classes or the efficient administration of justice, remains limited. In the report of the World Economic Forum from 2009 mentioned above, it recommends to the Argentine government to 'institutionalize solid fiscal policies, achieve more respect for the rule of law, and reduce the bureaucracy to increase the trust of potential investors on the Government' (in Galak 2009). Similarly, as it was mentioned above, the Argentine citizens themselves perceive their state as a weak actor. By contrast, international and global actors such as the IMF are regarded as wielding most of the political and economic power most of the time (López-Alves 2007, 72; see also Waisman 1997, 230).

The crisis that affected the Argentine state, at least until 2003, was a crisis of its instrumental capabilities to adapt to the changing domestic and international environments where it operated. This capacity depended on two combined factors: the quality of the norms that regulate its internal processes and its relations with the outside world, and the absence of pertinent resources (financial, human, and technical) at its disposal. The Argentine state traditionally depicted serious deficiencies in both realms.

In the domestic political arena, the dysfunctions of Argentine politics and the shortcomings of its policymaking process can be summarized as follows: Congress is not an important policymaking arena; presidents have substantial leverage in pursuing a unilateral agenda; provincial governors are very important (perhaps too important) in shaping national policies; the bureaucracy is not a very effective political body to delegate the technical implementation of policy bargains; the judiciary is not very present, to say the least; and non-governmental actors (such as business groups and unions) tend to follow unilateral and short-term strategies not conducive to long-term cooperation, due to the lack of a proper institutionalized environment for political bargains (Spiller and Tommasi 2007, 7).

The Argentine experience of 1982–2008 clearly manifests the need for institutional building in order to assure economic and political stability, and to cope better with the challenges and opportunities of globalization in a proper way. Without the building of institutions indispensable for efficient markets, social and economic development, and social integration and cooperation, deregulating policies had led to economic and social fragmentation and disintegration, with a conjunction of unemployment, poverty, and a regressive distribution of wealth.

Argentina has much to learn and to improve in this domain, as the institutional foundations of its policymaking process are still weak, so public policies lack credibility, stability, and coherence, and are often poorly implemented. In this sense, state capabilities have to be dramatically enhanced and improved, in order to fulfil the normative mandate of the state as an able, active 'transmission belt' between the forces of globalization and the social arena (Chudnovsky and López 2007, 177; García-Heras 2009, 285; and Nochteff and Abeles 2000, 13).

*The Argentine state in practice: implementing social policies to cope with poverty and inequality, 1982–2008*

In practice, the categorization of Argentina as a weak state has to be somehow qualified, since there have been some advances in the last few years, so we can record a variance in the behaviour of the Argentine state. These practices refer to social and economic policies to cope with poverty and inequality between 1982 and 2008.

Up to the 1970s, the relatively more egalitarian Argentine society, with a significant middle class, was the result of functioning institutions for social policy of the state. These institutions represented for the entire population the possibility of access to exercise social and economic rights through a powerful and universal mechanism of social integration. This mechanism was articulated through the universal provision of basic social services, such as health and education, and the possibility to reach relative conditions of equity in the distribution of wealth. The major relevant social policies included: education; health; access to water and sanitary services; a working pensions system; programmes for the reduction of poverty; provision of basic infrastructures; progressive labour policies; and the provision of basic municipal services, such as lighting and waste collection (see Carpio 2000, 53–4; and Cruces and Gasparini 2009b, 4).

By the mid-1970s, Argentina still located itself as a relatively developed welfare state with a high level of human development in terms of social security. Alongside Uruguay, Chile, Cuba, Brazil, and Costa Rica, Argentina still showed high values in terms of social indicators regarding institutions of social policy, pensions, and life expectancy.

Yet, following the military coup of 1976, there has been a steady deterioration of the distribution of wealth. The military government suspended labour negotiations, weakened the trade unions, cut the social expenses, and started a process of trade liberalization. Moreover, from 1975 on, the Argentine state transferred wealth from the public to the private realm by several means: nationalization of private debts (both domestic and external); hidden subsidies; and a subsidized sale of public enterprise to the private sector. The results were a sudden rise in poverty and inequality. For instance, the Gini coefficient rose in the Buenos Aires metropolitan area (*Gran Buenos Aires*) from 0.345 in 1974 to 0.430 in 1981 (see Cruces and Gasparini 2009a, 407; Escudé 2006a, 28–9; and Lo Vuolo 1998, 37).

With the return of democracy in 1983, the redefinition of the role of the state in the 1980s and into the 1990s led to the articulation of distinct social policies, stemming from a neoliberal ideology, which included the focalization of programmes of assistance to extreme poverty, replacing the universal social policies of the former welfare state. In the 1980s, we can register a rise in the activity of the trade unions with stronger labour institutions as well as an increase in social expenses. At the same time, the policies to eradicate poverty remained static. There was an expectation, according to neoliberal tenets, that in the long term growth would effectively deal with poverty; meanwhile, there was an immediate need to address only the cases of extreme poverty (see Cruces and Gasparini 2009a, 407; Dinatale 2004, 33; and Lo Vuolo et al. 1999, 283).

In the 1990s, there was a further deepening of the neoliberal social policies articulated not in a coherent way in the 1980s. As mentioned above, there was a significant process of retraction of the welfare state, including the dismantling of universal welfare assistance in favour of focused and focalized programmes. There was also a further weakening of labour institutions (less protection for the employed); trade unions became more vulnerable; programmes of monetary transfer grew in importance; and pensions were privatized. Consequently, the distribution of income became extremely unequal (see Cruces and Gasparini 2009a, 409; Lo Vuolo 1998, 39).

A sea change in the articulation of social policies took place only after the crisis of 2001–2 and the election of Néstor Kirchner. Since 2003, the Argentine government has adopted economic and social strategies that emphasize the rebuilding of the national economy with a view to reach growth with social inclusion – an appropriate goal in view of the lingering high degree of poverty and inequality in the country. Thus, the social policies implemented after 2003 brought an end to a long phase of social regression since the military dictatorship of 1976 and reversed the previous curve of the worsening in the distribution of income (Fernández Valdovinos 2005, 4; Kulfas 2010, 62; Novick 2010, 75; and Raus 2008, 85).

The two major elements in the new economic and social policies were decisive state intervention in the labour realm and the strengthening of social security. These pro-active policies were translated into encouraging employment and income transfer programmes. Parallel to the strengthening of the state, social security became again a crucial tool for the redistribution of wealth. According to an official flyer from the Argentine Ministry of Labour (whose statistics have been a subject of harsh criticism), 'the political project that started in 2003 focuses its public social policies upon quality labour registered within social security; a process of "inclusive development" to generate wealth to all the Argentines; reduction of unemployment from 25 per cent in 2003 to 7.3 per cent in 2011; and reduction of informal labour from 50 per cent to 34 per cent' (www.trabajo.gob.ar, my translation). Thus, the Kirchner administration radically changed the labour policies, leading to a redistribution of wealth via improvement of real wages by about 400 per cent between 2003 and 2008, reregulation of labour legislation, and collective bargaining with trade unions.

Furthermore, the economic expansion that took place in 2003–8 and the new structure of prices improved the redistributive impact of fiscal policies. As a result, social expenses grew significantly and taxes became much more progressive, due to export retentions and taxes of financial transactions. New social programmes of monetary transfers were implemented, including the programme for Unemployed House Holders (*Programa Jefes y Jefas de Hogar Desocupados (PJJHD)*) and, after 2009, universal assignation for families (see Cruces and Gasparini 2009b, 25).

As a result of these social policies, as well as other economic factors mentioned above, indicators of poverty and inequality dropped substantially between 2003 and 2008. For instance, there has been an overall reduction of poverty from 50.9 per cent in 2003 to 22 per cent in 2007. Moreover, according to official statistics, between 2004 and

2008, the Gini coefficient dropped by 14 per cent, mainly as a result of improvement in the income from registered labour, reaching levels similar to those previous to the crisis of 2001 (see Cruces and Gasparini 2009b, 22; Kulfas 2010, 64; and Novick 2010, 77).

At the same time, education and health indicators have not improved overall, and there has not been a rational and long-term investment in basic infrastructures to cope with poverty and inequality. Moreover, the distributive implications in terms of wealth of those progressive social policies are not entirely clear, since the informal sector is larger than 50 per cent of the labour market in Argentina (Cruces and Gasparini 2009b, 25).

## A comparative perspective: Argentina's Southern Cone neighbours: Brazil and Chile

In this section, I briefly explore the cases of Brazil and Chile, Argentina's closest neighbours and economic partners in the Southern Cone. These three nations are known together as the 'ABC countries' of South America, sharing parallel trajectories together with important contrasts. I assess the political economies of Brazil and Chile between 1982 and 2008 in terms of the formulation of economic policies vis-à-vis globalization and the distribution of wealth; the realities of poverty and inequality; the assessment of state–society relations; and the social policies formulated to address poverty and inequality.

### Brazil: an economic giant plagued by poverty and inequality

From 1929 to the early 1980s, Brazil was among the world's fastest-growing economies, and its GDP grew faster than in many other developing countries, at an average of about 6 per cent a year (see Maddison 1992, 43; and Panizza 2003, 72). The country's industrial sector is the most diversified and advanced in South America, with a huge domestic market for consumers and competitive industries in international terms. Thus, the Brazilian economic policy, which has favoured industrialization since the 1930s, has created a manufacturing sector with the highest productivity in the developing world (Maddison 1992, 72).

In spite of this encouraging economic reality, Brazil has been plagued by high indexes of poverty and a consistent pattern of social inequalities and gross inequalities of wealth, income, and education that were not substantially modified until the 2000s. There has also been a consistent growth in urban violence. Despite a steady improvement in social indicators such as education and health in the last thirty years, the indexes of income inequality are still very high, even according to Latin American standards (see Maddison 1992, 3–4; and Panizza 2003, 50).

Poverty and inequality are deeply embedded in the history and politics of Brazil. Even in the post-World War II period of high economic growth the poor benefited marginally. The high concentration of land distribution, the lack of a significant land reform, and the legacy of slavery still affect rural poverty and racial inequality. Moreover, the lopsided distribution of human capital (especially in education) and the deficient social security system have been crucial factors that explain the socio-economic disparities in the country. In addition, huge socio-economic disparities divide the country both in social and regional terms, such as the contrast between the very poor northeast and the industrial centre and south of the country (see Maddison 1992, 12–13 and 90–1; and Panizza 2003, 84–5).

Like many of its South American neighbours, Brazil experienced a period of military rule from 1964 to 1985. The problem of alleviating poverty and reducing inequality had not been a high priority of Brazilian governments, either during the military rule or in earlier periods. Their major priority had been to maximize the overall growth rate (Maddison 1992, 94). Similarly to the Argentine case, the simultaneity in the transition towards a popular democracy and an economic system oriented towards the global market, in a context of high inequality and fragile political institutionalization, made the 1980s and the 1990s uncertain in both economic and political terms. Moreover, the performance of the Brazilian economy had been mediocre until the second half of the 1990s. However, there has been a significant improvement under the administration of President Fernando Henrique Cardoso (1994–2002), followed by the very successful economic performance of President Lula da Silva (2003–10), with a high degree of continuity in terms of their economic and social policies.

*Brazilian economic policies, 1982–2008*  In the early 1980s the military regime, with its legitimacy and political power already jeopardized, had to deal with the second oil shock (prompted by the Iranian Revolution of 1979) and the debt crisis that exploded in 1982, following the defaults of Mexico and Argentina. After 1982, Brazil had made major capital transfers to service its foreign debt, while attempting unsuccessfully to break the spiral of inflation. The 1980s represented the 'lost decade' in terms of Brazil's meagre economic performance, as a direct consequence of external shocks and structural constraints. By 1981, 43.2 per cent of the Brazilian population, about 50 million people, lived under the poverty line. In the same year, Brazil showed a Gini coefficient of

0.587, where the richest 1 per cent sustained 12.7 per cent of the rent, while the poorest 20 per cent only 2.62 per cent.

After a period of failed stabilization plans and high inflation during the 1980s, the 1990s were known as the 'decade of market-oriented reforms'. The *real* (Brazilian new currency) stabilization plan of Cardoso in 1994 finally managed to tame inflation, which was still 2,148 per cent in 1993, reducing it to 66 per cent in 1995 and to only 6.9 per cent in 1997. This adjustment plan, together with liberalizing economic reforms and the influx of foreign investments, created expectations for a long-term growth. The economic reforms brought about a substantial reduction in tariff rates, the abolition of import regimes, a floating exchange rate, a series of privatizations, overall trade liberalization, and a significant easing of inward capital controls. As a result, the Brazilian economy grew at an average growth of about 4 per cent between 1994 and 1997. Concomitantly, the poverty index dropped from 30.2 per cent in 1990 to 20.9 per cent in 1997 and to 19 per cent by 2001; though an additional 14.5 per cent of the population was defined as indigent (absolute poverty). Moreover, the Gini coefficient in 2000 was still very high, at 0.609 (see Berumen and Guterres da Gama 2007, 106–8; Da Motta Veiga 2002, 58, 60–1; Panizza 2003, 81; and Rudra 2008, 185).

The Brazilian economy continued to grow into the 2000s. Moreover, there has been a lot of continuity in the articulation and implementation of neoliberal policies under the leadership of President Lula, after 2002, based on the positive performance and solid economic basis forged by the previous Cardoso administration. From the beginning of his government, Lula turned to a neoliberal direction, in spite of his ideological affiliation with the Workers' Party (PT) and its social-democratic credentials. That included the implementation of fiscal and monetary discipline and even far-reaching reforms in taxes and pensions (see Berumen and Guterres da Gama 2007, 109; and Carvalho 2003, 59).

*The evolving strength of the Brazilian state, 1982–2008* The Brazilian state can be located at the middle of a continuum between the Argentine case (a relatively weak state) and the Chilean one (a relatively strong one).

Until the mid-1990s, the reasons for the relative weakness of the Brazilian state were related to the lack of consensus to implement substantial reforms of the state and its institutions, whether in a neodevelopmentalist or neoliberal direction. Brazil has witnessed a process of institutional deterioration in the capacity of the state to impose law and order, curb corruption, and face organized crime. Alongside powerful but small economic and social sectors that are well inserted into the global economy, there were huge contingents of the Brazilian population who remained marginalized.

The arena of political power in the Brazilian state has been heterogeneous and segmented, alongside a steady expansion of its civil society. Brazil is a gigantic federal state whose power is split between the federal government and the component states, with a large regional variation. Moreover, the Brazilian state is not only divided on a vertical basis between the federal government and the regional states, but also on a horizontal axis, as fragmentation characterizes the federal government itself.

Paradoxically, by being a presidential multi-party democratic regime and a federal state, and with a very heterogeneous society, the system of political power in Brazil can gain substantial political legitimacy due to its intrinsic fragmentations, so that Brazilian federalism can be considered as a form of conflict management. Furthermore, the Brazilian state managed to develop an able and functional federal bureaucracy, insulated in organizational terms from its societal and political entourage (see Loureiro and Abrucio 2003, 578; Palermo 2001, 47; Panizza 2003, 64; and Souza 2003, 190–2).

The Brazilian society is complex and diverse, in both cultural and regional terms. Significant social differences lead to different forms of articulation in state–society relations. For instance, a modern and active civil society, in which NGOs challenge state action, coexists with paternalist and hierarchical patron–client relationships, in which the relative absence of the state has been replaced by parallel social orders. At the same time the Brazilian society has also experimented with a process of social exclusion, with a vast informal sector, high rates of unemployment, and persistent high levels of economic and cultural inequalities, leading to urban violence and to chaos (see Da Motta Veiga 2002, 83; Palermo 2001, 44; and Panizza 2003, 70).

Similarly to the Argentine case, there has been some variation in the evolving strength of the Brazilian state between 1982 and 2008. The 1980s represented a crisis of the Brazilian state in dealing with the debt problem and hyperinflation. Although democracy returned gradually, its consolidation took place within a fragile institutional context, plagued with problems of criminality, domestic violence, and corruption. At the same time, the Brazilian state benefited from the absence of regional or ethnic schisms, at least in political terms (see Da Motta Veiga 2002, 55; and Palermo 2001, 37).

There was a significant strengthening of the Brazilian state following the initial success of the stabilization plan of 1994–5, which implied the recovery of the state and the possibility of governing macroeconomic issues and implementing significant structural reforms. Thus, the relative success of the Cardoso administration in taming inflation and carrying on economic reforms reflected its governing capabilities in re-establishing the authority and relative unity of the Brazilian state. In socio-economic terms, this transpired also in a significant reduction in the indexes of poverty, though there was not much improvement in the distribution of income (see Palermo 2001, 39; and Panizza 2003, 88). Under the Lula administration, this pattern of state strengthening did continue.

*Brazilian social policies related to the distribution of wealth, 1982–2008* During the ISI period, Brazilian social policies were associated with a strong emphasis upon social security, labour market protections, and universal access to primary education. Yet, the social policies of the military regime after 1964 were regressive, especially its policy on wages. The military government imposed a system of forced savings as part of the social security system, so that the squeeze on wages was greater than the squeeze on labour compensation. The centralization of decisions and resources at the federal level, the inefficiencies of the social expenditures, the superposition and fragmentation of the programmes and their appropriation by the middle classes, and the poor quality of services and goods offered to the poorest made the Brazilian system of social security a mechanism to reproduce inequality (see Maddison 1992, 91; and Rudra 2008, 185).

The end of Brazil's military rule in 1985 played a significant role in explaining welfare reforms, such as new social insurance schemes, labour market protections, and education. There has been a clear change in the social policies with the launching of a new social agenda that includes the universalization of basic social services, regarded as basic citizens' rights; decentralization; assurance of a steady influx of resources to social programmes; and the creation of emergency funds regarding vulnerable groups. These progressive reforms were passed in the drafting of the new Constitution of 1988 (see Rudra 2008, 210).

Contrary to what Lula and the Workers' Party affirmed while they were in opposition, the Cardoso administration (1995–2002) made significant advances in the reform of the social security system. For instance, in the realm of universal social policies, there were important achievements in health and education. Moreover, income support programmes were expanded, such as *Bolsa Escola* that would evolve into Lula's *Bolsa Família* in 2003. These programmes, which were funded by the state and supported by the World Bank, target the poor and provide incentives to improve their health and education status (see Rudra 2008, 186, 192).

As with economic policies, there has also been a lot of continuity regarding social policies in the transition from the Cardoso to the Lula administrations. The Lula government argued that its 2003 reforms would redress broad inequalities and free up money for pro-poor social programmes, though the benefits were far from immediate. Paradoxically, the government from the left managed to reform the pensions system. Some advances in programmes such as *Bolsa Familia* have occurred, concomitant to the Brazilian boom and full insertion into globalization. Thus, Lula managed to introduce equity-enhancing reforms in the historically regressive social security system, alongside important reforms in primary education. Despite his rhetorics of change and departure from the past, Lula turned out to be as conservative and neoliberal as his predecessor, albeit with some significant social-democratic nuances regarding equity and poverty alleviation (see Dowbor 2003, 125; Rudra 2008, 204–5, 210).

Similarly to the Argentine case, we can trace in Brazil an interesting correlation between the strengthening of the state and more progressive social policies. At the same time, the effects of globalization upon the enactment of economic and social policies seem to be less evident in the Brazilian case. Thus, Brazil has been much less vulnerable to the volatility of the global economy, with regards to the restrictions stemming from the international scene and to the flux of financial capital. This is also related to the large size of the local market.

Conversely, much like Argentina, Brazil also suffered from the global shock of the debt crisis in the 1980s, and greatly benefited from the commodity boom and the bonanza years of the 2000s. In the mid-1990s, due to the effective leadership of Fernando Henrique Cardoso, the economy turned into a definitive positive direction, bringing about both growth and development. As in the Argentine experience, this brief analysis demonstrates the relevance of *Hypothesis 1* and *2*, and to a lesser extent *Hypothesis 4* (Brazil has been less vulnerable to economic globalization than Argentina).

*Chile: the odd country of Latin America? Growth and inequality*

The Chilean case is particularly interesting for several reasons. First, Chile developed an early scheme of a welfare state from the beginning of the nineteenth century, in terms of the development of its social security. Second, for the forty years preceding the 1973 military coup, Chile was politically unique in Latin America in maintaining a competitive electoral democracy, usually free of the corruption and political manipulations that seem to characterize many of its neighbours. Third, Chile underwent the earliest experience of radical neoliberal reforms in Latin America, catapulted by the Pinochet military coup d'état in September 1973 that overthrew socialist President Salvador Allende. Fourth, contrary to Argentina and many other Latin American countries, Chile has fully inserted itself into the globalization schemes and it has maintained its neoliberal economic policies, despite ups and downs, since the mid-1970s. As a consequence, the economic model adopted by the Chilean military junta has persisted throughout the transition to democracy in 1989 and ever since. Finally, and in contrast to many Latin American countries, Chile has a relatively strong state, with a vibrant and consolidated working democracy that applies an efficient and prosperous liberal economic model, while maintaining economic stability and sound fiscal and financial accounts (see Sznajder 2011, 2–3, 5; and Teichman 2001, 23–4).

Nevertheless, despite (or because of) its successful economic performance, Chile still confronts a serious problem of social inequality, which has always been the major Achilles' heel of the Chilean society. Although poverty has been reduced significantly in the last twenty years, as a result of growth and efficient social policies of the Chilean state, a truly redistribution of wealth has not taken place. As a result, perhaps the poor are less poor, but the rich are richer. Thus, although the relative distances between rich and poor have not changed significantly, the absolute distances have increased astronomically, due to the high rates of growth of the economy as a whole.

Although poverty has been significantly reduced since the late 1980s, dropping from 45.1 per cent (about 5 million people) in 1987 to about 21 per cent in 1997 (about 3 million people), not only has the socioeconomic gap widened but also the share of the national income earned by the lowest quintiles of Chilean society has decreased as well. For instance, by 1996, the average per capita income of the top 5 per cent was about one hundred times larger than the average for the poorest 5 per cent (see Ffrench Davis 2002, 229–30; Garretón 2002, 274; Oficina Internacional del Trabajo 1998, 56; Schatan 2001, 67, 74; and Sznajder 2011, 13).

The explanations for the persistence of the unequal distribution of income are directly related to the implementation and resilience of the neoliberal model. In other words, notwithstanding the rapid economic growth that took place over the last two decades, income distribution remained unchanged with the benefits of higher productivity favouring mainly the wealthiest through various means. Moreover, the opening of the economy helped to weaken the capacity for employment creation, due to increasing imports of industrial and agricultural goods. Furthermore, the worsening of labour conditions and increased unemployment kept inequality high. To sum up, the stability linked to the high levels of inequality in the distribution of income means that the reduction in poverty is due to the general rise in the average level of population well-being, instrumented through economic growth, rather than a result of a more egalitarian distribution of income (see Oficina Internacional del Trabajo 1998, 65; and Schatan 2001, 57, 72–3).

*Chilean economic policies, 1982–2008* After the Great Depression of 1929–31, which considerably weakened the traditional Chilean export sectors such as copper, nitrates, and other mineral resources, Chile favoured an economic policy based on state-led ISI. However, after more than forty years, the shortcomings of the application of the ISI model created the background for reforming and modernizing the Chilean economy in the 1970s (see Koch 1999, 5; and Sznajder 2011, 19).

Following the military coup of 1973, the new authoritarian regime adopted an economic policy of neoliberalism, attempting to find a particular solution to the lingering tension that affected the Chilean society between a high level of political development and a relatively low level of economic development (see González Meyer 2004, 61; and Sznajder 2011, 3). In the first decade of the military regime (1973–83), Chile opened its economy to the world market, though there was not significant economic growth in this period. The social implications of the neoliberal economic policies were quite devastating: a large increase in open and hidden unemployment, the deregulation of wages, de-industrialization, and significant growth of the informal sector.

These negative trends did not continue in the second part of the 1980s. Instead, the economy gradually recovered, and from approximately 1988 onwards, it began to expand. Unemployment was reduced, wages improved, and a certain level of re-industrialization took place, alongside a decrease of informal employment (see Koch 1999, 7).

Even after the return to electoral democracy in 1989 under the new government of the *Concertación* (a multi-party coalition of centre and centre-left political parties that opposed Pinochet), the implementation of neoliberal economic policies continued apace, with a certain dose of pragmatism (like in Brazil after 2002), and an attempt to bring about *reforms to the reforms*, especially with a vigorous expansion of the productive capacity, but without basically changing the neoliberal economic paradigm.

Due to the early implementation of important structural reforms in the late 1970s and 1980s and the maintenance of a coherent economic policy, Chile experienced in the 1990s significant advances in preserving its macroeconomic balance, sustainable growth, and political stability. As a result, Chile has stood up among the Latin American countries as a remarkable, if not unique, emerging economy, with one of the highest HDIs in the region, and a significant reduction of poverty and of indigence, finally joining the exclusive club of the OECD just a few years ago (see Garretón 2002, 271; and Oficina Internacional del Trabajo 1998, 15).

The preservation of the neoliberal economic model is explained by two major factors. First, the democratic *Concertación* wanted to maintain the same successful economic model that had produced accelerated rates of economic growth and reduced poverty. Second, the constitutional design imposed by the military rule in the 1980s left enough political enclaves that precluded any significant transformation of the lingering economic model. Thus, although civil liberties were restored and human rights began to be respected once again in Chile, the free-market philosophy was retained as the lynchpin of the national economic policies. Moreover, in spite of rapid economic growth, the extremely unequal distributions of income and wealth remained intact (see Ffrench Davis 2002, 219; Schatan 2001, 63; Sznajder 2011, 4; and Teichman 2001, 65).

*The evolving strength of the Chilean state, 1982–2008* In comparison with Argentina and Brazil, Chile is considered as a relatively strong and functional state that works properly, with an able judiciary and police and low levels of corruption. Its predominant socio-political matrix during the twentieth century can be characterized as both statist and democratic. The Chilean state has played a fundamental role in the development of the country, including the formulation of social policies to combat poverty. Nowadays, the state remains strong and has a significant impact upon the functioning of the neoliberal economy (see Garretón 2002, 247–8; González Meyer 2004, 68–9; and Oficina Internacional del Trabajo 1998, 49).

During the military regime (1973–89), the neoliberal economic doctrine promoted a substantial reduction in the social and economic role of the state with respect to its integrative and redistributive tasks. This state contraction was based on the belief that it might lead to a progressive distribution of wealth (see Garretón 2002, 252; and González Meyer 2004, 67).

With the return to democracy in 1989, there has been a strengthening in the functions and roles of the Chilean state. Since 1989, the state could not completely ignore its redistributive functions and the need for intervention, in order to ameliorate the vast inequalities stemming from the functioning of markets. With the free and popular suffrage back in place, there was now a political expression of a coalition of social sectors very different from those who supported the previous military regime. Especially after the (relatively moderate) economic crisis of 1997–8, there was a renewed role for the state in the economic realm, regarding the creation of jobs and the regulation of external shocks (see González Meyer 2004, 63, 67).

*Chilean social policies related to the distribution of wealth, 1982–2008* In the course of the period 1920–73 there was a clear trend towards social progress, sponsored by the Chilean state during the ISI period. The welfare state was gradually expanded and an entire infrastructure of social services was created in issue-areas such as education, health, and social security (see Koch 1999, 6; and Schatan 2001, 58).

Following the military coup of 1973, the state relinquished control of social benefits to a considerable extent. The adoption of neoliberal economic policies led to a shift of socio-political regulation from the state to the market. This was accomplished by a series of measures, such as the drastic reduction of the budget for social affairs; the transfer of basic social services such as health, pensions, and parts of the educational system to the private sector; the decentralization of the remaining social benefits policies to the local governments (*municipalidades*); and the introduction of market principles in the distribution of public spending. The social policies between 1973 and 1989 were oriented towards the elimination of extreme poverty, with a focus upon the marginal groups that could not satisfy their basic needs (see Frediani 1987, 39; Koch 1999, 6; and Oficina Internacional del Trabajo 1998, 44).

With the return of democracy in 1989, and despite the fact that the basic neoliberal economic model was maintained, there was a change in the formulation of social policies, as related to the distribution of wealth. There has been a clear shift in the focus regarding the priority for the promotion of social integration, including the reduction of poverty and inequality, through increased government spending on social welfare.

For instance, under President Aylwin in the early 1990s, two important laws with social implications were passed: first, a tax reform in order to raise taxes and finance needed improvements in education, health, family transfers, and pensions; and second, a labour reform, in order to return some of the bargaining power to the trade unions and the workers, and to reduce the social gaps of labour capabilities. As a result, by 1993, the unemployment rate was 4.4 per cent only, the lowest in twenty years, while the average wages increased by 11.7 per cent. Moreover, by 2000, only 21 per cent of the Chilean population was under the poverty line, compared to 45 per cent in 1987. The official position of the democratic government has been that its economic and social policies are geared towards achieving growth with equity (see Ffrench Davis 2002, 222, 228–30; García et al. 1994, 197; and Oficina Internacional del Trabajo 1998, 15).

Like the other 'ABC countries', the Chilean case proves that there might be an important correlation (if not causation) between the strength of the state and the formulation of social policies geared towards the reduction of poverty and inequality, where there has been much more success in reducing poverty than in curbing inequality. Moreover, among the three 'ABC countries', Chile is the most globalized one (according to the globalization index) and has the longest and most consistent adoption of a neoliberal model. There has been a striking continuity in the economic policies adopted by both military and civilian regimes (in the aftermath of the Pinochet military dictatorship), though there have also been important differences in the formulation of social policies. In terms of the relevance of the hypotheses of my *intermestic* model, *Hypotheses 1 and 2* are only partly corroborated, since despite the strength of the state and the enactment of effective social policies, the reduction of poverty has not been accompanied by a concomitant reduction in social inequalities.

## *Comparing the ABC countries*

This brief analysis of the other two 'ABC countries' helps us to draw some interesting comparisons between these three South American countries, in terms of similar patterns and differences with respect to variations in state strength and the external impact of globalization. A brief comparison is reflected in Table 5.4.

From the reading of Table 5.4 we can suggest the following conclusions:

1. In terms of state–society relations, we can locate Argentina, Brazil, and Chile along a continuum from the strongest case (Chile) to the weakest one (Argentina), with Brazil straddling a middle or intermediary position. It should be noticed as well that there has been some variation in the degree of state strength across these three decades. In other words, Argentina strengthened its state in the early 1990s, though the political and economic situation deteriorated gravely towards 2001. Only after 2003 has there been a significant resurgence in the power and resilience of the state. By comparison, the Brazilian state became stronger in 1994 with the enactment of the *real* plan and the advent of the Cardoso administration in 1995. There has been a significant

Table 5.4 *The 'ABC countries' at a glance, 1982–2008*

| Country/variable | Argentina | Brazil | Chile |
|---|---|---|---|
| **State–society relations** | | | |
| State–society relations | Relatively weak state | Intermediary strength | Relatively strong state |
| State strength in the 1980s | Weak | Medium | Strong |
| State strength in the 1990s | Stronger than in the 1980s in the early 1990s; then it deteriorated towards 2001 | Stronger than in the 1980s | Stronger than in the 1980s |
| State strength in the 2000s | Stronger than in the 1990s | Similar level to mid-1990s | Similar level to the 1990s |
| Military regime | 1976–83 | 1964–85 | 1973–89 |
| Transition to democracy | Abrupt (1982–3) | Gradual (1980s) | Gradual (1987–9) |
| **Impact of globalization** | | | |
| Impact of globalization | High | Low | Medium |
| Effect of globalization in the 1980s | High negative impact (debt crisis) | High negative impact (debt crisis) | Moderate negative impact (early 1980s) |
| Effect of globalization in the 1990s | Washington Consensus, filtered by national policies | Washington Consensus, filtered by national policies | Not much impact, continuity with the 1980s |
| Effect of globalization in the 2000s | High positive impact (commodity boom) until 2008 | High positive impact (commodity boom) until 2008 | High positive impact (commodity boom) until 2008 |
| Neoliberal economic policies | 1975–2001 | 1982–2008 | 1973–2008 |
| Continuity/ discontinuity of economic policies | Discontinuity after 2003 (under Kirchner) | Continuity (even under Lula after 2003) | Continuity (even after return to democracy in 1989) |
| Opening to world economy | Abrupt (1989–91) | Gradual | Abrupt (1973) |
| Effective social policies | Improvement since 2003 | Improvement since 1995 | Improvement since 1989 |
| **Results** | Reduction of poverty and inequality | Poverty reduced, inequality persists | Poverty reduced, inequality persists |

continuity in the level of state strength under the successive Lula administrations (2003–10).

2. In terms of exposure to globalization, all three countries have been integrated into the global economic processes, probably Chile the most, and Argentina and Brazil to a lesser extent. Conversely, Argentina has been the most vulnerable to the volatile flows of external financial waves and shocks, while Brazil has been the least vulnerable.

3. In general, if we compare the effects of globalization upon the 'ABC countries' in these three decades, we might conclude that, in the 1980s, all of them suffered from the debt crisis, Chile to a much lesser extent. In the Chilean case, the economic problems were caused mainly by the mismanagement of the liberal model until the mid-1980s. By contrast, in the 1990s, there has been a much more significant variance across the three economies, with Argentina and Brazil experiencing successful stabilization plans that killed inflation, first in Argentina (in 1991) and then in Brazil (1994). Towards the late 1990s, both countries were affected by external shocks, first Brazil (in 1997–9) and then, by a ripple effect of globalization, Argentina. Finally, in the 2000s, all three countries benefited from the commodity boom, the resurgence of their national economies, and a better enactment of fiscal and social policies.

4. As for the continuity of economic and social policies related to the distribution of wealth, Argentina stands out for the discontinuity between the Kirchner administration (2003–7) and the previous governments. Conversely, Chile has the highest degree of continuity between the democratic governments of the *Concertación* and the previous military regime of General Pinochet. As for Brazil, it is a peculiar case of continuity, despite the contrasting rhetorics and style, between the administrations of Fernando Henrique Cardoso (1995–2002) and Lula's left government (2003–10).

5. Finally, effective social policies to reduce poverty have been enacted in the three countries with various degrees of success in the last decade. At the same time, only Argentina experienced some reduction in the level of income inequality, while a very high Gini still characterizes Chilean and Brazilian social inequalities.

### Conclusions

Argentina's road to default and to economic and political crisis in 2001–2 can be considered as an extreme example of how the dynamics of globalization might have paramount, if not devastating, effects upon developing countries. At the same time, the decision of the Argentine government in

1991 to peg its national currency to the dollar (the 'convertibility plan') was a sovereign political choice that was not necessarily prompted by the guidelines of the 'Washington Consensus' or by the economic forces of globalization, but rather derived from the political constraints and political economy history of the country (a long trajectory of hyperinflation and economic and political instability).

The Argentine experience seems to demonstrate how the exposure to globalization by vulnerable economies might increase poverty and inequality within their societies, through two major causal mechanisms. First, increased competition derived from economic liberalization leaves behind the less efficient domestic actors, thus increasing unemployment and, by transition, exacerbating poverty. Second, economic vulnerability to external financial fluctuations creates financial problems that lower real incomes within the country and, by extension, increase poverty. As a result, exposure to globalization might enlarge the gap between domestic winners and domestic losers, thus increasing inequality.[7]

While it is a truism that globalization creates opportunities and risks, the key is how to manage it, where different countries have adopted different policies with diverse results (i.e., Argentina, Brazil, and Chile). In other words, while it is clear that international systemic realities (the global economic context) played a crucial role in the Argentine economic crisis of 2001–2, the policies put in place at home, first and foremost the adoption of the convertibility plan, were probably the overwhelming cause of the economic debacle (see Carranza 2005, 81; and Weintraub 2003, 121).

The Argentine crisis of 2001–2 is a cautionary tale that should be understood within the larger framework of an analysis of the Argentine political economy in the last three decades, since Argentina had adopted a neoliberal model and embraced globalization after a hiatus of several decades. The Argentine crisis was the result of a long process of institutional and political decay underway since the 1970s that finally exploded in 2001–2. And yet, even though the neoliberal model exhausted itself in the crisis of 2001–2, the logic of economic globalization continued afterwards. Paradoxically, the Argentine economic renaissance after 2002 has been based on a similar dynamic that characterized the first Argentine insertion in globalization in the first three decades of the twentieth century (Jozami 2003, 375). The globalization story goes on. At the same time, the Kirchner administration has adopted heterodox economic and social policies that challenge the continuity and validity of the neoliberal model.

---

[7] I want to thank Galia Press-Bar-Nathan for her insights on this point.

To what extent can we learn useful lessons from the Argentine story? Perhaps some interesting parallels could be drawn between the Argentine crisis of 2001–2 and the US (and, later on, global) financial crisis of 2008–9. In both cases, we learned about the greedy motivation to get monies, short-term high revenues, and high financial speculation, leading to an enormous psychological impact of herding behaviour, cascading panic, and economic debacle. Again, in both cases, we also realize the need for enhancing the political capacity of states and institutions to regulate the economy, and how important the image projected by the state internationally is. Of course, the major difference is that the Argentine crisis was after all a local crisis embedded within globalization, while the US financial crisis, by definition, became a global one. For both Argentina and the United States (and for every other country in the world), globalization creates incentives and opportunities, provides the structural context, and opens possibilities for potential winners and losers. But, ultimately, it is up to the political and social actors, within their respective polities, to choose their preferred path.

# 6    Regional comparisons and policy implications

It was a decade ago when Robert Gilpin formulated a challenging argument regarding the contradictory implications of the possible links between globalization and the distribution of wealth, considered in terms of poverty and inequality. In this book, I have followed Gilpin's challenge by arguing that, at times, the reduction of poverty might be accompanied by a concomitant increase in income inequality. More importantly, this book has directed a great deal of attention to the *political dimension* of the debate, which is particularly relevant for international relations scholars, by presenting an *intermestic* model to explain the dynamic interactions between the international arena and the domestic politics domain.

The current wave of globalization holds an enormous potential for improving the lives of millions of people around the world, by leading to growth, reducing poverty, and narrowing inequality. Yet, the results are far from clear or self-evident, where new efforts are essentially needed by states, in both bilateral and multilateral frameworks of cooperation at the regional and global levels, to realize this promise.

By the end of the day (and of this book), we might realize that globalization creates incentives and opportunities for different actors, as part of the structural setting and constraints within which the state and other political institutions at the national and regional levels make their crucial political choices. And, yet, it is very difficult to offer blanket generalizations about clear links between globalization and the distribution of wealth. It seems that the outcome is highly context-specific, whether at the state or the regional level, as a function of both the regional and international hierarchy of power and especially of the strength of the state vis-à-vis its own society.

The main argument formulated in this book has been that politics plays a crucial role in our effort to discern the problematic effects of globalization upon domestic societies, as well as a vital part of the effort to tame globalization and find proper solutions to its potential negative externalities, including poverty and inequality. Even if the effects of economic globalization along several social dimensions, especially the

198

reduction of poverty, are deemed benign, on balance, rather than malign, we still need *political institutions* to monitor and to cope with globalization in order to improve upon the positive potential outcomes to which globalization might lead.

In a nutshell, I argue in this book that states act as 'transmission belts', mediating the impact of globalization upon their own societies. Hence, variations in the effects of globalization upon the distribution of wealth should be best understood by examining the interplay of domestic politics and international affairs, as I showed empirically in Chapters 4 and 5. One of the major arguments in this respect is that globalization tends to promote greater inequality in weak states, since they are less likely than strong states to articulate and implement progressive and effective social and economic policies to cope successfully with poverty and inequality.

Political institutions, first and foremost national governments and state institutions, themselves should play an essential role not only in mitigating market failures and reducing poverty, but also in ensuring social justice and decreasing social inequalities. They should frame the economic and social policies that act as critical variables to reap the benefits of globalization and to cope with its adverse effects within their domestic societies. This truism has to be spelled out by referring to the state and other political actors and institutions as intermediary actors between the structural forces of economic globalization and the structural domestic characteristics of any given society, plagued sometimes by poverty and social inequalities.

For instance, as the cases of Latin America in general and of Argentina in particular have demonstrated, the vulnerability of developing countries to the risks associated with financial globalization are intrinsically related to the quality of their macroeconomic policies and the nature of domestic governance, such as their level of political corruption. At a second tier, regional institutions (as frameworks of multilateral cooperation) and international/global institutions could, and should, fulfil potentially positive roles in coping with globalization, though they carry their own political agendas, so they might also serve as 'transmission belts' between globalization and the states.

The research questions addressed in the book included the following. Why should we care about the distribution of wealth, in terms of poverty and inequality? What are their implications in normative and practical terms? What is the nature of the links between globalization and the distribution of wealth and what are their causal mechanisms, as suggested by Liberals, Radicals, and Realists?

In this concluding chapter, I address two additional questions to those formulated above. First, can we formulate a relevant comparison, not only between single countries (i.e., Argentina, Brazil, and Chile), but also across other developing regions in addition to Latin America, in terms of the links between globalization and the distribution of wealth? Although the *intermestic* model set out in Chapter 3 might be relevant, in principle, to all the countries and regions of the world, developed and developing alike, I rather prefer to focus the discussion upon the developing world. In other words, I extrapolate from the findings in the Latin American context briefly to ascertain similar and different situations in other regions of the developing world, including Southeast and East Asia, South Asia, sub-Saharan Africa, and the Middle East and North Africa.

Second, which lessons can be drawn from the difficult realities of Latin America in general, and of Argentina in particular? Which policy recommendations can be offered to cope with the twin problems of poverty and inequality, as related to the dynamics of economic globalization?

### Regional comparisons: Latin America in a comparative perspective

When processes of globalization have an impact upon specific geographical regions, it is obvious that there are differences in the level of economic globalization between different regions. In other words, the regional level becomes relevant as an alternative explanation to assess the causes for a certain regional distribution of wealth, in terms of poverty and inequality. Thus, if we group the developing countries into different regions, we might find that regional heterogeneity (across different regions) and common characteristics within a single region might have a greater effect on levels of poverty and inequality than economic globalization per se (see Heshmati 2003, 20).

Countries in the same region might sustain similar levels of globalization (for instance, in the Middle East, East Asia, and South Asia), though in other regions, such as in Latin America and in sub-Saharan Africa, there is also a large differentiation across individual countries in a given region (see Neutel and Heshmati 2006, 18–20). For the purpose of regional comparisons in the developing world, I refer here to five such regions: East Asia and Southeast Asia; South Asia; the Middle East and North Africa (MENA); sub-Saharan Africa; and Latin America (already described in Chapter 4) (see Milanovic 2005).

Table 6.1 offers a series of statistical indicators in relation to economic globalization, GDP per capita, total real GDP growth (in percentages), and trade (as a percentage of GDP). In addition, Table 6.1 presents several indicators for poverty and inequality for these five regions. Table 6.2 offers a more precise measurement of three different concepts

Table 6.1 *Regional statistical indicators, 1982–2008*

| | Economic globalization index[a] | | | | GDP per capita, PPP, constant 2005 international $ | | | | Total real GDP growth (%) | | | Trade (as a percentage of GDP) | | | |
|---|---|---|---|---|---|---|---|---|---|---|---|---|---|---|---|
| | 1982 | 1990 | 2000 | 2007 | 1982 | 1990 | 2000 | 2007 | 1982–9 | 1990–9 | 2000–7 | 1982 | 1990 | 2000 | 2007 |
| Latin America | 41.04 | 45.33 | 57.86 | 59.85 | 7879.1 | 7669.0 | 9027.2 | 10497.7 | 15.75 | 33.36 | 27.66 | 26.1 | 32.4 | 42.1 | 47.0 |
| Southeast and East Asia | 39.94 | 44.03 | 60.67 | 67.02 | 3196.7 | 3888.0 | 5168.6 | 6427.7 | 49.33 | 48.98 | 40.74 | 60.0 | 75.5 | 117.0 | 107.9 |
| South Asia | 17.32 | 18.91 | 30.72 | 44.42 | 957.0 | 1250.7 | 1724.4 | 2511.7 | 47.14 | 59.84 | 62.44 | 18.5 | 20.3 | 29.7 | 45.3 |
| Sub-Saharan Africa | 37.68 | 40.13 | 53.54 | 59.45 | 4241.5 | 3988.4 | 3942.9 | 4789.4 | 18.50 | 25.46 | 40.55 | 52.6 | 53.3 | 64.5 | 69.5 |
| Middle East and North Africa | 29.41 | 30.26 | 39.37 | 43.30 | 16611.5 | 12177.0 | 12501.5 | 14975.8 | 10.61 | 34.95 | 39.47 | 65.0 | 58.2 | 56.6 | 77.1 |

| | Gini index | | | Poverty headcount ratio at $1.25 a day (PPP) (% of population) | | | | Poverty headcount ratio at $2 a day (PPP) (% of population) | | | | Ranking in the Human Development Index (in parentheses is the number of countries in the index in that given year) | | |
|---|---|---|---|---|---|---|---|---|---|---|---|---|---|---|
| | 1989–91 | 1999–2001 | 2005–7 | 1981 | 1990 | 1999 | 2005 | 1981 | 1990 | 1999 | 2005 | 1990 (of 160) | 2000 (of 173) | 2007 (of 182) |
| Latin America | 54.00 | 54.13 | 51.62 | 12.87[b] | 11.32[b] | 10.89[b] | 8.22[b] | 24.61[b] | 21.88[b] | 21.81[b] | 17.12[b] | 55 | 64 | 66 |
| Southeast and East Asia | — | — | 40.20 | — | — | — | 16.8 | — | — | — | 38.7 | 82 | 88 | 98 |
| South Asia | 31.17 | 32.62 | 32.40 | 59.35 | 51.71 | 44.13 | 40.34 | 86.52 | 82.65 | 77.22 | 73.91 | 121 | 126 | 135 |
| Sub-Saharan Africa | — | — | 45.10 | 53.37 | 57.58 | 58.37 | 50.91 | 73.81 | 76.04 | 77.61 | 72.85 | 109 | 133 | 145 |
| Middle East and North Africa | 39.44 | 38.95 | 36.60 | 7.87 | 4.31 | 4.22 | 3.60 | 26.68 | 19.68 | 18.94 | 16.85 | 83 | 89 | 83 |

*Notes:* The aggregates are composed of weighted averages where the weights are based on the 2000 GDP in PPP values. All data is taken from the World Bank database for consistency.

The regions include the following countries (for the measurement, based on World Bank indicators).

*Latin America:* Argentina, Bolivia, Brazil, Chile, Colombia, Costa Rica, Dominican Republic, Ecuador, El Salvador, Guatemala, Honduras, Mexico, Nicaragua, Panama, Paraguay, Peru, Uruguay, and Venezuela (n = 18).

*Southeast and East Asia* (excluding China): Brunei Darussalam, Cambodia, Fiji, Indonesia, Kiribati, Lao PDR, Malaysia, Papua New Guinea, Philippines, Samoa, Thailand, Timor-Leste, Tonga, Vanuatu, and Vietnam (n = 15).

*South Asia:* Bangladesh, Bhutan, India, Maldives, Nepal, Pakistan, and Sri Lanka (n = 7).

*Sub-Saharan Africa:* Angola, Benin, Botswana, Burkina Faso, Burundi, Cameroon, Cape Verde, Central African Republic, Chad, Comoros, Congo, Democratic Republic, Congo, Republic, Cote d'Ivoire, Equatorial Guinea, Eritrea, Ethiopia, Gabon, Gambia, Ghana, Guinea, Guinea-Bissau, Kenya, Lesotho, Liberia, Madagascar, Malawi, Mali, Mauritania, Mauritius, Mozambique, Namibia, Niger, Nigeria, Rwanda, Senegal, Seychelles, Sierra Leone, South Africa, Sudan, Swaziland, Tanzania, Togo, Uganda, and Zambia (n = 44).

*Middle East and North Africa:* Algeria, Bahrain, Djibouti, Egypt, Iran, Jordan, Kuwait, Lebanon, Libya, Malta, Morocco, Oman, Qatar, Saudi Arabia, Syrian Arab Republic, Tunisia, United Arab Emirates, and Yemen (n = 18).

[a] The economic globalization index as described in Chapter 1 is standardized to a scale of one to a hundred, where a hundred is the maximum value. The higher the index value is indicates a greater level of globalization, in a composite measure of trade and foreign investment.

[b] Latin America and the Caribbean for the poverty headcount ratio indicators.

*Sources:* WDI (World Development Indicators), 2009, World Bank, and UN report: Human Development Index.

Table 6.2 *Regional Gini coefficients, 2005*

|  | Concept 1 Unweighted Gini (average by countries) | Concept 2 Population-weighted Gini | Concept 3 Regional Gini (inequality between individuals) | Number of countries (population in millions) |
|---|---|---|---|---|
| Latin America and the Caribbean | 53.1 | 54.4 | 57.5 | 18 (524) |
| Southeast Asia | 40.2 | 40.9 | 47.3 | 7 (496) |
| South Asia | 40.1 | 34.9 | 39.1 | 5 (1,431) |
| Sub-Saharan Africa | 45.1 | 41.9 | 48.0 | 29 (548) |
| MENA | 37.8 | 37.3 | 45.1 | 6 (208) |

*Notes:* The regions include the following countries (for the measurement of three concepts of Gini, based on World Income Distribution Database and personal correspondence with Branko Milanovic).

*Latin America*: Argentina, Bolivia, Brazil, Chile, Colombia, Costa Rica, Dominican Republic, Ecuador, El Salvador, Guatemala, Honduras, Mexico, Nicaragua, Panama, Paraguay, Peru, Uruguay, and Venezuela (n = 18).

*Southeast Asia*: Cambodia, Indonesia, Laos, Malaysia, Philippines, Thailand, and Vietnam (n = 7).

*South Asia*: Bangladesh, Bhutan, India, Nepal, and Pakistan (n = 5).

*Sub-Saharan Africa*: Angola, Cape Verde, Central African Republic, Comoros, Congo, Democratic Republic, Cote d'Ivoire, Djibouti, Ethiopia, Gabon, Gambia, Ghana, Guinea, Guinea-Bissau, Kenya, Lesotho, Liberia, Madagascar, Malawi, Mali, Mozambique, Niger, Nigeria, Senegal, Sierra Leone, Tanzania, Togo, Uganda, Zambia, and Zimbabwe (n = 29).

*Middle East and North Africa*: Egypt, Iran, Jordan, Morocco, Tunisia, and Yemen (n = 6).

*Sources:* World Income Distribution Database; personal communication with Branko Milanovic (2011).

of the Gini coefficient for the five regions in 2005, where all expenditures or incomes are on household per capita basis. The data is gathered from household surveys, not including all the countries in all the relevant regions.

From the reading of Tables 6.1 and 6.2, the following generalizations and conclusions can be drawn.

1. The ranking of the regions, in terms of economic globalization, puts East Asia and Southeast Asia at the top of the globalization index, Latin America second, sub-Saharan Africa third, South Asia fourth, and the Middle East and North Africa (MENA) at the bottom, as the least globalized region of the developing world.

2. In terms of GDP per capita, the Middle East and North Africa is the richest region due to its oil-producing countries (this shows how

skewed this indicator is). After MENA, come Latin America, South-east and East Asia, sub-Saharan Africa, and South Asia at the bottom as the poorest region of the world. Conversely, in terms of extreme poverty, sub-Saharan Africa is the poorest region in the developing world, followed by South Asia, East Asia and Southeast Asia. In comparative terms, Latin America and MENA experience lower levels of extreme poverty.

3. In terms of real growth from 1982 until 2008, the most successful story has been that of East Asia and Southeast Asia, with a record of 645 per cent, followed by South Asia, with 318.8 per cent. At the sluggish end of the scale we find sub-Saharan Africa (with 114 per cent), and at the bottom end, the Latin American region (with only 99.9 per cent). There is an interesting correlation, and possibly a causal link, between these trends of real economic growth and the positive fluctuations in terms of poverty reduction. This is the argument presented by Liberals (that growth will resolve poverty), according to the economic and social models sponsored by the World Bank and by the IMF. Thus, poverty has dramatically decreased in East Asia and Southeast Asia, despite the fact that this region currently sustains the fastest population growth in the world. Proxy indicators such as the increase in population with access to improved water sources and a longer life expectancy indicate a substantial poverty reduction and a concomitant improvement in human development. Poverty has also decreased in South Asia and remains relatively low in the MENA region. At the same time, the rates of poverty have not decreased, but rather increased, in sub-Saharan Africa, while in Latin America the reduction in poverty has become significant only in the last decade (see Berry and Serieux 2004, 153; and Glenn 2007, 166).

4. The globalization period of 1982–2008 bypassed many poor people in Latin America and in sub-Saharan Africa, while these regions did not register any significant economic growth until the early 2000s. At the same time, most poor people reside in South Asia (India, Pakistan, and Bangladesh) and in China. Particularly in India and China, there has been a significant increase in their incomes during the last three decades, with an impressive decline in poverty, but without a parallel decline in income inequality. Whether economic globalization can be credited with some or all of the reduction of poverty in China and India is a legitimate question; rapid growth of exports has certainly contributed to China's very fast growth, as well as India's thriving due to its services sector (see Berry and Serieux 2004, 156; and Bhalla 2002, 142).

5. If we examine income inequality across regions, by comparing per capita incomes with the average income of the developed countries

of the OECD, the picture is a mixed one with some encouraging trends, though there is still a large regional variation. Thus, over the last three decades, East Asia and Southeast Asia have improved their per capita income relative to the high-income OECD countries from a ratio of 1:10 to a ratio of 1:6. This is consistent with their impressive economic growth and the phenomenal reduction of poverty. Most of the successful stories in terms of upward mobility are found in East Asia and Southeast Asia with Taiwan, Singapore, Hong Kong, South Korea, and Malaysia (see Milanovic 2005, 78). By contrast, Latin America and the Middle East experienced relative stagnation. Finally, much of the increase in inequality relative to the high-income countries of the OECD is explained by the decline in income of the least-developed countries, most of which are located in the sub-Saharan African region (see Glenn 2007, 158).

6. In terms of the different measures of regional Gini as shown in Table 6.2, it is evident that Latin America is still the most unequal region in the world, followed by sub-Saharan Africa and Southeast Asia. Although South Asia shows very high levels of extreme poverty, inequality is lower than in other developing regions. As for the MENA region, the assessment of inequality depends on whether we take an unweighted measurement of the Gini coefficient or not on a regional basis.

Let us turn now to a brief discussion of each of the four regions (as Latin America has been discussed at length in Chapter 4), in terms of the possible links between globalization and the distribution of wealth.

### East Asia and Southeast Asia

By pooling together East Asia and Southeast Asia, we should be aware that this is a very economically heterogeneous region.[1] A better grouping divides the region into two: Japan and the 'tigers' (South Korea, Taiwan, Singapore, and Hong Kong) and the 'rest'. Then, the indexes of poverty and inequality might be very different.

With this caveat in mind, in comparative and relative terms, East Asia (including Southeast Asia) is the region that has benefited the most from economic globalization, exhibiting high growth rates and a labour-intensive pattern of production, leading to spectacular reductions in poverty, but not necessarily of inequality. Between 1981 and 2005,

[1] I would like to thank Nissim Otmazgin for his incisive comments and suggestions on this brief depiction of East Asia and Southeast Asia.

the percentage of poor people living below US$1.25 a day dropped from 78 per cent to just 17 per cent (Nissanke and Thorbecke 2010, 4). At the same time, in terms of inequality, the Gini coefficient has not dropped but rather further deteriorated.

The East Asian economies differ from their Latin American counterparts in their macroeconomic performance and their political environments, as well as in the role of the state as an active 'transmission belt', following a model of the 'developmental state' first introduced by Japan several decades ago (see Beeson 2009). According to the East Asian model, the state intervenes not only in cases of market failures or for moral and social incentives to help the poor, but rather to assist and contribute to economic growth. In comparative terms, the state is indeed strong but not much emphasis has been put on helping the poor or in reducing inequality. In this sense, the Chinese model (the alternative 'Beijing Consensus'), which could be considered as a variant of the 'developmental state', combines elements of neo-mercantilism, state interventionism, export-led growth, and a managed (not liberal) insertion into globalization, with impressive results in the reduction of poverty but not of inequality.

The East Asian region also enjoys some forms of regional cooperation and institutionalization, through regional frameworks such as ASEAN and APEC. At the same time, many analysts consider the level of formal institutionalization as rather low, with a preference for market-embedded mechanisms.

Overall, in the years preceding the East Asian financial crisis of 1997, the East Asian economies sustained robust macroeconomic fundamentals (see Desai 2008, 287). Moreover, the challenges posed by economic globalization to the Asian states are different from those of Latin America, since we find in the region particularly strong states, like South Korea and Taiwan, who managed through governmental intervention and wise economic policies to keep their Gini coefficients of income distribution relatively low.

As for China, which is sometimes considered as a category of its own, it experienced economic growth before adopting neoliberal policies and gradually embraced economic globalization while keeping government-led regulation. The bulk of poverty reduction took place during the phase of agricultural de-collectivization before 1980 (see Nissanke and Thorbecke 2010, 8). As a result of its high economic growth, some sectors of its population were lifted out of absolute poverty, but inequality increased concomitantly. Thus, the Chinese case demonstrates that there is no single 'right' political economy model in order simultaneously to reduce poverty and inequality. As for other successful East Asian economies, such as Malaysia, Thailand, Indonesia, and Singapore, their record is more ambivalent with respect to income inequality (Jomo 2001, 17).

### South Asia

In terms of economic globalization, South Asia is quite a peculiar region regarding international trade, capital flows, and economic management. In South Asia, as in other developing regions, economic globalization has given rise to new industries and created new employment opportunities, in sectors such as the Information Technology industry in India, and ready-made garment industries in Bangladesh and Sri Lanka.

As it can be observed in Table 6.1, the volume of trade (as a percentage of GDP) is relatively small in the region, though larger than in Latin America for the 2007 figures. The size of the manufacturing sector in South Asia is relatively small, compared to a much larger service sector in countries like India, if we include remittances. India's remarkable economic growth has been spearheaded by exports of modern services (outsourcing) rather than by exports of goods. Remittances and traditional service exports are also very important to Bangladesh and to Nepal.

With a population of about 1.5 billion people, South Asia made significant progress in the reduction of poverty during the 1980s and the 1990s. The number of extremely poor people fell from 475 million in 1981 to 462 million in 1990 and then to 428 million in 2001. In contrast to Latin America, however, the major socio-economic problem in the region is that of poverty, rather than inequality. Thus, the indexes of extreme poverty remain very high, about 40 per cent for both India and the region as a whole (see Glenn 2007, 181). The region is still plagued by widespread poverty, illiteracy, and low life expectancy. On a per capita basis, this remains the poorest region of the world.

The unequal distribution of the gains of economic growth in the last three decades might nowadays constitute an enormous political and economic challenge, undermining the progress in poverty reduction and leading to an increase in income inequality. There is a need for social inclusion of large marginalized sectors of the population (especially the agricultural sector), which has not clearly benefited from economic globalization. In this context, one of the most interesting initiatives taken in the last decade has been the recourse to micro-finance, as an instrument to promote economic and social inclusiveness.

In terms of regional cooperation, the existence of a South Asian Association for Regional Cooperation (SAARC) still remains in an embryonic stage due to the lingering conflict between India and Pakistan (see Khan and Larik 2007). Moreover, ethnic conflicts, civil wars, and military interventions have negatively affected the economic growth of many countries in the region.

### Sub-Saharan Africa

In contrast to the stereotyped image of sub-Saharan Africa as a region that has been marginalized from the global economy, I suggest that it is actually marginalized *within* the economic globalization. At the beginning of their independent political life, after the de-colonization wave of the 1960s, many countries of the region indeed adopted an inward-oriented development strategy (ISI) that isolated them from the global economy, leading to slow growth and stagnation.

Yet, since the 1980s, many African countries have adopted Structural Adjustment Programmes (SAPs), a set of macroeconomic reforms to 'shock' developing economies into equilibrium by liberalizing trade and cutting government social expenditures, under the auspices of the IFIs, first and foremost the IMF. Trade has become an important percentage of the region's GDP (69.5 per cent in 2007, as indicated in Table 6.1), though the influx of FDIs has remained quite limited (see Nissanke and Thorbecke 2010, 17–19).

The results from the integration of sub-Saharan Africa into economic globalization have been mixed, if not discouraging. The incidence of extreme poverty doubled from 212 million in 1982 to 388 million in 2005 (in terms of percentage of the region's population it slightly declined from 53 to 51 per cent). SAPs (but not necessarily globalization per se) actually increased poverty and inequality among women and children, among both rural and urban populations. The degree of income inequality in the region also increased sharply between the 1980s and the late 1990s. Moreover, figures for the 1980s indicate large disparities in income. Using GDP per capita and comparing the richest 20 per cent with the poorest 20 per cent, the inequality ratios of countries like South Africa and Zimbabwe only rival those of Latin America (Glenn 2007, 163).

In the sub-Saharan African case, the negative impact of the SAPs is a clear example of the failure of the global financial institutions to prepare properly the African states to benefit from globalization. Adding the problematic nature of the typical African state (weak if not failed) to the equation, we get a 'double failure' of the possible 'transmission belts' depicted in Chapter 3, a tragic failure of politics.[2]

[2] I would like to thank Galia Press-Bar-Nathan for her comments on this point.

The uneven integration of sub-Saharan Africa into the global economy, sometimes involving capital flight and brain drain rather than resource inflows, has not been a sufficient condition to bring about economic growth and poverty reduction. Sub-Saharan Africa remains stuck in a vicious cycle of low value-added exports, notably agricultural commodities and minerals, leaving the region exposed to international price fluctuations, attracting few technology inflows, and having few linkages back to the rest of the economy. Moreover, the African countries suffer from a significant lack of financial investment, technological innovation, infrastructure, and institutional capacity (see Bejan 2010; and Kayizzi-Mugewa 2003, 45). Moreover, the combination of three factors, i.e., the nature and pattern of the integration of the region into the global economy, the slow rate of structural transformation of its national economies, and the neglect of its agricultural sector, all together have precluded the generation of virtuous cycles of globalization-induced growth and poverty reduction (Nissanke and Thorbecke 2010, 19).

Moreover, as in Latin America, the regional variation *within* the sub-Saharan African region implies that the effects of globalization are mediated by the actions of individual states and their specific political and economic contexts. For instance, countries such as Uganda, Ghana, and Botswana have successfully managed to cope with economic globalization, as part of a political effort to recreate conditions for social development (Kayizzi-Mugewa 2003, 50; and Milanovic 2005, 78). By contrast, the majority of the African states are still considered as weak, patrimonial, and even predatory, if not failed, states, with low levels of institutional capacity and governance, not to mention the very low status of most of the countries in the regional and international hierarchy of power. As for the regional level, multilateral cooperation also remains virtual and ineffective.

### The Middle East and North Africa (MENA)

In comparison to other developing regions, the MENA region does not show significant indexes of poverty and inequality.[3] Yet, the extent of inequality, poverty, unemployment, and illiteracy has increased from the 1980s to the 2000s, elevating the number of people living in poverty from 80 million to 118 million. At the same time, the MENA region sustains the lowest level of economic globalization (according to the globalization

---

[3] I would like to thank Avraham Sela for his comments and suggestions regarding the Middle East.

index, only 43.3 in 2007, even lower than that of South Asia and sub-Saharan Africa).

MENA is very much an economically diverse region. As Avraham Sela argues (1998, 23), the extreme disparity of oil wealth and economic constraints between the Arab states in the Middle East has been a constant source of intra-regional tension. Overall, the economic and social performance of the region has been disappointing. Historically, dependence on oil wealth in several Persian Gulf countries and a legacy of central planning have played a major role in shaping the development strategies of many countries in the region, with a few recent exceptions (such as Egypt and Jordan) (see Abed and Davoodi 2003). The move towards liberalization of the economies since the late 1960s in countries such as Tunisia, Egypt, Jordan, and Yemen has led to the breaking of the social contract between states and societies, leading to an economic and social polarization, and an increasing gap between rich and poor people. This partly provides the political economy background for the ebullition of secular Arab regimes and societies in the Middle East, leading in December 2010–January 2011 to the so-called 'Arab Spring' and revolutionary movements and civil wars in Tunisia, Egypt, Libya, and Syria.

We do not have a clear sense of the future directions that a post-Arab Spring Middle East and North Africa will be undertaking, with reference to issues of poverty, inequality, and development (see Ajami 2012). It is clear that the 2011 Arab Spring revolutionary movements have included, among other issues, a clear demand for a civil state model that would respect human rights, lead to democracy, establish gender equity, and bring about social justice. At the same time, we still do not know the consequences and implications of the Arab Spring, as the euphoria of revolution is giving way to the on-the-ground realities of reconstruction and post-revolutionary politics, whether in the form of democracy, Islam, or some combination of both.

In the case of Egypt, for instance, while there has not been a dramatic departure from the socio-economic policies of the Mubarak government, at least in rhetorical terms there has been a noticeable tilt to the left with an increased government intervention in the economy and the equation of a free-market economy with corruption (see Said Aly 2012, 62). Moreover, the discourse of social justice and reducing poverty and inequality has been at the centre stage of Muslim Brotherhood parties, which won democratic elections in both Tunisia and Egypt.

One might argue that the key to understanding the lack of a clear relationship between globalization and the distribution of wealth in this region is political and cultural, rather than economic. There is a globalization deficit, a democratic deficit, and a human rights deficit. There are major structural domestic problems, as related to the nature of the societies, their stratification, lack of individual initiatives, and a cultural aversion to the adoption of capitalist and liberal competition. As Sela (2003) suggested, the implementation of a global economy in the region is very problematic because the expansion of capitalism has taken place within weak states that sustain strong social and cultural traditions that oppose globalization, such as Islam.

The MENA region, and in particular the Arab countries within it, have not benefited from globalization in the past decade. The region remains largely isolated from the global economy, its growth rate has stagnated, its shares of global trade and FDI has shrunk considerably, and it has created far too few jobs to match the enormous growth of its population and labour force (see Handoussa and Abou Shnief 2008, 227).

Like in Latin America and in sub-Saharan Africa, the explanations for the disappointing economic performance in the MENA region lead us back to the role of states and the importance of domestic politics, especially the fact that most of the countries in the region are neither democratic nor liberal, and that the state has been relatively weak. Sela characterizes many of the Arab countries (especially in the Gulf region, but not only there) as 'rentier states'. Their economy is based on rent rather than on taxation, states' penetration and leverage vis-à-vis their respective societies has remained superficial, and many political regimes remain authoritarian or autocratic, lacking political legitimacy from their populations (Sela 2003, 3, 7–8).

Moreover, unlike other developing regions, MENA suffers also from a particular configuration of political and geopolitical circumstances, such as the lingering Arab–Israeli conflict and the interference of foreign actors, including the United States and Russia (and, before it, the former Soviet Union). This has led to an enormous spending on the defence sector, at the expense of welfare allocations to health, education, and housing. Yet, this geopolitical argument is ancillary to the major domestic structural problems that affect the countries of the region, which led to the rising of opposition Islamic political movements (like the Muslim Brotherhood) that act as social actors that provide basic social services due to the social welfare vacuum left by the rentier states.

At the regional level, there are a few recent initiatives for multilateral cooperation, such as the Agadir Agreement and cooperation with the European Union, as a forum to address common social and economic issues. And, yet, the level of regional integration and institutionalization, perhaps with the exception of the Gulf Cooperation Council in the security realm, remains very low and only at the rhetorical level, like in the case of the Arab League (see Sela 1998).

*Testing the hypotheses of the* intermestic *model at the regional level*

Based on this brief analysis of the four developing regions, coupled with the longer discussion of the Latin American case in Chapters 4 and 5, we can now turn to the assessment of the four hypotheses of the *intermestic* model at the regional level. As a preliminary caveat, we should be aware of the large intra-regional heterogeneity in several regions (especially within Latin America, sub-Saharan Africa, and the Middle East).

Hypothesis 1: *strong and weak states* At the risk of over-generalizing, the relevance of this hypothesis is found in the correlation between the most successful developing region (East Asia and Southeast Asia) and the incidence of strong states. Conversely, weak and failed states are found mostly in sub-Saharan Africa and South Asia. In an intermediate range that includes both strong and weak states, we can aptly describe particular cases in Latin America and in the Arab Middle East.

In the case of Latin America (see Chapters 4 and 5) we find a continuum ranging from strong states, such as Chile, Uruguay, and Costa Rica, to relatively weak states, such as Argentina and Colombia, all the way to very weak if not failed states, such as Bolivia and Haiti. In an intermediate category, we might locate countries like Brazil. The Argentine state has been usually considered as being weak in relation to its society by disregarding the protection of private property rights, malfunction of its judiciary, its failure in the implementation of proper public policies, legal inefficiency, and political corruption. But even in the Argentine case, we can trace an interesting variation in terms of state strength across time, with a significant improvement after 2003 (see Chapter 5).

As for the Middle East, before the 'Arab Spring' of 2011, Egypt was considered as a relatively strong state, alongside cases of other non-Arab nation-states, such as Turkey, Iran, and Israel. At the same time, most of the rentier states in the region are usually considered as weak ones.

Hypothesis 2: *state strength and good governance* In a similar vein, we find a strong correlation between the presence of strong states and the enactment of adequate socio-economic policies that reflect 'good governance' and a more effective treatment of poverty and inequality. For East Asia, Taiwan, South Korea, and to a limited extent China are all relevant examples. In South Asia, it is clear that India has made significant progress in a positive direction. In Latin America, we can contrast the 'good governance' policies adopted in Chile, Brazil, and Uruguay with those of Argentina and Venezuela. In sub-Saharan Africa, the positive exceptions seem to be first and foremost Botswana and, to some extent, Ghana, Uganda, Rwanda, and Senegal, in contrast to those of weak and failed states such as Congo or Nigeria. For the Middle East, Jordan and Tunisia might be relatively positive outliers in an otherwise quite discouraging picture.

Hypothesis 3: *the relevance of regional institutions* There is a large variance in the level of institutionalization and international (regional) cooperation coping with economic issues in general, and those related to globalization, poverty, and inequality in particular. The most institutionalized region seems to be Southeast Asia (through ASEAN), followed by Latin America (with different regional and sub-regional frameworks of cooperation). In South Asia, SAAEC is quite ineffective. In sub-Saharan Africa there are several sub-regional frameworks of cooperation (such as ECOWAS), while MENA has the Arab League and some economic fora for cooperation. Yet, the presence of those regional frameworks does not guarantee that states will cope better with the challenges of globalization, so the evidence here is quite inconclusive. Moreover, one can argue that a high level of institutionalization (such as in the European Union) might lead to a contagion effect in which one of the member-states experiences an economic crisis, such as the Greek and Irish cases in 2009 and 2010, or the most recent 'Eurocrisis' of 2011.

Hypothesis 4: *the relevance of international institutions* In the implementation of this hypothesis we again find a large inter-regional (and at some times intra-regional) variation. It seems that the two regions more affected by the presence of the international/global institutions, such as the World Bank and the IMF, have been sub-Saharan Africa and Latin America, and to some extent also South Asia. In the cases of the Middle East and of East Asia and Southeast Asia, the hypothesis seems to be less relevant, except for the IMF intervention in the East Asian financial crisis of 1997 (regarding South Korea, Indonesia, and Thailand).

This hypothesis is directly linked to the logic of *Hypothesis 1*. In other words, the presence of international/global institutions is more intrusive and paramount when facing weak states. By contrast, stronger states might be able to resist the intrusion of those institutions. Table 6.3 summarizes the findings across the five regions. To assess the overall effects of those hypotheses, I incorporate data on poverty and inequality from the previous two tables.

Table 6.3 *Testing the hypotheses of the* intermestic *model at the regional level*

| Hypothesis/results | Latin America | East Asia and Southeast Asia | South Asia | Sub-Saharan Africa | Middle East and North Africa |
|---|---|---|---|---|---|
| 1 – Strong states Weak states | Chile, Brazil Most | Taiwan, South Korea | India? Most | Botswana Most | Egypt Most |
| 2 – Good governance | Chile, Brazil, Uruguay | Taiwan, South Korea | India? | Botswana | Tunisia and Jordan, to some extent |
| 'Bad governance' | Most | | Most | Most | Most |
| 3 – Regional institutions | Relevance mostly rhetorical | Some relevance | Quite irrelevant | Token relevance | Token relevance |
| 4 – Global/international institutions | Relevant, especially in the 1980s | Some relevance in the late 1990s | Some relevance (of the World Bank) | Relevance, especially in the 1980s and 1990s, emphasis of the World Bank | Not much relevance |
| Extreme poverty (indigence), 2005 | 8.2% | 16.8% | 40.3% | 50.9% | 3.6% |
| Absolute poverty, 2005 | 17.12% | 38.7% | 73.91% | 72.85% | 16.85% |
| Inequality (measured as Gini unweighted, 2005) | 0.531 | 0.402 | 0.401 | 0.451 | 0.378 |

The results depicted in Table 6.3 indicate that *Hypotheses 1 and 2* seem to be the most relevant to assess the political dimension of the links between globalization and the distribution of wealth, compared to *Hypotheses 3 and 4*, which shift the analysis from the domestic or *intermestic* arena to the international one. The hypotheses related to the regional and international structures still display some relevance, though they seem to be less salient, and the empirical findings can be contradictory and puzzling. On the basis of these hypotheses and the empirical results, I suggest several policy implications and recommendations.

## Policy implications and recommendations

According to Joseph Stiglitz, 'Poverty has become an increasingly important development priority. The existence of a correlation between growth and poverty reduction should come as no surprise. But the correlation does not prove that trickle-down strategies are the best way to attack poverty' (Stiglitz 2002, 82). Thus, the policy implications of our concern about globalization and the distribution of wealth remain, at this stage, open-ended and moot. I list four possible policy implications under the following headings: (1) how to cope with poverty and inequality?; (2) the relevance of politics; (3) the relevance of ideas and norms; and (4) ethics and prudence converge after all.

### *How to cope with poverty and inequality?*

As I mentioned in Chapter 2, the links between globalization and the distribution of wealth lead us to take a normative stance, linking the actual unsatisfactory state of affairs to a better future as envisioned in our normative analysis.[4] For instance, advocating social democracy is a clear normative stance. In Chapter 2, I identified the normative and prudential arguments that justify our concern about the relationship between globalization, poverty, and inequality. The next step should be turning to the policy-oriented debate about the real causes of poverty and inequality, and, concomitantly, to the possible mechanisms for their reduction and eventual eradication.

The theoretical and policy debate has tended to be polarized around two explanatory models of poverty (described in Chapter 1): the structural (mainly political) and the behavioural (mainly economic) approaches. The structural model emphasizes institutional systems of

---

[4] I would like to thank Richard Sandbrook for his comments on this point.

inequality, macroeconomic impacts, and political strategies of exploitation and exclusion. Conversely, the behavioural model focuses on the personal attributes and behaviour of poor people in economic terms (see Pinker 1999, 1–2).

From a structural point of view, poverty and social inequality should be tackled only by the intervention of national governments in the free play of competitive (global) market forces, through deliberated policies of redistributive justice, pro-poor growth initiatives, and the provision of international aid. Alternatively, from a behavioural standpoint, the solution to poverty and to inequality lies in encouraging the action of the free forces of globalization, including the growth of competitive markets and the reduction of the role of governments and of international aid. This is the traditional Liberal interpretation and faith in a general 'harmony of interests' that will generate wealth and prosperity through the invisible and the invincible hand of the market. Eventually, according to this Liberal interpretation (denied by Stiglitz in the quote above), affluence and prosperity will trickle down to the poor.

During the last decade, both the IMF and the World Bank formulated significant poverty-reduction strategies. For instance, already in 2000, the Commission of the International Monetary Fund (IMFC) emphasized that a lasting breakthrough in combating poverty would be achieved only if the poorest countries were able to build the fundamentals for sustained growth themselves. It stated that the Poverty Reduction and Growth Facility (PRGF) initiative provided an essential framework for supporting countries' growth strategies and for enabling debt relief under the enhanced Heavily Indebted Poor Countries Initiative to be translated into poverty reduction.

The core of these initiatives focused on the country's 'ownership' of the strategies to reduce poverty, and on the issue of effective or good governance. In other words, borrowing countries should prepare poverty reduction strategy policy papers in a process that would involve the active participation of their civil societies, non-governmental organizations, donors, and international institutions. To be effective, the recommended policies should emerge out of national debates involving the voices of the poor and marginalized sectors (see International Monetary Fund, September 2000, 16). In addition to designing national strategies to eradicate poverty, the issue of effective governance should be stressed.

For globalization to contribute to alleviating rather than increasing poverty, more attention should be paid to preparing vulnerable groups and the poorest countries to cope with competition in a more successful way. This requires first of all a stronger transformative capacity for states in the form of domestic institutions, particularly those involved in the restructuring through investment and reallocation of resources – investing in human capital, education and training, entrepreneurial capacity and infrastructure, and articulating adequate labour market policies (Kohl 2003, 115).

In more specific terms, turning back to the experiences of Latin America in general, and of Argentina in particular, what particular policy recommendations can be suggested to address the twin problems of poverty and inequality? To start with, it will be necessary to adopt two major policies: achieving and maintaining macroeconomic stability in order to lead to a broad-based economic growth; and attaining high levels of investment in physical and especially in human capital, including the creation of social safety nets for the most vulnerable groups in society affected by globalization. In this context, the strategy of placing major emphasis upon education, health, progressive labour policies regarding minimal wages, and training is crucial to the pursuit of sustained growth with social equity, aimed on a universal basis of social security rather than only to targeted populations affected by extreme poverty.

Education remains the key to address inequality, considering the fact that Latin America has a very unequal distribution of education or human capital, and the highest skill differentials in the world. In order for people to take advantage of the opportunities provided by globalization-induced economic growth, they must be educated and healthy. If human capital is unequally distributed, as it is the case in most of Latin America, then the maldistribution of physical assets and of income will be exacerbated, resulting in further and cumulative social inequalities (see Altimir 1996, 69; Berry 2004, 15; Birdsall and Szekely 2003, 50; Burki and Perry 1997, 97; Gafar 1998, 594; Mamalakis 1996, 9; and Morley 2003, 64).

### The relevance of politics

This long list of policy recommendations about how to alleviate poverty and reduce inequality, in Latin America as well as in other regions, assumes a large, paramount role for states to play. If globalization is rather a limited phenomenon, as Gilpin suggested more than ten years ago, then the real big question remains what states can do to alleviate poverty and inequality in the context of globalization. In other words, the domestic effects of economic globalization are largely determined by the states themselves, and by their interactions with their societies (see Gilpin 2000, 322). While economic globalization and poverty are both global issues and processes that have transcended nationalism (for instance, they affect people transnationally), the actions of states remain transcendental in dealing with these two phenomena. It is still the case that states, rather than global agents and non-state actors, remain the major guarantors (and transgressors) of justice and freedom.

One way to approach this question about the role states should play is to ask which policies have some positive potential to bring about economic and social benefits vis-à-vis economic globalization, and how political institutions might affect their feasibility. For instance, land redistribution helped reduce poverty and narrow inequality gaps in successful economies in East Asia, such as Taiwan and South Korea. Nowadays, it could be an emphasis in pro-poor policies and investment in human capital (especially in education) as suggested above.[5]

Even if we conclude that globalization increases inequality in many developing countries, its effects tend to be small, and other, largely domestic, factors have much more importance. Thus, the impact of global forces on individual economies depends on the particular characteristics of a country, especially the design of its economic and social policies and the strength of its domestic institutions responsible for resource allocation (Kohl 2003, 112). In a nutshell, it is politics all the way down.

The natural tendency in international relations in general, and in the public discourse of Latin America in particular, has been to underline the role of external forces in determining a developing country's economic future through the constraints of structural *dependencia* (for Radicals), or, alternatively, through the invisible hand of the economic forces of globalization (for Liberals). Yet, it is my contention that we should focus the discussion upon the specific national policies to determine the political context through which globalization might affect poverty and inequality in positive or pernicious directions. For instance, the fact that the 2008–9 economic crisis might be interpreted for Latin America as one of 'pain but no panic' might be attributed, first and foremost, to the useful lessons Latin American countries managed to discern from their turbulent economic past and the successful economic and social policies implemented in coping with that crisis (see *Economist*, 2 May 2009, 47–9).

At the same time, it is clear that globalization does place significant limitations on the range of options available for governments to articulate their economic and social policies. For instance, in the case of Latin America, we have seen that all three 'ABC countries' suffered to a large extent from the external shocks of globalization and the debt crisis of the 1980s, leading to the 'lost decade'. Conversely, in the 2000s, Argentina, Brazil, and Chile largely benefited from the commodity boom and the positive terms of trade within the framework of globalization. Thus, globalization might also create new opportunities and spaces for

[5] I would like to thank Albert Berry for his comments on this point.

policy engagement. In sum, globalization changes the ways in which policies at various levels (sub-national, national, regional, international, and global) can be deployed. In many respects, it widens rather than restricts the range of policy options (Goldin and Reinert 2007, 229).

In practical terms, the relevance of politics has to be emphasized not only at the domestic level, but also at the international one. For instance, one of the most important lessons that emerged from the globalization crises of Latin America in general and of Argentina in particular is that there are fundamental problems in the construction and sustainability of international or global governance. Thus, the current structure of global governance has not kept pace with changes in the world economy and does not sufficiently promote development and poverty reduction (see Kohl 2003, 116; and Stiglitz 2008, 80). This insufficiency or malfunction has become even more evident in the most recent financial crisis of 2008–9 initiated in the United States, which sustains interesting parallels with the Argentine crisis of 2001–2 (the major difference being of course that the contagion from the US mortgage crisis developed into a global financial crisis, while the Argentine case remained localized and marginalized).

*The relevance of ideas and norms*

Although the definition of globalization adopted in this book focuses on the economic and material dimensions, we have to keep in mind the relevance of ideas, norms, culture, and ideologies in the framing of specific policies and strategies by different states in different regions.[6] In other words, the globalization of trade and finance is also relevant for the realm of ideas and ideologies; hence the need to differentiate between processes of globalization per se and the *ideology* that sustains these processes, whether it is neoliberalism, the 'Washington Consensus', the 'post-Washington Consensus', or even the 'Beijing Consensus'.

From the short discussion of the different regions in the developing world, in addition to the much longer analysis of the Latin American case, we have learned that cultural and ideological factors significantly matter. For instance, in the Latin American context, the ideologies of *desarrollismo* ('developmentalism') and of neoliberalism affected the changing responses of states to the challenges of globalization. *Desarrollismo* sustained the ISI economic policies between 1930 and the mid-1970s, while neoliberalism provided the ideological lynchpin for the social and

[6] I would like to thank Avraham Sela, Yaacov Vertzberger, and Lior Herman for stressing to me the relevance of ideas and norms.

economic policies addressing globalization since the mid-1970s (see Sikkink 1991).

In a similar vein, in the Middle East, the Islamic response to globalization – primarily on cultural grounds – might indicate that the basic assumptions about a structural and homogeneous effect of globalization is not very relevant in the case of Arab Muslim societies, in contrast to non-Islamic societies (Sela 2003, 3). However, the recent events of the 'Arab Spring' might change our preconceptions regarding the impossibility of political democratization in the region. What remains to be seen, following the unfinished revolutionary processes in countries like Tunisia and Egypt, is whether there might be, after all, a possible coexistence between Islam and democracy in the current age of globalization, like in the case of Turkey.

*Ethics and prudence converge after all*

As I argued in Chapter 2, the analysis of the links between globalization and the distribution of wealth is not just a futile academic exercise for the sake of theorizing in international relations. It carries policy implications and practical consequences, especially in relation to the political volatility catapulted by the question of social inequality. Coping with poverty is a moral obligation; addressing inequality might be sound and practical politics, even if there is an apparent trade-off between political concerns and economic efficiency. To a certain extent, the legitimacy and success of globalization have come to depend on its perceived effects upon poverty and inequality, especially in the developing world.

The importance attributed to the domestic and international distribution of wealth, as defined in terms of poverty and inequality, should not be framed exclusively in normative or 'prudential' terms. It is actually both. In coping with poverty and inequality we should (and must) be prudent and moral at the same time. It is a matter of both moral and practical concern, both at the domestic and at the international levels.

A practical way of translating these lofty conclusions is to advocate, in policy terms, a 'third way' or social-democratic path to cope with economic globalization. Countries such as Costa Rica, Mauritius, Chile, Brazil, and Uruguay have managed quite well under globalization; they have adopted social-democratic policies that were actually a blessing in disguise for globalization forces, attracting foreign capital and investments, while at the same time developing functioning welfare structures, quite extraordinary in the Latin American and African settings. Thus, ethics and prudence can after all converge as is illustrated in these successful cases of developing economies (see Sandbrook et al. 2007).

## Conclusions: globalization, the distribution of wealth, and the North–South divide

To what extent can the different interpretations about the links between globalization and the distribution of wealth be reconciled within the context of North–South relations? The answer, it seems to be, is far from being simple. The gap between the rich and developed countries and the poor and less-developed nations does not provide us with clear guidelines about how to understand and interpret these links. In other words, the debate about whether globalization brings about or reduces poverty and inequality does not reflect the North–South divide, but rather the ideological cleavages both *within* the North and *within* the South about the best way to cope with globalization and its social, political, and economic consequences.

For instance, the most strident and vocal critiques of globalization do not come from the South, but rather from certain intellectual circles in affluent North America and Europe. Hence, the debates reflect a North–North ideological gap (for instance, a transatlantic rift about different versions of globalization, confronting the United States and some European countries, at least until the 2008–9 global economic crisis), or even a domestic debate within the United States or in any given European country. After all, globalization might increase poverty and inequality within the developed world as well.

Similarly, while there have been many protests about the effects of globalization in the United States and Europe, it should be pointed out that many voices from the South avidly look for foreign investments and international trade. Chile and Brazil are clear examples of globalized countries, showing a significant continuity in their liberal economic policies, in spite of the transition from military regime to democracy (Chile), or from centre-right to centre-left and social-democratic governments (Brazil).

In some cases, such as with the Latin American economic elites, there is a sense of resentment regarding the marginalization of the Third World from the world economy following the end of the Cold War, rather than a complaint about the pernicious effects of economic globalization upon the developing world. Hence, if we take Latin America as a recent and interesting example, the political and economic emphasis remains a continuing quest for the insertion of the region into the global economy, even and despite the leftist credentials and the vociferous rhetoric of political leaders ranging from the virulent Chavez in Venezuela to the more moderate Lula in Brazil.

Furthermore, different approaches to globalization, poverty, and inequality divide countries within the global South. While China, India, and the newly industrializing countries of East Asia and Southeast Asia have successfully managed to integrate themselves into the global economy, many African, Middle Eastern, and Southern Asian countries have remained relatively detached from processes of globalization. In the Latin American context, the turn to the left in the recent decade echoes a fascinating debate about the need to transcend the 'Washington Consensus' of the late 1980s and the 1990s, but without abandoning the basic tenets of a liberal economy and the promotion of globalization, as was clearly demonstrated in the cases of Chile after 1989 and Brazil since 2003.

To sum up, there is an empirical (factual) North–South gap in terms of economic indicators and economic development, but this divide does not systematically correlate with an ideological or theoretical divide. Hence, we can find the most radical opponents of globalization in the North, and the most orthodox adherents of neoliberalism in the South (such as Carlos Menem and Domingo Cavallo in Argentina in the 1990s), alongside agnostic Realists across the board in both developed and developing nations.

Thus, the phenomenon studied in this book remains partly undetermined. Some aspects of globalization make poverty worse, others reduce poverty, others increase inequality, and still others have no effects at all. In sum, while the socio-economic gap between the developed and developing countries correlates with the North–South divide, we remain puzzled and confused when we attempt to explain that divide by turning to alternative theories and ideologies, in order to discern the very complicated and inconclusive links between globalization and the distribution of wealth.

The practical conclusion remains that we should search for a political focus to discern those links, as presented in my *intermestic* model. The argument here, based on a rather minimalist definition of globalization, points in the direction of the paramount role for national governments and states as potential culprits and saviours regarding poverty and inequality. Regional and international/global institutions are also relevant, but, to a lesser extent, by setting the structural context where the game of domestic politics takes place.

# References

Abed, George T. and Davoodi, Hamid R. 2003. 'Challenges of growth and globalization in the Middle East and North Africa', Washington, DC: International
Monetary Fund. www.imf.org/external/pubs/ft/med/2003/eng/abed.htm.

Aisbett, Emma. 2007. 'Why are the critics so convinced that globalization is bad
for the poor?', in Harrison, Ann (ed.), *Globalization and Poverty*. University
of Chicago Press, pp. 33–75.

Ajami, Fouad. 2012. 'The Arab Spring at one: a year of living dangerously',
*Foreign Affairs* 91 (2): 56–65.

Altimir, Oscar. 1996. 'Economic development and social equity: a Latin American perspective', *Journal of Interamerican Studies and World Affairs* 38 (2/3):
47–71.

1998. 'Inequality, employment, and poverty in Latin America: an overview', in
Tokman, Victor E. and O'Donnell, Guillermo (eds.), *Poverty and Inequality
in Latin America: Issues and New Challenges*. University of Notre Dame Press,
pp. 1–35.

Altimir, Oscar and Beccaria, Luis. 2001. 'El persistente deterioro de la distribución del ingreso en la Argentina', *Desarrollo Económico* 40 (160): 589–
618.

Anan, Kofi. 2000. *We the Peoples: The Role of the United Nations in the 21st Century*.
New York: United Nations Department of Public Information.

Aninat, Eduardo. 2000. 'Latin America and the challenge of globalization',
*Reforma*, 4 July. www.imf.org/external/np/vc/2000/070400.htm.

Banerjee, Abhijit Vinakat, Bénabou, Ronald, and Mookherjee, Dilip (eds.). 2006.
*Understanding Poverty*. Oxford University Press.

Bárcena, Alicia. 2010. 'Challenges and opportunities for a state role in the post-
crisis', *Pensamiento Iberoamericano* 6 (June).

2011. 'Spreading the wealth', *Finance and Development* (March): 20–1.

Beccaria, Luis. 1998. 'La distribución del ingreso durante la reconversión pro-
ductiva en la Argentina', *Revista Argentina del Régimen de la Administración
Pública*: 15–25.

Beeson, Mark. 2009. 'Developmental states in East Asia: a comparison
of the Japanese and Chinese experiences', *Asian Perspectives* 33 (2):
5–39.

Bejan, Michael. 2010. 'Explaining African under-development', Department of
Government, Georgetown University, seminar paper.

Beker, Víctor Alberto. 2000. 'Economic reform, job destruction and unemployment: the case of Argentina, 1990–1994', unpublished manuscript, Universidad de Belgrano.

Berry, Albert. 1997. 'Poverty policy in Latin America during the 1980s', *Review of Income and Wealth* 43 (1): 119–29.

2001. 'Las causas de la pobreza rural en América Latina y política para reducirla, con referencia especial al Paraguay', in Galeano, Luis and Rivarola, Domingo (eds.), *Pobreza y cambio social*. Asunción, Paraguay: Centro Paraguayo de Estudios Sociológicos, pp. 15–44.

2003a. 'Who gains and who loses? An economic perspective', in Sandbrook, Richard (ed.), *Civilizing Globalization: A Survival Guide*. Albany, NY: State University of New York Press, pp. 15–25.

2003b. 'Respuestas de política a los problemas de pobreza y desigualdad en el mundo en desarrollo', *Revista de la CEPAL* 79: 101–15.

2004. 'Confronting the challenge of rural poverty in Latin America', in Allarcón, Diana (ed.), *Priorities and Strategies in Rural Poverty Reduction: Experiences from Latin America and Asia*. Washington, DC: Inter-American Development Bank, pp. 3–23.

2007a. 'Attacking poverty: the institutional base', in Mace, Gordon, Thérien, Jean-Philippe, and Haslam, Paul (eds.), *Governing the Americas: Assessing Multilateral Institutions*. Boulder, CO: Lynne Rienner, pp. 213–33.

2007b. 'The economic and social effects of economic integration in Latin America: a review of the literature and some policy implications', unpublished manuscript.

Berry, Albert and Serieux, John. 2004. 'All about the giants: probing the influences on world growth and income inequality at the end of the 20th century', *CESIFO Economic Studies* 50 (1): 133–70.

Bertucci, Hugo Abel. 2001. *Porqué nos pasa lo que nos pasa a los Argentinos?* Buenos Aires: Dunken.

Berumen, Sergio A. and Guterres da Gama, Milton Silva. 2007. 'Una visión crítica del desempeño de la economía brasileña en el proceso de globalización, 1991–2006', *Revista de Ciencias Sociales* 117–18: 105–16.

Bhagwati, Jagdish. 2000. *The Wind of Hundred Days*. Cambridge, MA: MIT Press.

2004. *In Defense of Globalization*. New York: Oxford University Press.

2008. 'Globalization with a human face', in Zedillo, Ernesto (ed.), *The Future of Globalization: Explorations in Light of Recent Turbulence*. London: Routledge, pp. 34–9.

Bhalla, Surjit. 2002. *Imagine There's No Country*. Washington, DC: Institute for International Economics.

Birdsall, Nancy and Szekely, Miguel. 2003. 'Bootstraps, not band-aids: poverty, equity and social policy', in Kczynski, Pedro Pablo and Williamson, John (eds.), *After the Washington Consensus: Restarting Growth and Reform in Latin America*. Washington, DC: Institute for International Economics, pp. 49–73.

Blackmon, Pamela. 2008. 'Rethinking poverty through the eyes of the International Monetary Fund and the World Bank', *International Studies Review* 10 (2): 179–202.

Blustein, Paul. 2005. *And the Money Kept Rolling In (and Out): Wall Street, the IMF, and the Bankruptcy of Argentina*. New York: Public Affairs.

Bourguignon, François and Morrison, Christian. 2002. 'The size distribution of income among world citizens, 1820–1990', *American Economic Review* 92 (4): 727–44.

Bouzas, Roberto. 2002. 'La Argentina después de las reformas', in Bouzas, Roberto (ed.), *Realidades nacionales comparadas*. Buenos Aires: Altamira, pp. 13–53.

——— 2005. 'Globalización y políticas nacionales: cerrando el círculo', *Desarrollo Económico* 45 (179): 323–48.

Bouzas, Roberto and Ffrench Davis, Ricardo. 2004. 'Globalization and equity: a Latin American perspective', unpublished manuscript.

Bulmer-Thomas, Víctor, Coatsworth, John H., and Cortés Conde, Roberto. 2006. 'Introduction', in Bulmer-Thomas, Víctor, Coatsworth, John H., and Cortés Conde, Roberto (eds.), *The Cambridge Economic History of Latin America*, vol. II. Cambridge University Press, pp. 1–11.

Burki, Shahid Javed and Perry, Guillermo E. 1997. *The Long March: A Reform Agenda for Latin America and the Caribbean in the Next Decade*. Washington, DC: World Bank.

Callaghy, Thomas M. 2001. 'The challenges of attacking inequality: the view from poor country debt', paper presented at the ISA Annual Meeting, Chicago, 20–4 Feb.

Calvo, Guillermo. 2003. 'La crisis argentina: una explicación', in Bruno, Carlos and Chudnovsky, Daniel (eds.), *Porqué sucedió? Las causas económicas de la reciente crisis argentina*. Buenos Aires: Siglo Veintiuno de Argentina, pp. 11–27.

Cardoso, Fernando H. and Faletto, Enzo. 1979. *Dependency and Development in Latin America*. Berkeley, CA: University of California Press.

Carpio, Jorge. 2000. 'Aportes para la construcción de la agenda social', in García Laboyle, Javier (ed.), *Pobreza, desigualdad y exclusión social en la Argentina: propuestas y políticas*. Buenos Aires: Caritas, pp. 49–62.

Carranza, Mario E. 2005. 'Poster child or victim of imperialist globalization? Explaining Argentina's December 2001 political crisis and economic collapse', *Latin American Perspectives* 32(6): 65–89.

Carvalho, Carlos Eduardo. 2003. 'El gobierno de Lula y el neoliberalismo relanzado', *Nueva Sociedad* 187: 59–73.

Castañeda, Jorge C. 2008. 'Where do we go from here?', in Jorge C. and Morales, Marco A. (eds.), *Leftovers: Tales of the Latin American Left*. New York: Routledge, pp. 231–43.

Castañeda, Jorge C. and Morales, Marco A. (eds.). 2008. *Leftovers: Tales of the Latin American Left*. New York: Routledge.

Castro, Jorge. 2000. *La gran década: del abismo al crecimiento*. Buenos Aires: Sudamericana.

Centeno, Miguel Angel. 2002. *Blood and Debt: War and the Nation-State in Latin America*. University Park, PA: Pennsylvania State University Press.

Chen, Shaouhua and Ravallion, Martin. 2001. 'How did the world's poor fare in the 1990s?', *Review of Income and Wealth* 47 (3): 359–76.

Chossudovsky, Michel. 1997. *The Globalization of Poverty: Impacts of IMF and World Bank Reforms*. London: Zed.

Chudnovsky, Daniel and López, Andrés. 2007. *The Elusive Quest for Growth in Argentina*. New York: Palgrave.

Chudnovsky, Daniel, López, Andrés, and Pupato, Germán. 2003. 'Las recientes crisis sistémicas en países emergentes: las peculiaridades del caso argentino', in Bruno, Carlos and Chudnovsky, Daniel (eds.), *Porqué sucedió? Las causas económicas de la reciente crisis argentina*. Buenos Aires: Siglo Veintiuno de Argentina, pp. 17–109.

Clark, Ian. 1999. *Globalization and International Relations Theory*. Oxford University Press.

Collier, Ruth Berins, and Collier, David. 1991. *Shaping the Political Arena: Critical Junctures, the Labor Movement, and Regime Dynamics in Latin America*. Princeton University Press.

Cruces, Guillermo and Gasparini, Leonardo. 2009a. 'Desigualdad en Argentina: una revisión de la evidencia empírica: primera parte', *Desarrollo Económico* 48 (192): 395–437.

2009b. 'Desigualdad en Argentina: una revision de la evidencia empírica: segunda parte', *Desarrollo Económico* 49 (193): 3–29.

Dallmayr, Fred. 2002. 'Globalization and inequality: a plea for global justice', *International Studies Review* 4 (2): 137–56.

Da Motta Veiga, Pedro. 2002. 'Brasil a inicios del nuevo milenio: herencias y desafíos de la transición', in Bouzas, Roberto (ed.), *Realidades nacionales comparadas*. Buenos Aires: Altamir, pp. 55–90.

De Ferranti, David, Perry, Guillermo E., Ferreira, Francisco H.G. and Walton, Michael. 2004. *Inequality in Latin America: Breaking with History?* Washington, DC: World Bank.

De Janvry, Alain and Sadoulet, Elisabeth. 2001. 'Has aggregate income growth been effective in reducing poverty and inequality in Latin America?', in Lustig, Nora (ed.), *Shielding the Poor: Social Protection in the Developing World*. Washington, DC: Brookings Institution, pp. 21–39.

De la Dehesa, Guillermo. 2007. *What Do We Know about Globalization? Issues of Poverty and Income Distribution*. Malden, MA: Blackwell.

De la Escosura, Leandro Prados. 2007a. 'When did Latin America fall behind?', in Edwards, Sebastian, Esquivel, Gerardo, and Márquez, Graciela (eds.), *The Decline of Latin American Economies: Growth, Institutions, and Crises*. University of Chicago Press, pp. 15–57.

2007b. 'Inequality and poverty in Latin America: a long-run explanation', in Hatton, Timothy J., O'Rourkey, Kevin H., and Taylor, Alan M. (eds.), *The New Comparative Economic History: Essays in Honor of Jeffrey G. Williamson*. Cambridge, MA: MIT Press, pp. 291–315.

Del Cueto, Carla Muriel, and Luzzi, Mariana. 2008. *Rompecabezas: transformaciones en la estructura social argentina, 1983–2008*. Los Polvorines: Universidad Nacional de General Sarmiento.

Derber, Charles. 1998. *Corporate Nations*. New York: St Martin's Press.

Desai, Padma. 2008. 'Explorations in light of financial turbulences from Asia to Argentina', in Zedillo, Ernesto (ed.), *The Future of Globalization: Explorations in Light of Recent Turbulence*. London: Routledge, pp. 284–315.

De Soto, Hernando. 2000. *The Mystery of Capital: Why Capitalism Triumphs in the West and Fails Everywhere Else*. New York: Basic Books.

Dinatale, Martín. 2004. *El festival de la pobreza: el uso político de planes sociales en la Argentina*. Buenos Aires: Ediciones La Crujía.

Dollar, David and Kraay, Aart. 2002. 'Spreading the wealth', *Foreign Affairs* 81 (1): 120–33.

2004. 'Trade, growth and poverty', *Economic Journal* 114 (493): 22–49.

Dowbor, Ladislau. 2003. 'Brasil: tendencias de la gestión social', *Nueva Sociedad* 187: 114–27.

Doyle, Michael W. 2000. 'Global economic inequalities: a growing moral gap', in Wapner, Paul and Ruiz, Lester Edwin J. (eds.), *Principled World Politics: The Challenge of Normative International Relations*. Lanham, MD: Rowman and Littlefield, pp. 79–97.

Dreher, Axel. 2006. 'Does globalization affect growth? Evidence from a new index of globalization', *Applied Economics* 38 (10): 1091–110.

Dreher, Axel, Gaston, Noel, and Martens, Pim. 2008. *Measuring Globalization: Gauging its Consequences*. New York: Springer.

ECLAC. 2009. *Social Panorama of Latin America, 2008*. Santiago de Chile: ECLAC/CEPAL.

Edwards, Sebastian, Esquivel, Gerardo, and Márquez, Graciela. 2007. 'Introduction', in Edwards, Sebastian, Esquivel, Gerardo, and Márquez, Graciela (eds.), *The Decline of Latin American Economies: Growth, Institutions, and Crises*. University of Chicago Press, pp. 1–11.

Escudé, Carlos. 2002. 'Argentina, a "parasite state" on the verge of disintegration', *Cambridge Review of International Affairs* 15 (3): 453–67.

2006a. *Festival de licuaciones: causas y consecuencias de la pobreza en Argentina*. Buenos Aires: Lumiere.

2006b. 'From captive to failed state: Argentina under systemic populism, 1975–2006', *Fletcher Forum of World Affairs* 30 (2): 125–35.

Fajnzylber, Fernando. 1990. *Unavoidable Industrial Restructuring in Latin America*. Durham, NC: Duke University Press.

Falk, Richard. 2009. *Achieving Human Rights*. New York: Routledge.

Fernández Valdovinos, Carlos G. 2005. 'Growth, poverty, and social equity in Argentina', *En Breve* 82: 1–4.

Ferrer, Aldo. 1998. 'Desarrollo y subdesarrollo en un mundo global: los dilemas de América Latina', in Emmerij, Louis and Nuñez del Arco, José (eds.), *El desarrollo económico y social en los umbrales del siglo XXI*. Washington, DC: Inter-American Development Bank, pp. 198–205.

1999. *De Cristóbal Colón a Internet: América Latina y la globalización*. Buenos Aires: Fondo de Cultura Económica.

2008. *La economía argentina: desde sus origines hasta principios del siglo XXI*, 4th edn. Buenos Aires: Fondo de Cultura Económica.

Ffrench Davis, Ricardo. 2002. 'Chile: entre el neoliberalismo y el crecimiento con equidad', in Bouzas, Roberto (ed.), *Realidades nacionales comparadas*. Buenos Aires: Altamira, pp. 219–44.

Filgueira, Fernando. 2008. *El desarrollo maniatado en América Latina: estados superficiales y desigualdades profundas*. Buenos Aires: CLACSO.

Finnemore, Martha. 1996. *National Interest in International Society*. Ithaca, NY: Cornell University Press.

Fiorucci, Flavia. 2004. 'Fascinated by failure: The "bestseller" explanations of the crisis', in Fiorucci, Flavia and Klein, Marcus (eds.), *The Argentine Crisis at the Turn of the Millennium*. Amsterdam: Aksant, pp. 150–72.

Fischer, Stanley. 2003. 'Globalization and its challenges', unpublished manuscript.

Fishlow, Albert. 1998. 'América Latina en el siglo xxi', in Emmerij, Louis and Nuñez del Arco, José (eds.), *El desarrollo económico y social en los umbrales del siglo XXI*. Washington, DC: Inter-American Development Bank, pp. 449–62.

Frank, Robert H. 2010. 'Income inequality: too big to ignore', *New York Times*, 17 October.

Franko, Patrice M. 2007. *The Puzzle of Latin American Development*, 3rd edn. Lanham, MD: Rowman and Littlefield.

Friedman, Thomas L. 1996. 'Answers needed to globalization dissent', *Houston Chronicle*, 8 February: 30.

2005. *The World Is Flat: A Brief History of the Twenty-First Century*. New York: Farrer, Strauss, and Giroux.

Gacitúa, Estanislao and Davis, Shelton H. 2001. 'Introduction: poverty and social exclusion in Latin America and the Caribbean', in Gacitúa, Estanislao and Sojo, Carlos (eds.), *Social Exclusion and Poverty Reduction in Latin America and the Caribbean*. Washington, DC: World Bank, pp. 13–22.

Gafar, John S. 1998. 'Growth, inequality and poverty in selected Caribbean and Latin American countries, with emphasis on Guyana', *Journal of Latin American Studies* 30 (3): 591–617.

Gal, Orit. 2007. 'Between compassion and fear: doctrinal shifts in the World Bank, 1973–2003'. Ph.D. dissertation. Jerusalem: Hebrew University of Jerusalem, Department of International Relations.

Galak, Oliver. 2009. 'El foro de Davos advirtió sobre la falta de confianza en el país', *La Nación* 9, September, Section 2, p. 1.

Galiani, Sebastián, Heymann, Daniel, and Tommasi, Mariano. 2003. 'Expectativas frustradas: el ciclo de la convertibilidad', *Desarrollo Económico* 43 (169): 3–43.

Gambina, Julio C. and Crivelli, Agustín. 2005. 'Liberalización de la economía argentina: ruptura o continuidad?', in Reyno, Jaime Estay (ed.), *La economía mundial y América Latina: tendencias, problemas y desafíos*. Buenos Aires: CLACSO, pp. 391–411.

García, Ligia, Rivera, Eugenio, and Vega, Juan Enrique. 1994. 'Chile: posibilidades y riesgos de una integración activa en el Mercado mundial', in Hurtene, Thomas (ed.), *Cambio de rumbo en el Cono Sur*. Caracas: Nueva Sociedad, pp. 195–226.

García-Heras, Raúl. 2009. 'Economic stability and sustainable development in Argentina', *Latin American Research Review* 44 (1): 279–90.

Garretón, Manuel Antonio. 2002. 'El difícil reintento de un proyecto de país: la sociedad chilena a comienzos de siglo', in Bouzas, Roberto (ed.), *Realidades nacionales comparadas*. Buenos Aires: Altamira, pp. 245–300.

Gaudin, Andrés. 2006. 'The Kirchner factor', in Prashad, Vijay and Ballué, Teo (eds.), *Dispatches from Latin America: On the Frontlines against Neoliberalism*. Cambridge, MA: South End Press, pp. 77–85.

Gerchunoff, Pablo and Llach, Lucas. 2009. 'Equality or growth: a 20th century Argentine dilemma', unpublished manuscript.

Gill, Stephen. 2002. 'Constitutionalizing inequality and the clash of globalizations', *International Studies Review* 4 (2): 47–65.

Gilpin, Robert. 1987. *The Political Economy of International Relations*. Princeton University Press.

2000. *The Challenge of Global Capitalism: The World Economy in the 21st Century*. Princeton University Press.

Glade, William. 1996. 'Institutions and inequality in Latin America: text and subtext', *Journal of Interamerican Studies and World Affairs* 38 (2/3): 159–71.

Glenn, John. 2007. *Globalization: North–South Perspectives*. London: Routledge.

Godio, Julio. 2002. *Argentina: en la crisis está la solución: la crisis global desde las elecciones de octubre de 2001 hasta la asunción de Duhalde*. Buenos Aires: Biblos.

Goldin, Ian and Reinert, Kenneth. 2007. *Globalization for Development: Trade, Finance, Aid, Migration, and Policy*. New York: Palgrave.

González Meyer, Raúl. 2004. 'Tres décadas de un nuevo orden económico: Chile, 1973–2003', *European Review of Latin American and Caribbean Studies* 77: 61–77.

Goodin, Robert. 2003. 'Globalizing justice', in Held, David and Koenig-Archibugi, Matthias (eds.), *Taming Globalization: Frontiers of Governance*. Cambridge: Polity, pp. 68–92.

Gordon, David and Spicker, Paul (eds.). 1999. *The International Glossary on Poverty*. London: Zed.

Gourevitch, Peter. 1978. 'The second image reversed: the international sources of domestic politics', *International Organization* 32 (4): 881–912.

Grinspun, Pablo Ariel. 2003. *Crisis Argentina y globalización: la vigencia de Raúl Prebisch*. Buenos Aires: Grupo Editor.

Haass, Richard and Litan, Robert. 1998. 'Globalization and its discontents', *Foreign Affairs* 77 (3): 2–6.

Handoussa, Heba and Abou Shnief, Heba. 2008. 'The Middle East: challenges and opportunities of globalization', in Zedillo, Ernesto (ed.), *The Future of Globalization: Explorations in Light of Present Turbulence*. London: Routledge, pp. 227–52.

Harris, Richard L. 2008. 'Dependency, underdevelopment, and neoliberalism', in Harris, Richard L. and Nef, Jorge (eds.), *Capital, Power, and Inequality in Latin America and the Caribbean*. Lanham, MD: Rowman and Littlefield, pp. 49–95.

Harris, Richard L. and Nef, Jorge. 2008a. 'Capital, power, and inequality in Latin America and the Caribbean', in Harris, Richard L. and Nef, Jorge (eds.), *Capital, Power, and Inequality in Latin America and the Caribbean*. Lanham, MD: Rowman and Littlefield, pp. 1–23.

2008b. 'Globalization and regionalization in the Americas', in Richard L. Harris and Jorge Nef (eds.), *Capital, Power, and Inequality in Latin America and the Caribbean*. Lanham, MD: Rowman and Littlefield, pp. 273–319.

Harrison, Ann (ed.). 2007. *Globalization and Poverty*. University of Chicago Press, pp. 1–30.

Hartlyn, Jonathan. 2002. 'Democracy and consolidation in contemporary Latin America: current thinking and future challenges', in Tulchin, Joseph S. (ed.), *Democratic Governance and Social Inequality*. Boulder, CO: Lynne Rienner, pp. 103–30.

Hecht Oppenheim, Lois. 2000. 'Globalization, regionalism and sub-national fragmentation in Latin America', paper presented at the 18th World Congress of IPSA, Quebec City, Canada, 1–5 August.

Helwege, Ann. 1995. 'Poverty in Latin America: back to the abyss?', *Journal of Interamerican Studies and World Affairs* 37 (3): 99–125.

Helwege, Ann and Birch, Melissa. 2007. 'Declining poverty in Latin America? A critical analysis of new estimates by international institutions', paper presented at the LASA Annual Meeting.

Hershberg, Eric. 2002. 'Why Argentina crashed – and is still crashing', *NACLA Report on the Americas* 36 (1): 3–33.

Heshmati, Almas. 2003. 'The relationship between income inequality and globalization', working paper, UNU/WIDER, 25 April.

Hillal Dessouki, Ali E. 1993. 'Globalization and the two spheres of security', *Washington Quarterly* 16 (4): 109–17.

Hilton, Isabel. 2001. 'Forget Cancún: globalization has destroyed the real Latin America', *Guardian*, 8 August.

Hoffman, Kelly and Centeno, Miguel Angel. 2003. 'The lopsided continent: inequality in Latin America', *Annual Review of Sociology* 29: 363–90.

Holm, Hans-Henrik and Sorensen, Georg. 1995. 'Introduction', in Holm, Hans-Henrik and Sorensen, Georg (eds.), *Whose World Order? Uneven Globalization and the End of the Cold War*. Boulder, CO: Westview, pp. 1–17.

Holsti, Kalevi J. 1996. *The State, War, and the State of War*. Cambridge University Press.

Hurrell, Andrew. 1999. 'Security and inequality', in Hurrell, Andrew and Wood, Ngaire (eds.), *Inequality, Globalization, and World Politics*. Oxford University Press, pp. 248–71.

Hurrell, Andrew and Woods, Ngaire. 1999. 'Introduction', in Hurrell, Andrew and Woods, Ngaire (eds.), *Inequality, Globalization, and World Politics*. Oxford University Press, pp. 1–7.

Iglesias, Enrique. 1992. *Reflections on Economic Development: Toward a New Latin American Consensus*. Washington, DC: Inter-American Development Bank.

   1997. 'The new Latin America and the Inter-American Development Bank', in Diehl, Paul F. (ed.), *The Politics of Global Governance: International Organizations in an Interdependent World*. Boulder, CO: Lynne Rienner, pp. 233–42.

Insulza, José Miguel. 2010. 'Poverty and inequality make democracy more fragile', ECLAC, 30 March.

International Monetary Fund. 1998. 'Should equity be a goal of economic policy?', *Economic Issues* 16: 1–12.

   1999 and 2000. *IMF Survey* 28 and 29.

Ish-Shalom, Piki. 2008. 'Render unto Caesar that which is Caesar's: on the joint pursuit of morality and security', *American Behavioral Scientist* 51 (9): 1285–302.

Jomo, K.S. 2001. 'Globalization, liberalization, poverty and income inequality in Southeast Asia', OECD Development Center, Working Paper No. 185.

Jozami, Aníbal. 2002. 'La declinación argentina', *Archivos del Presente* 27 (7): 9–13.

2003. *Argentina: la destrucción de una nación*. Barcelona: Mondadori.

Kacowicz, Arie M. 1994. *Peaceful Territorial Change*. Columbia, SC: University of South Carolina Press.

1998. *Zones of Peace in the Third World: South America and West Africa in Comparative Perspective*. Albany, NY: State University of New York Press.

1999. 'Regionalization, globalization, and nationalism: convergent, divergent, or overlapping?', *Alternatives* 24: 527–56.

2005. *The Impact of Norms in International Society: The Latin American Experience, 1881–2001*. University of Notre Dame Press.

2007. 'Globalization, poverty, and the North–South divide', *International Studies Review* 9 (4): 565–80.

Kaplinsky, Raphael. 2005. *Globalization, Poverty, and Inequality: Between a Rock and a Hard Place*. London: Polity.

Katzenstein, Peter. 1978. 'Introduction: domestic and international forces and strategies of foreign economic policy', in Katzenstein, Peter (ed.), *Between Power and Plenty: Foreign Economic Policies of Advanced Industrialized States*. Madison, WI: University of Wisconsin Press, pp. 3–22.

Kaufman, Robert R. 2003. 'Latin America in the global economy: macroeconomic policy, social welfare, and political democracy', in Kohli, Atul, Moon, Chung-in, and Sorensen, George (eds.), *States, Markets, and Just Growth: Development in the 21st Century*. Tokyo: United Nations University Press, pp. 97–126.

Kay, Cristóbal. 2008. 'Latin America's rural transformation: unequal development and persistent poverty', in Harris, Richard L. and Nef, Jorge (eds.), *Capital, Power, and Inequality in Latin America and the Caribbean*. Lanham, MD: Rowman and Littlefield, pp. 24–48.

Kayizzi-Mugewa, Steve. 2003. 'Globalization, growth and income inequality: the African experience', in Kohl, Richard (ed.), *Globalization, Poverty, and Inequality*. Paris: OECD, pp. 45–51.

Keating, Michael. 2008. 'Globalization and inequality: substantial differentials within nation-states', MA thesis. George Mason University.

Kedar, Claudia. 2009. 'The routinization of dependency: Argentina and the IMF, 1944–1977'. Ph.D. dissertation (in Hebrew). Tel-Aviv, Israel: Tel-Aviv University, Institute for Latin American History and Culture.

Khan, Haider A. and Larik, Zulfikar. 2007. 'Globalization and regional cooperation in South Asia: a political and social economy approach', University of Denver, GSIS, February/March.

Kim, Hae S. 2000. 'The effect of global dependency on the quality of life in developing countries', paper presented at the XVIII Congress of IPSA, Quebec, 1–5 August.

Klein, Marcus. 2004. 'Stumbling on the verge of the abyss (without falling into it): Argentina and its crisis of the millennium', in Fiorucci, Flavia and Klein,

Marcus (eds.), *The Argentine Crisis at the Turn of the Millennium*. Amsterdam: Aksant, pp. 1–14.

Klein, Naomi. 2008. *The Shock Doctrine: The Rise of Disaster Capitalism*. Toronto: Knopf Canada.

Kliksberg, Bernardo. 2001. *The Social Situation of Latin America and its Impact on Family and Education*. Washington, DC: OAS.

2005. 'Un tema ético central: el impacto de la pobreza sobre la familia en América Latina', in Kliksberg, Bernardo (ed.), *La agenda ética pendiente de América Latina*. Washington, DC: Inter-American Development Bank, pp. 69–94.

Koch, Max. 1999. 'Changes in Chilean social structure: class structure and income distribution between 1972 and 1994', *European Review of Latin American and Caribbean Studies* 66: 5–18.

Koenig-Archibugi, Matthias. 2003. 'Introduction: globalization and the challenge to governance', in Held, David and Koenig-Archibugi, Matthias (eds.), *Taming Globalization: Frontiers of Governance*. Cambridge: Polity, pp. 1–17.

Kohl, Richard. 2003. 'Conclusions to the conference volume', in Kohl, Richard (ed.), *Globalization, Poverty, and Inequality*. Paris: OECD, pp. 109–16.

Korzeniewicz, Roberto Patricio and Smith, William C. 2000. 'Poverty, inequality, and growth in Latin America: searching for the high road to globalization', *Latin American Research Review* 35 (3): 7–54.

Krasner, Stephen D. 1978. *Defending the National Interest: Raw Materials, Investments and U.S. Foreign Policy*. Princeton University Press.

Kuczynski, Pedro Pablo. 2003a. 'Setting the stage', in Kuczynski, Pedro Pablo and Williamson, John (eds.), *After the Washington Consensus: Restarting Growth and Reform in Latin America*. Washington, DC: Institute for International Economics, pp. 21–32.

2003b. 'Reforming the state', in Kuczynski, Pedro Pablo and Williamson, John (eds.), *After the Washington Consensus: Restarting Growth and Reform in Latin America*. Washington, DC: Institute for International Economics, pp. 33–47.

Kulfas, Matías. 2010. 'Crecer o distribuir: un planteo equivocado', *Desafíos para un Proyecto Nacional* 1: 60–73.

Larson, Mikael. 2003. 'Poverty and globalization in Argentina: the linkages between the application of a neo-liberal economic model and the increase in poverty in the 1990s', Department of Government, Georgetown University, seminar paper.

Latin American Herald Tribune. 2009. 'Global economic crisis adds nine million to ranks of Latin American poor', 3 December.

Lazebnik, Yulia. 2005. 'Globalization, poverty, and inequality', Jerusalem: Hebrew University of Jerusalem, Department of International Relations, seminar paper.

Leonard, Andrew. 2006. 'Argentina's tango with globalization', www.salon.com/2006/12/14/argentina_4/.

Levy Yeyati, Eduardo and Valenzuela, Diego. 2007. *La resurrección: historia de la poscrisis argentina*. Buenos Aires: Sudamericana.

Lewis, W. Arthur. 1978. *The Evolution of the International Economic Order*. Princeton University Press.

Li, He. 1997. 'Democracy in Latin America: does globalization matter?', paper presented at the 1997 Annual Meeting of APSA. Washington, DC, 28–31 August.

Lischinsky, Bernardo. 2002. 'El rompecabezas de la deuda externa', *Archivos del Presente* 8 (29): 129–40.

Llach, Lucas. 2004. 'A depression in perspective: the economics and the political economy of Argentina's crisis of the millennium', in Fiorucci, Flavia and Klein, Marcus (eds.), *The Argentine Crisis at the Turn of the Millennium*. Amsterdam: Aksant, pp. 40–63.

Lloyd-Sherlock, Peter. 1997. 'Policy, distribution and poverty in Argentina since redemocratization', *Latin American Perspectives* 24 (6): 22–55.

López-Alves, Fernando. 2007. 'Uncertainty, the construction of the future, and the divorce between citizens and the state in Latin America', in López-Alves, Fernando and Johnson, Diane E. (eds.), *Globalization and Uncertainty in Latin America*. New York: Palgrave, pp. 47–76.

López-Alves, Fernando and Johnson, Diane E. 2007. 'Introduction: uncertainty and globalization', in López-Alves, Fernando and Johnson, Diane E. (eds.), *Globalization and Uncertainty in Latin America*. New York: Palgrave, pp. 1–24.

Loser, Claudio M. 2008. 'The macroeconomic environment of competition', in Haar, Jerry and Price, John (eds.), *Can Latin America Compete? Confronting the Challenges of Globalization*. New York: Palgrave, pp. 27–43.

Loureiro, María Rita and Abrucio, Fernando Luiz. 2003. 'Política y reformas fiscals en el Brasil reciente', in Palermo, Vicente (ed.), *Política brasileña contemporanea: de Collor a Lula en años de transformación*. Buenos Aires: Siglo Veintiuno Argentina, pp. 573–610.

Lo Vuolo, Rubén M. 1997. 'La retracción del estado de bienestar en la Argentina', unpublished manuscript.

    1998. 'Lecciones de un presente reaccionario y el campo de las posibilidades de las políticas socials y económicas', *Revista Argentina del Régimen de la Administración Pública*: 37–50.

Lo Vuolo, Rubén M., Barbeito, Alkberto, Palassi, Laura and Rodríguez, Caria. 1999. *La pobreza . . . de la política contra la pobreza*. Buenos Aires: Miño y Davila.

Lowi, Theodore J. 2002. 'Progress and poverty revisited: toward construction of a statist third way', in Tulchin, Joseph S. (ed.), *Democratic Governance and Social Inequality*. Boulder, CO: Lynne Rienner, pp. 41–74.

Lumsdaine, David H. 1993. *Moral Vision in International Politics: The Foreign Aid Regime, 1949–1989*. Princeton University Press.

Lustig, Nora. 2009. 'Poverty, inequality, and the "New Left" in Latin America', paper presented at the Woodrow Wilson Latin American Program, Washington, DC.

MacLachlan, Colin M. 2006. *Argentina: What Went Wrong*. New York: Praeger.

Maddison, Angus. 1989. *The World Economy in the 20th Century*. Paris: OECD.

    1992. *The Political Economy of Poverty, Equity, and Growth: Brazil and Mexico*. Oxford University Press.

    1995. *Monitoring the World Economy, 1820–1992*. Paris: OECD.

Maira, Luis. 2008. 'Pobreza y desigualdad: nuevos temas en la agenda internacional de América Latina', in Lagos, Ricardo (ed.), *América Latina: integración o fragmentación*. Buenos Aires: Edhasal, pp. 491–526.

Mallo, Susana. 2003. 'Argentina: un destino no esperado', paper presented at
the 24th Congress of LASA, Dallas, TX, 26–9 March.

Mamalakis, Markos J. 1996. 'Introduction: poverty and inequality in Latin America', *Journal of Inter-American Studies and World Affairs* 38 (2/3): 1–13.

Mandle, Jay. 2003. *Globalization and the Poor*. Cambridge University Press.

Mann, Michael. 2004. 'La crisis del estado-nación en América Latina', *Desarrollo
Económico* 44 (174): 179–98.

Mansbach, Richard W. and Rhodes, Edward. 2003. *Global Politics in a Changing
World*. Boston, MA: Houghton Mifflin.

Margheritis, Ana. 2003. 'Introduction: foreign policy and domestic restructuring
in Latin America: recent achievements and future challenges', in Margheritis, Ana (ed.), *Latin American Democracies in the New Global Economy*. Miami,
FL: North–South Center, pp. 1–27.

Martin, Hans-Peter and Schumann, Harold. 1997. *The Global Trap: Globalization
and the Assault on Democracy and Prosperity*. London: Zen.

Mastanduno, Michael, Lake, David A. and Ikenberrry, G. John. 1989. 'Toward
a Realist theory of state action', *International Studies Quarterly* 33: 457–74.

Mathews, Jessica T. 2002. 'September 11, one year later: a world of change',
*Carnegie Endowment for International Peace Special Edition* 18: 1–12.

Mehmet, Ozay. 2006. 'Race to the bottom: the impact of globalization on labor
markets: a review of empirical and theoretical evidence', in Ghosh, B.N. and
Guven, Hail M. (eds.), *Globalization and the Third World: A Study of Negative
Consequences*. New York: Palgrave, pp. 148–61.

Meyer, Carrie A. 2000. 'Globalization and inequality in Latin America', unpublished manuscript.

Migdal, Joel. 1988. *Strong Societies and Weak States: State–Society Relations and
State Capabilities in the Third World*. Princeton University Press.

Miguez, Eduardo. 2005. 'El fracaso argentino: interpretando la evolución
económica en el corto siglo XX', *Desarrollo Económico* 44 (176): 483–509.

Milanovic, Branko. 2005. *Worlds Apart: Measuring International and Global
Inequality*. Princeton University Press.

 2007. 'Global income inequality: what it is and why it matters', in Jomo, K.S.
and Baodout, Jacques (eds.), *Flat World, Big Gaps: Economic Liberalization,
Globalization, Poverty and Inequality*. London: Zed, pp. 1–23.

 2011. 'More or less', *Finance and Development*, September: 7–11.

Miller, Benjamin. 2007. *States, Nations, and the Great Powers: The Sources of
Regional War and Peace*. Cambridge University Press.

Mills, Melinda. 2009. 'Globalization and inequality', *European Sociological Review*
25 (1): 1–8.

Mittelman, James H. 1996a. 'The dynamics of globalization', in Mittelman,
James H. (ed.), *Globalization: Critical Reflections*. Boulder, CO: Lynne Rienner, pp. 1–19.

 1996b. 'How does globalization really work?', in Mittelman, James H.
(ed.), *Globalization: Critical Reflections*. Boulder, CO: Lynne Rienner,
pp. 229–41.

2004. 'What is critical globalization studies?', *International Studies Perspectives* 5: 219–30.

Mittelman, James H. and Tambe, Ashwini. 2000. 'Reconceptualizing global poverty: globalization, marginalization, and gender', in Wapner, Paul and Ruiz, Lester Edwin J. (eds.), *Principled World Politics: The Challenge of Normative International Relations*. Lanham, MD: Rowman and Littlefield, pp. 166–85.

Morales, Marco A. 2008. 'Have Latin Americans turned left?', in Castañeda, Jorge C. and Morales, Marco A. (eds.), *Leftovers: Tales of the Latin American Left*. New York: Routledge, pp. 19–41.

Morley, Samuel A. 2003. 'Distribution and growth in Latin America in an era of structural reform: the impact of globalization', in Kohl, Richard (ed.), *Globalization, Poverty, and Inequality*. Paris: OECD, pp. 63–9.

Moser, Caroline. 1998. 'Urban poverty and violence: consolidation or erosion of social capital?', in Burki, Shahid Javed, Aiyer, Sri-Ram and Hommes, Rudolf (eds.), *Poverty and Inequality: Development in Latin America and the Caribbean, 1996*. Washington, DC: World Bank, pp. 83–9.

Munck, Ronaldo. 2007. 'Globalization, poverty, and inequality', *Review of Radical Political Economics* 39 (4): 599–605.

Nandy, Ashis. 2002. 'The beautiful, expanding future of poverty: popular economics as a psychological defense', *International Studies Review* 4 (2): 107–21.

Nel, Philip. 2000. 'Equity as "global public good"?', paper presented at the IPSA, Quebec, 1–5 August.

Neutel, Marcel and Heshmati, Almas. 2006. 'Globalization, inequality and poverty relationships: a cross-country evidence', *Discussion Paper Series IZA DP*, no. 2223: 1–39.

Nissanke, Machiko and Thorbecke, Erik (eds.). 2006. *The Impact of Globalization on the World's Poor*. New York: Palgrave.

2007. 'Linking globalization to poverty', *Policy Brief* 2: 1–8.

2010. 'Linking globalization to poverty in Asia, Latin America, and Africa', *Policy Brief* 3: 1–32.

Nochteff, Hugo and Abeles, Martín. 2000. *Economic Shocks without Vision: Neo-Liberalism in the Transition of Socio-Economic System: Lessons from the Argentine Case*. Frankfurt: Ververt Verlag.

Noriega, Roger. 2009. 'Latin America and the economic crisis', *AEI Outlook Series* 2: 1–5.

Novick, Marta. 2010. 'Herramientas para pelear contra la desigualdad', *Desafíos para un Proyecto Nacional* 1: 74–85.

Nudelsman, Susana. 2006. 'Latin America in the era of globalization', paper presented at the LASA Annual Meeting, San Juan, Puerto Rico, 15–18 March.

Nürnberger, Klaus. 1999. *Prosperity, Poverty, and Pollution*. London: Zed.

Nussbaum, Martha C. and Sen, Amartya (eds.). 1993. *The Quality of Life*. Oxford University Press.

Ocampo, José Antonio. 1998. 'Globalización y su impacto en las economías', in Aravena, Francisco Rojas (ed.), *Globalización, América Latina y la diplomacia de Cumbres*. Santiago de Chile: FLACSO, pp. 65–80.

O'Donnell, Guillermo. 1988. 'State and alliance in Argentina, 1956–1976', in Bates, Robert H. (ed.), *Toward a Political Economy of Development: A Rational Choice Perspective.* Berkeley, CA: University of California Press, pp. 176–205.

—— 1998. 'Poverty and inequality in Latin America: some political reflections', in Tokman, Victor E. and O'Donnell, Guillermo (eds.), *Poverty and Inequality in Latin America.* University of Notre Dame Press, pp. 49–71.

OECD. 2008. *Latin American Economic Outlook 2009.* Paris: OECD.

Oficina Internacional del Trabajo. 1998. *Chile: crecimiento, empleo, y el desafío de la justicia social.* Geneva: OIT.

Oliveto, Guillermo. 2011. 'Viaje a la Argentina real', *La Nación*, 20 September.

O'Neil, Shannon K. (ed.). 2008. *US–Latin American Relations: A New Direction for a New Reality.* New York: Council on Foreign Relations.

Palermo, Vicente. 2001. 'Racionalidad política y gestión económica de gobiernos representatives en Argentina y Brasil: los planes de convertibilidad y Real', *Ciclos en la Historia, la Economía y la Sociedad* 21: 35–83.

Panizza, Francisco. 2003. 'Política y economía de Brasil contemporáneo', in Palermo, Vicente (ed.), *Política brasileña contemporánea: de Collor a Lula en años de transformación.* Buenos Aires: Siglo Veintiuno Argentina, pp. 49–89.

Paradiso, José. 2002. 'La declinación argentina', *Archivos del Presente* 27 (7): 14–16.

Pasha, Mustapha Kamal and Murphy, Craig N. 2002. 'Knowledge, power, and inequality', *International Studies Review* 4 (2): 1–6.

Perry, Guillermo E. and Serven, Luis. 2002. 'La anatomía de una crisis multiple: qué tenía Argentina de especial y qué podemos aprender de ella', *Desarrollo Económico* 42 (167): 323–75.

Pinker, Robert. 1999. 'Do poverty definitions matter?', in Gordon, David and Spicker, Paul (eds.), *The International Glossary on Poverty.* London: Zed, pp. 1–5.

Pogge, Thomas. 2005a. 'World poverty and human rights', *Ethics and International Affairs* 19 (1): 1–7.

—— 2005b. 'Severe poverty as a violation of negative duties', *Ethics and International Affairs* 19 (1): 55–83.

Polino, Héctor. 1998. 'Algunas reflexiones sobre la reconstrucción del Estado', *Revista Argentina del Régimen de la Administración Pública*: 33–6.

Porto, Guido G. 2007. 'Globalization and poverty in Latin America: some channels and some evidence', *World Economy* 30 (9): 1430–56.

Potter, Brian. 2003. 'The death of the universal development model: sustaining growth through different domestic norms', in Margheritis, Ana (ed.), *Latin American Democracies in the New Global Economy.* Miami, FL: North–South Center, pp. 265–79.

Powers, Nancy R. 1995. 'The politics of poverty in the 1990s', *Journal of Interamerican Studies and World Affairs* 37 (4): 89–137.

Prasad, Eswar S., Rogoff, Kenneth, Wei, Shang-Jin, and Kose, M. Ayhan. 2007. 'Financial globalization, growth, and volatility in developing countries', in Harrison, Ann (ed.), *Globalization and Poverty.* University of Chicago Press, pp. 457–516.

Price, John and Haar, Jerry. 2008. 'Introduction: can Latin America compete?', in Haar, Jerry and Price, John (eds.), *Can Latin America Compete? Confronting the Challenges of Globalization*. New York: Palgrave, pp. 1–25.

Ramaswamy, Sushila. 2000. 'Eclipse of dependency theory: the reasons for history's verdict against it', paper presented at the IPSA Congress, Quebec, 1–5 August.

Ramos, Joseph R. 1996. 'Poverty and inequality in Latin America: a neo-structural perspective', *Journal of Interamerican Studies and World Affairs* 38 (2/3): 141–58.

Rapley, John. 2004. *Globalization and Inequality: Neoliberalism's Downward Spiral*. Boulder, CO: Lynne Rienner.

Rapoport, Mario. 2006. *El viraje del siglo XXI: deudas y desafíos en la Argentina, América Latina y el mundo*. Buenos Aires: Norma.

Raus, Diego. 2008. 'América Latina: la difícil coyuntura: la política entre las posibilidades y los límites: notas sobre el caso argentino', in Moreira, Carlos, Raus, Diego and Gómez Leyton, Juan Carlos (eds.), *La nueva política en América Latina: rupturas y continuidades*. Montevideo: Ediciones Trilce, pp. 73–95.

Ravallion, Martin. 2003. 'The debate on globalization, poverty, and inequality: why measurement matters', *Policy Research Working Paper Series* 3038. Washington, DC: World Bank.

Rawls, John. 1971. *A Theory of Justice*. Cambridge, MA: Harvard University Press.

1999. *The Law of Peoples*. Cambridge, MA: Harvard University Press.

2005. *Political Liberalism*. New York: Columbia University Press.

Repetto, Fabián. 2000. 'Gestión pública, actores e institucionalidad: las políticas frente a la pobreza en los años 90', *Desarrollo Económico* 39 (156): 597–618.

Reynolds, Lloyd George. 1996. 'Some sources of income inequality in Latin America', *Journal of Interamerican Studies and World Affairs* 38 (2/3): 39–46.

Risse, Mathias. 2005. 'Do we owe the global poor assistance or rectification?', *Ethics and International Affairs* 19 (1): 9–18.

Risse-Kappen, Thomas. 1995. 'Bringing transnational relations back in: introduction', in Risse-Kappen, Thomas (ed.), *Bringing Transnational Relations back in: Non-State Actors, Domestic Structures and International Institutions*. Cambridge University Press, pp. 3–33.

Robinson, Bill. 2004. 'The crisis of global capitalism: how it looks from Latin America', in Freeman, Alan and Kagarlitsky, Boris (eds.), *The Politics of Empire: Globalization in Crisis*. London: Pluto Press, pp. 154–8.

Robinson, James A. 2003. 'Where does inequality come from? Ideas and implications for Latin America', in Kohl, Richard (ed.), *Globalization, Poverty, and Inequality*. Paris: OECD, pp. 71–5.

Robinson, Mary. 2002. 'Ethics, human rights, and globalization', second global ethic lecture, Global Ethic Foundation, Tübingen University, 21 January.

Rohter, Larry. 2004. 'Argentina's economic rally defies forecasts', *The New York Times*, 26 December.

Rojas Aravena, Francisco. 2005. 'Ingobernabilidad', *Nueva Sociedad* 198: 56–73.

Rojas-Suarez, Liliana. 2009. 'Growing pains: an economic growth framework for Latin America', Washington, DC: Center for Global Development.

Romero, Alberto. 2002. *Globalización y pobreza*. Bogotá: UMA.

Romero, Luis Alberto. 2004. 'The Argentine crisis: a look at the 20th century', in Fiorucci, Flavia and Klein, Marcus (eds.), *The Argentine Crisis at the Turn of the Millennium*. Amsterdam: Aksant, pp. 15–39.

Rosenthal, Gert. 1989. 'Some thoughts on poverty and recession in Latin America', *Journal of Interamerican Studies and World Affairs* 31 (1–2): 63–73.

Rouquié, Alain. 1987. *The Military and the State in Latin America*. Berkeley, CA: University of California Press.

Rudra, Nita. 2008. *Globalization and the Race to the Bottom in Developing Countries: Who Really Gets Hurt?* Cambridge University Press.

Sachs, Jeffrey. 2005. *The End of Poverty: Economic Possibilities of Our Time*. New York: Penguin Press.

2008. *Common Wealth: Economics for a Crowded Planet*. New York: Penguin Press.

Said Aly, Abdel Monem. 2012. *State and Revolution in Egypt: The Paradox of Change and Politics*. Boston, MA: Brandeis University, Crown Center for Middle Eastern Studies.

Saiegh, Sebastián. 2004. 'The sub-national connection: legislative coalitions, cross-voting, and policymaking in Argentina', in Fiorucci, Flavia and Klein, Marcus (eds.), *The Argentine Crisis at the Turn of the Millennium*. Amsterdam: Aksant, pp. 107–26.

Sáinz, Pedro. 2007. 'Equity in Latin America since the 1990s', in Jomo, K.S. and Baudot, Jacques (eds.), *Flat World, Big Gaps: Economic Liberalization, Globalization, Poverty and Inequality*. London: Zed, pp. 242–71.

Sala-i-Martin, Xavier. 2006. 'The world distribution of income: falling poverty and... convergence, period', *Quarterly Journal of Economics* 121 (2): 351–97.

Salama, Pierre. 2003. 'Nuevas paradojas de la liberación en América Latina: los casos de Argentina, Brasil y México', in Durán Juarez, Juan Manuel, Woo Morales, Ofelia, and Martínez, Jorge Ceja (eds.), *La globalización en América Latina a la luz del nuevo milenio*. Guadalajara, Mexico: Universidad General, pp. 79–121.

Salvucci, Richard J. (ed.). 1996. *Latin America and the World Economy: Dependency and Beyond*. Lexington, MA: D.C. Heath.

Sanchez, Omar. 2003. 'Globalization as a development strategy in Latin America?', paper prepared for delivery at the 2003 Annual Meeting of LASA, Dallas, Texas, 27–9 March.

Sandbrook, Richard. 2003. 'Introduction: envisioning a civilized globalization', in Sandbrook, Richard (ed.), *Civilizing Globalization: A Survival Guide*. Albany, NY: State University of New York Press, pp. 1–11.

Sandbrook, Richard, Edelman, Marc, Heller, Patrick, and Teichman, Judith. 2007. *Social Democracy in the Global Periphery: Origins, Challenges, Prospects*. Cambridge University Press.

Schatan, Jacobo. 2001. 'Poverty and inequality in Chile: offspring of twenty-five years of neoliberalism', *Development and Society* 30 (2): 57–77.

Scholte, Jan Aaart. 2000. 'Globalization and equity', paper presented at the 41st Annual Convention of the ISA, Los Angeles, 14–18 March.

Sela, Avraham. 1998. *The Decline of the Arab–Israeli Conflict: Middle East Politics and the Quest for Regional Order.* Albany, NY: SUNY Press.

— 2003. 'Globalization, Islam and the state in the Middle East', lecture to the South American Friends of Hebrew University, Punta del Este, Uruguay, January.

Sen, Amartya. 1981. *Poverty and Famines: An Essay on Entitlement and Deprivation.* Oxford: Clarendon Press.

— 1999. *Development as Freedom.* New York: Anchor Books.

— 2009. *The Idea of Justice.* Cambridge, MA: Harvard University Press.

Serrano, Franklin. 2003. 'Outlook for South and Central America: economic stagnation and state decline', in Pettifor, Ann (ed.), *Real World Economic Outlook: The Legacy of Globalization: Debt and Deflation.* New York: Palgrave, pp. 84–9.

Sersale, Carlos. 2002. 'La declinación argentina', *Archivos del Presente* 27 (7): 24–7.

Shambaugh, George E. 2004. 'The power of money: global capital and policy choices in developing countries', *American Journal of Political Science* 48 (2): 281–95.

Sikkink, Kathryn. 1991. *Ideas and Institutions: Developmentalism in Brazil and Argentina.* Ithaca, NY: Cornell University Press.

Sil, Rudra and Katzenstein, Peter. 2005. 'What is analytical eclecticism and why do we need it? A pragmatic perspective on problems and mechanisms in the study of world politics', paper presented at the Annual Meeting of the APSA, Washington DC, 1 September.

Singer, Hans W. 2002. 'Foreword', in Gray Rich, Patricia (ed.), *Latin America: Its Future in the Global Economy.* New York: Palgrave, pp. ix–xiii.

Smith, Peter. 2008. *Talons of the Eagle: Dynamics of US–Latin American Relations,* 3rd edn. Oxford University Press.

Soros, George. 2002. *On Globalization.* New York: Public Affairs.

Souza, Celina. 2003. 'Democratización, federalismo y gasto social en el Brasil', in Palermo, Vicente (ed.), *Política brasileña contemporánea: de Collor a Lula en años de transformación.* Buenos Aires: Siglo Veintiuno Argentina, pp. 155–94.

Speth, James Gustave. 1999. 'The plight of the poor: the US must increase development aid', *Foreign Affairs* 78 (3): 13–17.

Spicker, Paul. 1999. 'Definitions of poverty: eleven clusters of meaning', in Gordon, David and Spicker, Paul (eds.), *The International Glossary on Poverty.* London: Zed, pp. 150–62.

Spiller, Pablo T. and Tommasi, Mariano. 2007. *The Institutional Foundations of Public Policy in Argentina: A Transaction Cost Approach.* Cambridge University Press.

Stallings, Barbara. 2003. 'Rapporteur's report on Latin American regional session', in Kohl, Richard (ed.), *Globalization, Poverty, and Inequality.* Paris: OECD, pp. 77–9.

Stein, Howard. 2008. *Beyond the World Bank Agenda: An Institutional Approach to Development*. University of Chicago Press.

Stewart, Frances and Berry, Albert. 1999. 'Globalization, liberalization, and inequality: expectations and experience', in Hurrell, Andrew and Woods, Ngaire (eds.), *Inequality, Globalization, and World Politics*. Oxford University Press, pp. 150–86.

Stiglitz, Joseph E. 2002. *Globalization and its Discontents*. New York: W.W. Norton.

2007. *Making Globalization Work*. New York: W.W. Norton.

2008. 'The future of globalization: lessons from Cancún and recent financial crises', in Zedillo, Ernesto (ed.), *The Future of Globalization: Explorations in Light of Recent Turbulences*. London: Routledge, pp. 70–81.

Suter, Christian. 2009. 'Inequality beyond globalization: searching for the missing pieces of the puzzle: introduction to the special issue', *International Journal of Comparative Sociology* 50 (5–6): 419–24.

Sznajder, Mario. 2011. 'Citizenship and the contradictions of free market policies in Chile and Latin America', unpublished manuscript.

Teichman, Judith A. 2001. *The Politics of Freeing Markets in Latin America: Chile, Argentina, and Mexico*. Chapel Hill, NC: University of North Carolina Press.

2001–2. 'Latin America in the era of globalization: inequality, poverty, and questionable democracies', University of Toronto, *CIS Working Paper*. www.utoronto.ca/cis/working-papers/2001-2.pdf.

2002. 'Latin America in the era of globalization: facing the challenges of second-stage reform', paper presented at the ISA Annual Meeting, New Orleans, 23–7 March.

Townsend, Peter. 1993. *The International Analysis of Poverty*. New York: Harvester Wheatsheaf.

UNDP. 2000. *Overcoming Human Poverty: Report 2000*. New York: United Nations Press.

2009. 'Crisis update no. 2: the global financial crisis: social implications for Latin America and the Caribbean', 10 February. www.jm.undp.org/files/CrisisUpdateNo2.pdf.

United Nations Economic and Social Council. 2009. *Latin America and the Caribbean: Economic Situation and Outlook, 2008–2009*. New York: United Nations.

Väyrynen, Raimo. 2008. 'Poverty, inequality, and global politics', paper prepared for the WISC/ISA Conference, Ljubljana, Slovenie, 23–6 July.

Veigel, Klaus F. 2009. *Dictatorship, Democracy and Globalization: Argentina and the Cost of Paralysis, 1973–2003*. University Park, PA: Pennsylvania University Press.

Wade, Robert Hunter. 2002. 'Globalization, poverty and income distribution: does the liberal argument hold?', *Working Paper Series DESTIN LSE* No. 02–33, 2 July.

2004. 'Is globalization reducing poverty and inequality?', *World Development* 32 (4): 567–89.

Waisman, Carlos. 1987. *Reversal of Development in Argentina: Postwar Counter-revolutionary Policies and their Structural Consequences*. Princeton University Press.

1997. 'El fin del mercantilismo: Argentina y Chile como casos paradigmáticos', in Di Tella, Torcuato (ed.), *Argentina–Chile: desarrollos paralelos?* Buenos Aires: GEL, pp. 213–31.

Walker, R.B.J. 2002. 'International inequality', *International Studies Review* 4 (2): 7–24.

Weede, Erich. 2000. 'The impact of globalization: creative destruction and the prospect of capitalist peace', paper presented at the IPSA Congress, Quebec, Canada, 1–5 August.

Weintraub, Sidney. 2003. 'Mexican and other recent Latin American financial crises: how much systemic, how much policy?', in Margheritis, Ana (ed.), *Latin American Democracies in the New Global Economy*. Miami, FL: North–South Center, pp. 109–21.

Williamson, John. 2003. 'An agenda for restarting growth and reform', in Kuczynski, Pedro Pablo and Williamson, John (eds.), *After the Washington Consensus: Restarting Growth and Reform in Latin America*. Washington, DC: Institute for International Economics, pp. 1–19.

Wolf, Martin. 2004. *Why Globalization Works*. New Haven, CT: Yale University Press.

Wolfensohn, James D. 2000. 'Wolfensohn calls on governors to cooperate to build a more equitable world', *IMF Survey* 29 (19): 308–9.

Wolff, Jonathan and de-Shalit, Avner. 2007. *Disadvantage*. Oxford University Press.

Woods, Ngaire. 1999. 'Order, globalization, and inequality', in Hurrell, Andrew and Woods, Ngaire (eds.), *Inequality, Globalization, and World Politics*. Oxford University Press, pp. 8–35.

World Bank. 2001. *Attacking Poverty: World Development Report, 2000/2001*. New York: Oxford University Press.

2007. *Global Economic Prospects: Managing the Next Wave of Globalization*. Washington, DC: World Bank.

2009. *World Development Report 2010: Development and Climate Change*. New York: Oxford University Press.

# Index